Kirsten Kleine, Susanne Müller, Aretha Perkuhn, Nina Samson

In Stock For You

English for Packing and Logistics Staff

4. Auflage

Bestellnummer 11321

Bildungsverlag EINS
westermann

Die in diesem Produkt gemachten Angaben zu Unternehmen (Namen, Internet- und E-Mail-Adressen, Handelsregistereintragungen, Bankverbindungen, Steuer-, Telefon- und Faxnummern und alle weiteren Angaben) sind i. d. R. fiktiv, d. h., sie stehen in keinem Zusammenhang mit einem real existierenden Unternehmen in der dargestellten oder einer ähnlichen Form. Dies gilt auch für alle Kunden, Lieferanten und sonstigen Geschäftspartner der Unternehmen wie z. B. Kreditinstitute, Versicherungsunternehmen und andere Dienstleistungsunternehmen. Ausschließlich zum Zwecke der Authentizität werden die Namen real existierender Unternehmen und z. B. im Fall von Kreditinstituten auch deren IBANs und BICs verwendet.

Die in diesem Werk aufgeführten Internetadressen sind auf dem Stand zum Zeitpunkt der Drucklegung. Die ständige Aktualität der Adressen kann vonseiten des Verlages nicht gewährleistet werden. Darüber hinaus übernimmt der Verlag keine Verantwortung für die Inhalte dieser Seiten.

service@bv-1.de
www.bildungsverlag1.de

Bildungsverlag EINS GmbH
Ettore-Bugatti-Straße 6-14, 51149 Köln

ISBN 978-3-427-**11321**-8

westermann GRUPPE

Vorwort

Das Lehrbuch "In Stock For You" ist für Schülerinnen und Schüler im Bereich Fachlagerist und Fachkraft für Lagerlogistik sowie im Berufsvorbereitungsjahr für diesen Berufszweig konzipiert.

Orientiert am Gemeinsamen Europäischen Referenzrahmen für Sprachen ist "In Stock For You" auf dem Niveau A2/B1 einzuordnen.

Die Heterogenität und Interkulturalität in den Klassen – mit den damit verbundenen unterschiedlichen oder gar nicht vorhandenen Englischkenntnissen – machen es erforderlich, in kurzer Zeit einerseits Grundlagen zu vermitteln oder zu wiederholen und andererseits ergänzendes Fachwissen anzubieten.

Das vorliegende Buch möchte diesen Anforderungen gerecht werden. Die Texte und Aufgaben entstanden aus jahrelanger praktisch-beruflicher und didaktisch-pädagogischer Erfahrung im Bereich Logistik. Bei der Erstellung der Aufgaben wurde viel Wert auf die Praxisrelevanz und Authentizität gelegt. Zudem sind die Aufgaben auf unterschiedlichen Niveaustufen angesiedelt und umfassen verschiedene Kompetenzen, um allen Stufen gerecht zu werden und möglichst viele Lerntypen anzusprechen.

Ab dieser vorliegenden vierten Auflage beginnt jede Unit mit einem Überblick über die Lernziele (skills and competencies), die Inhalt der jeweiligen Unit sind. Dazu ist eine Unit-übergreifende Aufgabe an den Anfang gestellt, die sich nach Erarbeitung der Unit beantworten lässt.

Die wichtigsten Vokabeln zu jeder Unit sind jeweils am Ende dieser übersichtlich aufgelistet.

Weiterhin sind alle Aufgaben mit Icons zu den Fertigkeiten versehen, die in der Aufgabe angesprochen werden (Lese-, Hörverständnis, schriftliche und mündliche Sprachproduktion). Dadurch erhalten die Lernenden einen schnellen und guten Überblick über die Fähigkeiten, die mit den Aufgaben geschult werden.

Jede Unit ist zudem mit mindestens einem Hörtext ausgestattet. Gleichzeitig wurde darauf geachtet, insbesondere die kommunikativen Fertigkeiten durch die Aufgabengestaltung zu schulen. Die Activity-Aufgaben sind derart konzipiert, dass sie Redeanlässe schaffen und speziell die Eigenständigkeit und Kreativität der Lernenden fördern. Abgerundet wird jede Einheit durch ein gezieltes Vokabeltraining. Im Lehrerhandbuch finden Sie weitere Hörverständnisaufgaben zu Unit 1 sowie eine Vielzahl ergänzendes Material zu allen Units. Teilweise werden Ihnen auch Alternativen zu bestimmten Aufgaben geboten, damit Sie sie besser auf Ihre Lerngruppe anpassen und ohne weiteren Vorbereitungsaufwand auf unterschiedlichen Niveaustufen unterrichten können.

Unit 1 fungiert lernfeldübergreifend, um eine schnelle Einschätzung der unterschiedlichen Niveaus und einen motivierenden Einstieg ins Thema "Logistik" zu gewährleisten. Die anschließenden Units sind den jeweiligen Lernfeldern zugeordnet. Diese Aufteilung kann auch dem Inhaltsverzeichnis entnommen werden. Neu in dieser Auflage ist die Unit "Skill Files Literature", die einen literarischen Bezug zu dem Berufsfeld bietet.

Das Lehrwerk wird ergänzt durch einen Grammatikteil, der als Nachschlagewerk zu den Grammatikaufgaben der einzelnen Units dient. In allen Units werden die Schüler auf die entsprechenden Seiten in den Skill Files Grammar verwiesen, für den Fall, dass sie Hilfe bei der Bearbeitung benötigen.

Weiterhin findet sich in den Skill Files das umfangreiche Kapitel "Business Communication". Hier werden die Lernenden noch einmal gezielt in ihren kommunikativen Fähigkeiten geschult. Gleichzeitig werden berufsrelevante Themen durch eine motivierende Geschichte miteinander verknüpft, sodass der berufliche Alltag authentisch widergespiegelt wird.

Viel Freude am Lernen und in Ihrem Beruf wünscht Ihnen das Autorenteam

BuchPlusWeb

Die vorliegende Auflage umfasst ein Unit-based Vocabulary sowie ein englisch-deutsches Gesamtvokabelverzeichnis. Um das selbstständige Arbeiten auch in schwachen Lerngruppen zu fördern, kann es sinnvoll sein, auch ein deutsch-englisches Gesamtvokabelverzeichnis anzubieten. Deshalb haben wir für Sie im Internet ein solches bereitgestellt.

Inhaltsverzeichnis

WELCOME TO YOUR NEW JOB

Skills and Competencies

UNIT 1

Dear student,

after working with this unit you will be able to…

- tell others about your apprenticeship and other working experiences.
- use new vocabulary regarding your new job as warehouse operator or warehouse logistics operator.
- talk about numbers and dates.
- describe your daily routine.
- tell the time in more than one way.
- use the simple present and present progressive (present continuous) in the right way.

In each unit you will find a vocabulary training section which may help you to prepare for a class test.

Enjoy!

INDIVIDUAL TASK

Jan has to describe his everyday work including his working hours in his report portfolio. His colleague Rory McLake is from England and has to do the same as part of an exchange programme. He asks Jan to help him with the translation of all the German words.

Describe a typical week at work as if you would do for your report portfolio. Add your working hours, too.

Introducing yourself

In the break Jan, Klaus, Laura and Pjotr are meeting in the cafeteria at their school. Jan greets his friend Laura.

Jan: Hello Laura, that's a surprise. How are you? What are you doing here?
Laura: Hi Jan. I'm fine, thanks, and you? I'm doing an apprenticeship to become a warehouse logistics operator. Are you doing an apprenticeship, too, Klaus?
Klaus: No, I don't have an apprenticeship, yet. At the moment I'm trying to get one to become a warehouse operator. By the way, are you from Jan's company? What is your name again? Peter?
Pjotr: Hi! No, my name is Pjotr. I work with Jan at the same company. How old are you, Klaus?
Klaus: I'm 16 years old. I will get my forklift truck driver's license this year. But I'm not allowed to drive it until I'm 18. How old are you, Laura?
Laura: I'm 18. I'll be 19 next month. I will have a big party then and I need some people to help me because I have some pretty heavy stuff to move. Does anyone of you do sport? Jan, you maybe?
Jan: I like watching movies and going out with friends, but I'm not the sporting type. Pjotr, you look as if you like sport.
Pjotr: That's right. I like weight lifting at the gym and jogging. That's why I like to load and unload containers at our company. Do you like that, too, Klaus?
Klaus: No, I don't like working with containers. I like to pack boxes. In my free-time I play football and I like Hip Hop music, if that's any help, Laura.
Laura: Music is important. I like electronic music and I play the guitar. What is your favourite music, Jan?
Jan: I like Black music and R'n'B. What about you, Pjotr?
Pjotr: I know that it is not everyone's favourite, but I like Metal. Oh, the school bell is ringing. We better go back to our classes. Goodbye everyone and maybe we could talk about your party in the next break, Laura?
Laura: Yeah, that would be nice. Bye, all.
Klaus: See ya.
Jan: Goodbye.

Comprehension

Task 1

Audio

First, listen to the dialogue of the friends Laura, Jan, Klaus and Pjotr.
What are their ages, hobbies, jobs and likes in music? Read the text to check your answers.

Task 2

Find typical phrases for when you meet someone for the first time.

Task 3

Work with a partner.
Both of you copy the table and interview each other.
Fill in the table with the information given by your partner.
One of your class collects all papers and mixes them.
After that he or she reads one out and everyone may guess who is described.

name:	**age:**
	hobbies:
	music:
	job:
	further work experience:
	favourite clothes:

Getting started in a new job

Today is Jan's first day at work. He is looking forward to his apprenticeship. School is over and a new part of his life is beginning. Jan gets up early, has breakfast and takes the bus to the industrial estate. After a seven-minute walk he arrives at *Y-Store – Worldwide Logistics*, a British company with a British boss. First Jan has to go to the office. Mrs Smith works in the personnel department and he needs to give her some documents: the result of his initial medical examination and his social insurance identity card. He has also to tell her his tax identification number. Otherwise he will not receive any money for his work.

The door of the office is open. Mrs Smith is talking to someone on the phone. The second phone is ringing but nobody is there to pick it up because she is on her own. Maybe her colleague is ill, or is going to come later, so she is very busy. Mrs Smith gestures to Jan to take a seat. Jan sits down and waits. He is nervous. It is seven o'clock already and his boss is coming to pick him up from the office. Five minutes later, she finally finishes the phone call and turns to him.

"Hello, Jan. Good morning! Welcome to Y-Store. I'm sure you'll have a successful time with us, so good luck with everything! By the way, do you have the documents we need with you?"

Jan gets up. "Good morning, Mrs Smith. Yes, I do", he answers in English, which is the company language.

"Great!"

Jan gives her the documents and waits while Mrs Smith looks at them.

"Well, everything is okay for you to start work here", she says. "Mr Green is our chief storekeeper or store superintendent if you like. He will fetch you any minute now. If you'd like a cup of coffee while you wait for him, you'll find a coffee machine at the end of this corridor."

Jan is desperate to have a coffee, so he chooses one with milk and sugar to overcome his weariness.

It is twenty-five past seven when a tall man enters the office.

"Hello, good morning, everybody. Ah, you must be Jan! I'm your new boss."

Jan stands up to shake his hand.

"Pleased to meet you, Mr Green."

"Call me Pete – we're quite informal here," his boss smiles. "Hey, Janet, you look worried. Is everything alright here?" he says to Mrs Smith.

"Yes", she answers, "but I'm waiting for a call from Cindy. She hasn't arrived yet."

"I'm sure she'll call you very soon. Right, Jan, let's go to the warehouse. A lorry is already waiting at the ramp. It has just arrived with a lot of goods. We have to unload it, check the boxes and store the goods. Your first task will be to watch the others and help them as soon as you can. We have another apprentice here, Pjotr. I think you already know each other. He is waiting for your assistance. So let's get to work!"

"Yes, great. Pjotr and I met at vocational school. Bye, Mrs Smith", says Jan and gets started with his first day at work.

Task 4

Read the text about Jan's first day at work carefully. Copy and answer the following questions on the text. Write full sentences.

a. Why does Jan have to go to the personnel department?
b. Who works in the personnel department?
c. What is she doing when Jan enters the office?
d. Why is she alone in the office?
e. Who is Mr Green?
f. What is Mr Green's profession called in German?
g. What will Jan's first task be?

Task 5

Find out what the following words mean in German and explain their meaning.

a. initial medical examination
b. social insurance identity card
c. tax identification number

Task 6

Copy and complete the sentences with words from the box:

colleague · apprentice · successful · store · busy
lorry · to work · to unload · goods · job

a. Jan is pleased to have a ...
b. Somebody who is being trained in a company is called a trainee or an ...
c. When somebody has a lot to do, he or she is ...
d. Things you trade in are called ...
e. A big vehicle for transporting goods is called a ...
f. When you take goods from the lorry, you ... it.
g. A big hall where goods are stored is called a ...
h. To earn your money, you have to ...
i. Somebody who works with me is my ...
j. People who do well in their career are ...

Job descriptions

Warehouse Operator and Warehouse Logistics Operator

Duration of apprenticeship
2 years or 3 years in company and part-time vocational school

Field of activity
Warehouse operators and warehouse logistics operators work in industrial, trading, forwarding and service companies. They do everything related to the transfer and storage of goods. Warehouse logistics operators work in the field of warehouse logistics, too.

Occupational skills
Warehouse operators or warehouse logistics operators, for example
- accept goods and check the delivery
- unpack goods, sort and place them into storage according to efficient warehouse systems
- pick and pack goods for delivery
- load and unload lorries
- use storage equipment such as forklift trucks or handtrucks
- use foreign language terminology where necessary

Warehouse logistics operators also
- handle storage documentary and also forwarding documents
- plan and organise cargo tours
- use foreign language terminology

Task 7

Read the texts above carefully and answer the following questions by writing keywords:

1. What is the name of your profession?
2. How long is the duration of your apprenticeship?
3. Which field of activity is your company related to?
4. Which occupational skills have you achieved so far?

Numbers, dates and times

What's the time?

Task 8

Copy the times and write down the times in words.

1	12:00	2	00:00
3	07:15	4	10:30
5	14:45	6	08:35
7	18:47	8	17:21
9	13:24	10	21:13

Listening

My daily routine

Task 9

a. **This is Laura Märtens. She is an apprentice and wants to become a warehouse logistics operator. Listen to her daily routine.**

Hello, my name is Laura Märtens. This is my daily routine. I get up at quarter to five in the morning.

I go to work by train. I need one hour to get there.

At quarter past seven I'm at work. The first thing I do is to get myself some coffee. After that, I check the incoming goods.
Then I pick the new orders:
I check our stock records, extract the needed goods, pack them, label them and send them to the outgoing goods department.
From time to time I'm in the customer service department, where I have to answer the phone and do the correspondence.

I have two breaks:
My first break is at nine o'clock in the morning and I have lunch in my second break at half past one in the afternoon.

My work ends at half past five.

When I'm home I usually phone a friend so we can meet. Sometimes we go to the cinema and sometimes we watch a show on TV.

I go to bed at about ten o' clock in the night. That's why I'm always tired.

b. **What does your daily routine look like? Write a text about your typical day at work.**

Grammar

Simple Present and Present Progressive (Present Continuous)

Task 10

Copy the sentences and fill in the correct form of the simple present.

a. I ... (to work) in a warehouse.
b. David ... (to be) a warehouse operator.
c. Mrs Smith ... (to go) to work at 8 a.m.
d. We ... (to be) a logistics company.
e. Our company ... (to store) goods.
f. Where ... you ... (to work)?
g. I ... (not, to drive) a forklift truck.
h. Which languages ... you ... (to speak)?
i. The colleague ... (not, to come) to work on Fridays.
j. Jan ... (to take) the bus to work, because he ... (not, to have) a car.

Task 11

Copy the sentences and fill in the correct form of the present progressive (present continuous).

a. At the moment, Mrs Smith ... (to talk) on the phone.
b. We ... (to check) the new goods right now.
c. I ... (to read) the newspaper.
d. Tim is not here. He ... (to load) the goods onto the lorry.
e. Look, it ... (to rain).
f. The lorry ... (to wait) at the ramp.
g. "... you ... (to drink) a cup of coffee?" – "No, it's tea."
h. I ... not ... (to work) at the moment, it's my break.
i. "What ... (to do) there?"
j. "I ... (to read) the labels."

Task 12

Copy the sentences and fill in the right form of the simple present or the present progressive (present continuous).

a. Today he ... (not, to be) in the office. At the moment he ... (to give) a conference in the meeting room.
b. I ... (to talk) on the phone right now. Can you please wait for a moment?
c. Don't forget to cover the goods. It ... (to rain).
d. Lorries ... (normally, to transport) the goods.
e. Usually, I ... (to work) as a warehouse logistics operator at Y-Store Logistics in Hamburg, but this summer I ... (to work) for them in England.
f. Sorry, I can't talk to you, we ... (to have) a lesson right now.

Task 13

Copy the sentences and translate them from German into English.

a. Ich arbeite in einem großen Lager.
b. Brauchst du Hilfe?
c. Frau Perlman ist immer noch am Telefon.
d. Er gibt ihr die Pickliste und geht zurück ins Büro.
e. Meine Firma hat viele englische Kunden.
f. Tut mir leid, ich muss zur Arbeit.
g. Das Geschäft ist am Montag nicht geöffnet.
h. Im Pausenraum gibt es auch eine Pantryküche mit Mikrowelle.
i. Wir haben einen neuen Gabelstapler im Lager.
j. Dürfen wir eine Pause machen?

For help see Skill Files Grammar pages 130f.

Activity

Interview and Poster

Task 14

Work with a partner:
Interview your partner about his or her work. Take turns and present your work to the class on a poster like in the example below.

name

name of the company
company's address
company's post code

class

working hours:
e.g. He works from ... o'clock until ... o'clock.

breaks:
e.g. He has a break from ... o'clock until ... o'clock.

occupational skills achieved so far:
e.g. He learned to unload lorries.
He started to practise for his driver's license for the forklift truck.

further work experience:
e.g. He had an internship at ... (name of company) as ... (profession)

Vocabulary trainer

Matching Words

Task 15

Copy the words below and match the correct English and German words.

apprenticeship	Sekretärin
warehouse operator	Lagermeister
goods	Fachkraft für Lagerlogistik
personnel department	kontrollieren
secretary	Ware
lorry	entladen
ramp	LKW
to check	Personalabteilung
to unload	Rampe
warehouse logistics operator	Ausbildung
chief storekeeper	Fachlagerist

Word Bank

apprenticeship · apprentice · warehouse logistics operator · warehouse operator · goods · forklift truck · to pick · to label · to check · to load and to unload · to extract to pack and to unpack · lorry · industrial, trading, forwarding and service companies · delivery · forwarding document · cargo · vocational school · stock records · customer service department · outgoing goods department

RECEIVING A NEW SHIPMENT

Skills and Competencies

UNIT 2

Dear student,

after working with this unit you will be able to …

- name different departments in the warehouse.
- describe the process of receiving a new shipment.
- express the flow of goods.
- check incoming packages and goods.
- name different important warehousing documents.
- identify problems with a delivery.
- use the simple past in the right way.

At the end of this unit you will find a vocabulary training section which may help you to prepare for a class test.

Enjoy!

INDIVIDUAL TASK

Klaus wants to study for a class test. He has to identify every station in the warehouse which handles goods. He has to know the names of every department and needs to be able to describe what is done there.

Klaus has problems with texts, so his friend Laura tells him to draw a picture, because that could help him to memorize the departments.

Draw a picture containing all the stations that deal with goods in the warehouse.
Name each department.
Describe how the goods are handled in the departments. Use keywords.

A new delivery

Jan is working in the truck dispatch when a driver of a forwarding agency enters with a delivery note and an invoice. Jan checks if the shipment is for the company by checking the address on the delivery note. After the delivery note is stamped and signed, he sends the driver to a non-occupied ramp.
In the incoming goods department, Pjotr unloads the lorry and performs a visual check. For the receipt of goods he has to check again that the packages are for the company, that there is no damage and that the number of packages is correct. If everything is alright the delivery note is signed with "goods delivered in apparently good condition". The driver then leaves with a copy of the delivery note.
In the quality control department a random sampling is performed for the immediate product testing by the chief storekeeper, Mr Green. He checks the goods for identity, quantity, quality and condition. A check is then carried out to ensure that it is the correct part, the correct quantity of goods and if there is any damage to them. It is also checked if the quality corresponds to what was ordered. To do this, he needs the following forwarding documents: delivery note and packing list. The order of the company is also needed for a comparison.

Mr Green compares the contents with the delivery note and the order. He finds out that one item is missing and one part has not been ordered. So he writes a letter to the supplier asking him to deliver the missing part within a fortnight. The part that has not been ordered is sent back. Meanwhile, the goods are transported to the shelves in the store by Pjotr, with the help of a hand truck.
Finally, the goods are entered into the stock list by the accountant, Mrs Phills in the accounts department. She enters the article number of the parts and adds the quantity that arrived. Later the invoice is compared with the order and the offer to check whether the prices are correct.

Comprehension

Task 1

Read the text carefully. Divide the text into different units of meaning. Sum up the units of meaning.

Task 2

Copy the following questions on the text and answer them.
Write keywords if not mentioned otherwise. Write down the lines where you found the information.

a. Which persons are involved in the receipt of goods and in which department do they work?

b. What is checked when the shipment is received and how is it done? Write about six sentences.
c. What is the checking called that is performed in question 2?
d. What is checked in the quality control department: goods or packages?
e. What is the difference between the receipt of goods and the immediate product testing?
f. What are the items checked for in the quality control department? Name the four aspects and describe their meaning. Write one full sentence for each aspect.
g. What is it called when a single item is picked out of a shipment and gets checked?
h. Which documents are needed for the receiving, checking and storing of goods?

Task 3

Answer the questions below.
Therefore copy the mind map and fill in the information given in the text "A new delivery".

a. Which persons are involved with a new delivery and where do they work?
b. Which documents are needed to check the delivery?
c. What do you check on the packages?
d. What do you check on the goods? And what do the keywords mean?

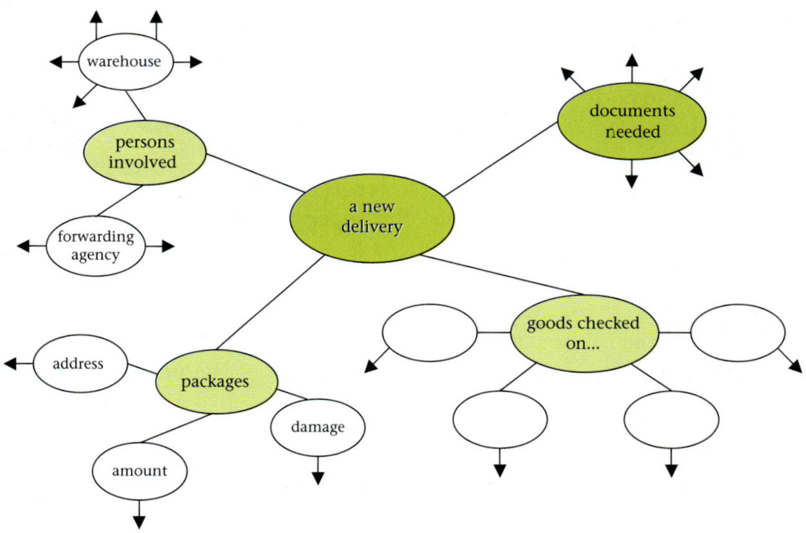

Problems with the delivery

Sometimes problems may occur with a delivery as mentioned in the text. You have to be very careful when you do the receipt of goods or the immediate product testing.

Task 4

Find the problems with the shipment in the text.

Which aspects of the following four have been harmed: identity, quality, quantity or condition?

Listening

Task 5

Listen to the different situations and decide which problem is described.

fault	corresponding aspect
over-delivery/short delivery	quantity
damage	condition
wrong article	identity
feature/quality	quality

Flow of goods – departments in the warehouse

You already know that there are a lot of different departments in the warehouse. For example, Laura told you in Unit 1 that she sometimes has to work in the customer service department, where she has to deal with the customers of her company. Jan only worked in the truck dispatch once. Not every company has a truck dispatch. Most of them are located in the port.
There are some other departments which may be more common to you. A flow of goods describes to which departments goods are taken while they stay in the warehouse.

Comprehension

Task 6

The departments of the flow of goods are mixed up.

a. Put the departments in the right order.
   Begin with the department where the packages arrive and end with the one where the packages leave the warehouse. You already know these words from Unit 1.

outgoing goods department · picking department · incoming goods department · packing department · storage · quality control department

b. Now assign the following activities to the department in which they take place.
   Attention: There can be more than one activity for each department!

pack extracted goods · extract goods from shelves with picking list · label packages · check goods on identity, quality, quantity, condition · check shipment on address, amount and damage · ship packages to customer · store goods · receipt of goods · care of goods · immediate product testing

c. Translate the complete flow of goods into German.

The accounts department

This department may not be very well-known to you, but it is very important for every day work and, of course, for your wages.
The accounts department can be divided into different subsections. Accountants manage all money matters of a company.
For example:

- In the wages department the wages of all employees are administered
- In the financial department they deal with invoices and reminders.
- In the inventory department the stock is checked regularly, orders and picking lists are made and complaints are dealt with.

Task 7

a. The text "A new delivery" tells you more about the inventory department. Describe what is also done in this department.
b. Which of the employees' documents does the wages department need? See Unit 1 for help where Jan goes to the personnell department to give his documents to Mrs Smith on page 11.

Grammar

Simple Past

Task 8

Copy the sentences and fill in the correct forms of the simple past.

a. Last week, I ... (to work) overtime.
b. The delivery ... (to be) late.
c. We ... (not, to get) the goods on time.
d. ... you ... (to check) the delivery that ... (to come) this morning?
e. The lorry ... (to leave) the warehouse at 10 a.m.
f. I ... (to get) an order from a new customer on Monday.
g. Sorry, but we ... (not, to order) this item.
h. "... (to be) the delivery alright?"
i. "Yes, I ... (to sign) the delivery note."

Task 9

Form questions in the simple past on an extra sheet.

a. when / you / get/ the goods?
b. the colleague / check / all the boxes?
c. where / the boss / go?
d. how / the driver / transport / the pallets?

e. you / see / the container/ yesterday?
f. when / the boss / order / the items?
g. what / you / do / in the office?
h. you / know / the size of the goods?
i. why / you / call / the customer?

For help see Skill Files Grammar page 133f.

Activity

Writing an essay

Task 10

a. Write an essay...

What kind of goods are delivered?
How do you perform the receipt of goods?
How is the immediate product testing carried out?
Who enters the new articles into the stock list?
Who is involved in the receiving and checking of goods?

b. First, ask your chief storekeeper for permission to take pictures during work.

Take pictures of the different situations when you receive a new shipment.
Follow the questions above when taking the pictures to visualise your essay.
Make a poster with your text and your photographs and present it to the class.

Vocabulary Trainer

Word Search

Task 11

Fifteen words are hidden in the word search puzzle. Copy the word puzzle and find the words. Who of you is quickest?
The words are arranged diagonally, horizontally or vertically.

C	N	C	L	Q	W	K	R	P	V	C	J	J	T	T
W	C	J	M	Z	E	F	F	D	Q	H	K	P	L	L
F	X	E	T	T	Q	K	I	I	N	V	O	I	C	E
R	T	P	H	E	D	P	T	T	V	H	P	E	G	T
I	O	E	D	B	X	V	H	T	R	Z	G	T	H	S
C	O	R	R	E	S	P	O	N	D	A	F	G	A	U
D	I	F	I	L	E	O	O	F	K	E	I	O	M	P
E	V	O	R	Y	L	B	N	C	R	N	D	Q	O	P
L	V	R	F	K	O	T	A	A	T	F	A	K	U	L
I	I	M	S	Y	F	P	L	R	Z	H	M	H	N	I
V	R	Y	A	B	F	C	O	G	B	C	A	B	T	E
E	B	S	P	R	E	F	F	J	V	V	G	Y	L	R
R	P	Q	B	D	R	S	H	I	P	M	E	N	T	Y
Y	X	A	R	S	C	O	N	T	E	N	T	S	Q	M
E	H	D	S	X	Q	W	L	X	Z	O	R	D	E	R

fortnight · correspond · shipment · supplier · invoice · declare · package · damage · contents · delivery · order · item · amount · offer · perform

Task 12

Form a sentence with each of the words you find.

Word Bank

forwarding agency · forwarding document · delivery note · invoice · order · to sign · incoming goods department · picking department · quality control department · packing department · accounts department · quality · quantity · identity · condition · damage · shipment · flow of goods

SAFETY AT WORK
Skills and Competencies

UNIT 3

Dear student,

after working with this unit you will be able to ...

- identify the five types of safety signs.
- name different safety signs.
- understand the importance of safety measures at work.
- identify adequate safety measures.
- write an accident report.
- give instructions for safety measures with modal verbs.

At the end of this unit you will find a vocabulary training section which may help you to prepare for a class test.

Enjoy!

INDIVIDUAL TASK

Laura has to give a talk at school. The topic is how safety signs at work can prevent dangerous accidents. For starters she wants to show pictures of accidents. She asks Klaus if he could have a look at the pictures and guess, which safety signs could have prevented the accidents. After all, he is the expert in reading and understanding the meaning of safety signs.

Have a look at Laura's pictures on the next page.
Which safety sign(s) could have prevented the following accidents?

1

2
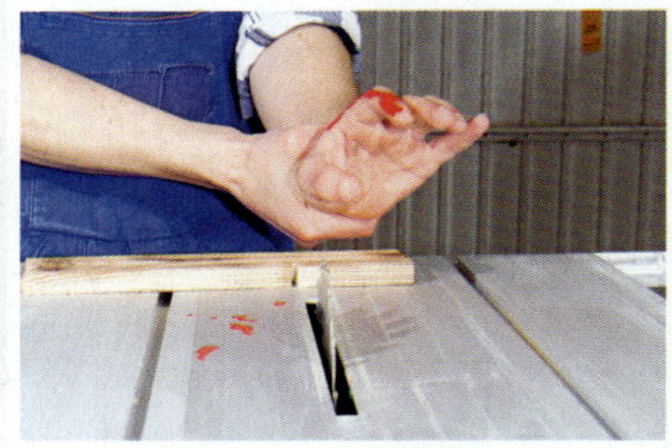

3

4

5

Safety First

Comprehension

Task 1

Describe what you see in the pictures on the next page and try to tell the story of poor Klaus' first day at work.

Listening

Task 2

Now listen to the story of Klaus and try to list all the mistakes he made on an extra sheet of paper. Also write down what his boss, Mr Schwartz, should have done better.

Comprehension

Error analysis

Klaus talks to his friend Jan about his miserable day. To avoid making the same mistakes again, Jan suggests doing an error analysis.
Klaus made several mistakes while working in the incoming goods department.
Help Klaus and Jan with their error analysis.

Task 3

Now formulate some advice to prevent the mistakes Klaus made, which you found in task 2. Write full sentences.

Safety Signs

Klaus learned a hard lesson: some accidents result from carelessness, others are a result of a lack of protection. Nevertheless, it is most important to protect not only the equipment in the warehouse but also the people working there.
Safety signs like the one Klaus ignored are a way of warning of special danger or of giving necessary instructions. So they help to prevent dangerous accidents. One has to know the signs to fully understand them. There are five different types of signs: prohibition signs, warning signs, mandatory signs, emergency signs and fire safety signs.
Prohibition signs are round signs with a white background and a red border and crossbar. They mean that something is forbidden. Warning signs are triangular signs with a yellow background, black border and a black symbol. They warn about special danger. Mandatory signs are round signs with a blue background and a white symbol. They show you what protective equipment you have to wear, like safety boots or a hard hat. Emergency signs are square or rectangular signs with white symbols on a green background. For example, they tell you where to go in case of a fire. Fire safety signs are square signs with white symbols on a red background. They indicate where the fire fighting equipment or the alarm, for example, can be found.

Task 4

Make a list of the five types of safety signs as in the example.
Write down what they look like and what their function is.
Then translate the sentences into German.

safety signs	description	function
prohibition signs	round signs, white background, red border and crossbar runde Zeichen ...	mean that something is forbidden bedeuten, dass ...
mandatory signs	...	...
warning signs	...	...
emergency signs	...	...
fire safety signs	...	...

Task 5

Match the pictures with the correct English expression that you find in the box.
Find the correct German translation.
Also write down which type of sign it is.

fire alarm · wear safety gloves · danger! high voltage! · fire extinguisher · no pedestrians · manual fire alarm · wear hard hat · no industrial trucks · slippery when wet · fire hose · wear safety boots · emergency call · no stacking · beware of explosives · wear ear protection · no cardiac pacemaker · beware of floating load · eye shower · gathering point · heart defibrillator · use safety belt · no smoking · beware of industrial trucks · wear goggles · emergency exit · no open fire · first-aid kit · fire fighting equipment · inflammable

Grammar

Giving instructions with modal verbs

GEBOTE: (müssen)	**You must** **You have to**	go to school. go to school.
VERBOTE: (nicht dürfen)	**You must not** **You are not allowed to** **(It is not allowed to**	smoke in the classroom. smoke in the classroom. smoke in the classroom.)

This sign says "You must wear safety boots".

Or you can say "…"

This sign says: "You must not light a fire here".

You can also say "…"

Task 6

Now please write down an instruction for the following safety signs:

For help see Skill Files Grammar pages 138f.

Activity

How to behave in case of an accident

Klaus will never forget his first day at work. He will have to live with his broken leg for a while. Nevertheless, he was lucky. Under the circumstances, he could have been even more badly injured. Now he will follow all the rules and safety instructions.

Even if all the rules are obeyed, some accidents still happen. The question is: What should you do when you witness an accident? There is some helpful advice you should learn by heart to act correctly in case of an accident.

You must perform first-aid if you can, and call emergency, if the one who has had the accident cannot do it alone. Give the following information when you call emergency:

- what happened
- where it happened
- how many people are involved
- who is calling and how you can be reached and then
- wait for questions

Task 7

Generate a role play in which you call emergency because a colleague has had an accident.
Work in pairs and present the role play to your classmates.
Follow the above advice when calling emergency.
Use one of the following situations or invent one on your own:

a. Your colleague has had an accident with a forklift truck. The truck skipped to one side and he is lying unconscious under it. You saw what happened and call emergency. (2 people required: the caller and the operator)
b. You cut your finger very deeply while you were cutting the stretch foil. You're trying to stop the bleeding with a tissue and get a colleague to call emergency for you. (3 people required: the caller, the one who had the accident and the operator)
c. Your foot was run over by a fast armature. It really hurts, you have to sit down, because you can't put any weight on it. You get your mobile phone and call emergency. (2 people required: the one who had the accident and the operator)
d. You tried to lift a sack weighing 45 kilograms. Suddenly your back hurts really bad and you can't straighten up again. After five more minutes you call emergency as you still can't move. (2 people required: the one who had the accident and the operator)
e. You saw a colleague unpacking dangerous goods. Suddenly one of the cans slipped and some liquid came pouring out. Your colleague wasn't wearing safety gloves, so the liquid ran over his hand. Now he is crying and shouting - it really seems to hurt. You call emergency for him. (2 people required: the caller and the operator)

Vocabulary Trainer

Accident report

Task 8

Klaus has to write an accident report for the health insurance.
Help him to fill out the form by describing how the accident at the beginning of this unit happened.
Therefore copy the accident report form on the next page.

Accident Report

Name: ______________________________

Address: ______________________________

____

Company: ______________________________

Address: ______________________________

____

Job title: ______________________________

Course of events

Date of accident: ____________ Time of accident: ____________

Place of accident: ______________________________

Were you doing your work while the accident happened? ☐ yes ☐ no

Any witnesses? yes ☐ no ☐

Names of the witnesses: ______________________________

____

Please describe the course of events of the accident:

____

____

____

____

____

____

____

date & signature

Word Bank

safety sign · mandatory sign · fire safety sign · prohibition sign · emergency sign · warning sign · accident · equipment · to protect · gloves · hard hat · goggles · gathering point · emergency (exit) · safety belt · industrial truck · inflammable · cardiac pacemaker · heart defibrillator · fire extinguisher · accident report

DIFFERENT TYPES OF WAREHOUSES AND THEIR EQUIPMENT

UNIT 4

Skills and Competencies

Dear student,

after working with this unit you will be able to …

- decide which warehouse is appropriate for which goods.
- name the different types of warehousing.
- identify various racking systems.
- talk about different types of forklift trucks and their equipment.
- know the correct English terms for tools and equipment around the warehouse.
- list different handling and hoisting equipment.
- explain what is meant by *FiFo*, *LiFo* and *HiFo*.
- decide when to use the simple present and simple past.

At the end of this unit you will find a vocabulary training section which may help you to prepare for a class test.

Enjoy!

INDIVIDUAL TASK

Pete Green, the chief storekeeper, is assigned to plan the new storage area at Y-Store. He talks to his apprentices Jan, Pjotr and Rory about it and asks them about their opinion.

Jan: "This isn't easy. What kind of goods will be stored …"
Klaus: "Can the goods be stacked in their packages or do they need special care?"
Rory: "And isn't this here some kind of dangerous good? Doesn't it need to be stored in a special place?"

Jan: "Pfft, there are awful lots of possibilities. How does the warehouse even need to be built? Open, half-open, closed?"
Klaus: "Will we have bulk cargo or what?"
Rory: "I think, we should start with the goods and how they need to be handled. Then let's decide on the construction of the warehouse."
Klaus: "And then we can decide, which racks and therefore which handling and hoisting equipment we need."
Pete: "Perfect, I knew, I can count on you, boys."
Jan: "What are you waiting for? Let's get to work."

Have a look at the goods in the pictures.

What kind of warehouse does Y-Store need to build for these goods?
Choose one good and decide:

- how the warehouse has to be built,
- which type of storage and therefore
- which racks and
- which handling and hoisting systems are needed.

Give a short presentation talking about your ideas and explaining them.

Different types of warehouses

Dividing warehouses according to types of businesses

There are different types of businesses in the economy which require different types of warehouses. For example, there are trading companies, service companies and production companies. The latter are divided into industrial companies and crafts enterprises. Trading companies are also divided into wholesale trade and retail trade.
Trading companies provide goods and sell them to their customers, while production companies make goods themselves. Service companies offer different services like transportation, for example.

What kinds of warehouses do different types of businesses need?

As already mentioned, industrial companies manufacture goods. Therefore they need the following types of storage:

- *goods receiving warehouse:* the components for building/ producing the goods are received in the incoming goods department. After the visual check they are either

forwarded to the production directly or placed in the storage.
- *material warehouse:* basic materials, auxiliary materials and consumables can be stored together or separately.
- *spare parts warehouse:* this warehouse stores tools and spare parts which are used up fast.
- *production warehouse:* this warehouse is divided into *manual warehouse* and *intermediate warehouse,* and is located in the production area. Components that are needed for the production are transferred from the material warehouse to the manual warehouse. Semi-finished goods are stored in the intermediate warehouse.
- *dispatch warehouse:* this is a general term for finished goods warehouses, distributing warehouses and special storage areas. In the first one, the finished goods are stored before they get packed in the distributing warehouse. Special storage areas are needed for office materials or materials for packing.

Trading companies need other warehouses. Wholesale companies need the following types of warehouses:
- *order picking warehouse:* here all the goods are kept for picking customers' orders.
- *commission warehouse:* in this warehouse foreign goods are stored before they are sold under the name of the owner. The stock keepers are called commission agents. They are never the owners of the goods but rather intermediaries.
- *consignment warehouse:* goods that belong to the supplier are stored in the consignment warehouse of the customer. They belong to the supplier until the customer extracts the goods. An invoice is then created.

Retail companies need the following types of warehouses:
- *sales warehouse:* some stores are built as sales warehouses. There customers can buy the goods, which are advertised and stored ready to hand.

- *sample warehouse:* in this warehouse, customers can decide upon a sample before purchasing a product. After the purchase contract is concluded the item can be delivered or picked up in the reserve warehouse.
- *reserve warehouse:* before goods are stored in the sales warehouse, they are received, checked and labelled in the reserve warehouse. As mentioned above, customers can also collect their goods here.

How to build a warehouse – Dividing warehouses according to construction

Warehouses need to meet a great range of demands. When designing a warehouse, the company has to consider the goods that will be stored as well as other aspects, like the logistics of storage and shops.
First, the company must decide whether they will store the goods in their *own warehouse* or in a *third-party warehouse.*
Then they need to know if the goods are only used in one place or if the company oper-

ates in different cities or countries. Hence they decide to build either *central* or *decentralized warehouses*.

Of course, the types of goods are also very important. How does the warehouse need to be built? Open, half open or closed? An example of an *open warehouse* is the *open-air storage* where goods are kept in the open without surrounding walls or a ceiling. When it comes to *closed warehouses,* we distinguish between *flat store, floor store, highrise rack store, tank store, airhall store* and *special warehouses*.

A *flat store* is a one-floor warehouse not higher than seven metres in which goods can be stored in shelves or on the floor. When consisting of multiple floors, the warehouse is called a *floor store*. There you need elevators and stairs to connect the floors. There are two different ways to build a *highrise rack warehouse:* one, you build the rack first and then the walls, or two, you first construct the building and then you put the rack inside. The first type of construction is called *silo construction*, while the second one is called rack *installation construction*.

A *bunker / silo / tank* store is needed if you want to store solid, liquid or gaseous substances. An *airhall* store is inflated like a balloon. It can only be entered through airlocks. Due to its fast and cheap construction, it is often used as emergency storage. If goods require special handling because they are hazardous, likely to be stolen or anything, a *special warehouse* is needed.

Next you have to decide whether it is more suitable to store your goods in a *floor* storage or in a *rack storage*. If your racks are the deciding factor, there are several kinds of racking systems, all of which will be explained later in this unit.

The last aspects to consider are the types of handling and hoisting equipment, such as forklift trucks, handtrucks or conveyors, for example.

Task 1

a. Create a chart with all the different warehouses divided according to the types of businesses like in the example below.

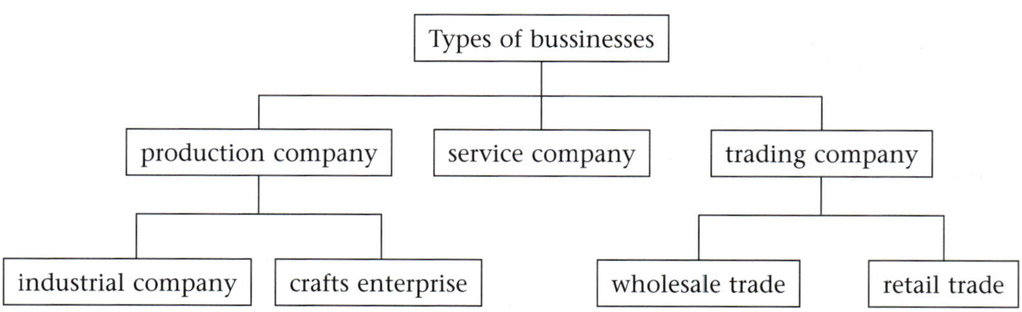

b. Find the English expressions in the text above for the German terms inside this box:

Konsignationslager · Handlager · Musterlager · Wareneingangslager · Werkzeug-/Ersatzteillager · Zwischenlager · Auslieferungs-/Versandlager · Absatzlager · Materiallager · Reservelager · Kommissionslager · Produktionslager · Fertigwaren-/Erzeugnislager · Verkaufslager · Sonderlager

c. How are the different types of businesses called in German? Add the expressions to the chart.

Task 2

Describe the difference between having your *own warehouse* and using a *third-party warehouse* and name the German expressions for both.

Task 3

What are the advantages and disadvantages of having your *own warehouse* compared to using a *third-party warehouse*? Make a list.

Task 4

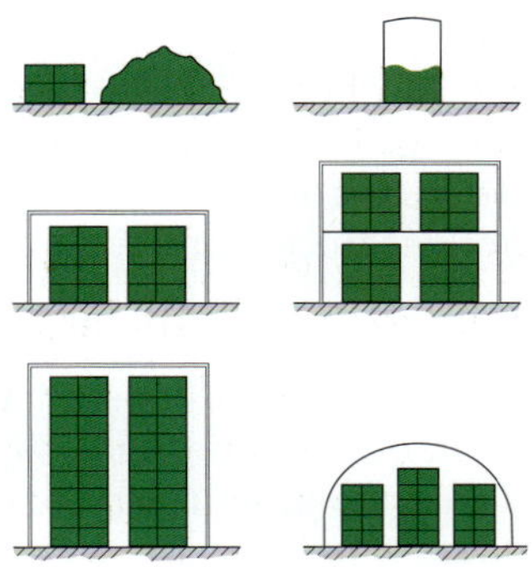

a. Look at the pictures and name them with the English terms for the warehouses from the text.
b. Now match the following German words with the English terms.

Tanklager · Traglufthallenlager · Hochregallager · Silolager · offenes Lager / Freilager · Etagenlager · Bunkerlager · Flachlager

Task 5

Which goods can be stored in the following warehouses? Find examples.

a. flat store
b. special warehouse
c. tank store

Task 6

What are the German expressions for the following words? Explain their meaning.

a) on-floor storage
b) rack storage

Lifting, transporting and stacking goods

Different types of equipment in the warehouse

To operate a warehouse different equipment is necessary. Some warehouses need more equipment than others. On the one hand it depends on the kind of goods which should be stored and on the other hand it also depends on how modern the warehouse is.

The equipment can be classified into the following types:

Handling and hoisting equipment
Continuous acting handling and hoisting equipment normally works nonstop. These items have unchanging routes of transport. This equipment is for example: *conveyor, slide, bucket elevator, belt conveyor*

Sporadic acting handling and hoisting equipment is for lifting, stacking and transporting goods. This equipment, which has to be operated by authorized personnel, is divided into two different types:

Hoisting devices
elevator, hoisting platform, overhead crane, gantry crane

Ground conveyor
forklift truck, hand forklift truck, rack access equipment

Tools
There are a lot different tools that you need in warehouses. Some are used more often than others. It depends on what kind of warehouse you work at.
Often tools are needed to check, to open and to pack goods properly. In special warehouses, tools are needed for example to pull out coffee samples or to block and secure goods.

Comprehension

Task 7

a. **What are the advantages and disadvantages of continuous acting handling and hoisting equipments? Make a list.**
b. **What are the advantages and disadvantages of sporadic acting handling and hoisting equipments? Make a list.**
c. **Compare the two systems and decide when which system should be used.**

Tools and equipment

Task 8

Find the right English names for the tools and the equipment out of the box below. What are the German terms?

1
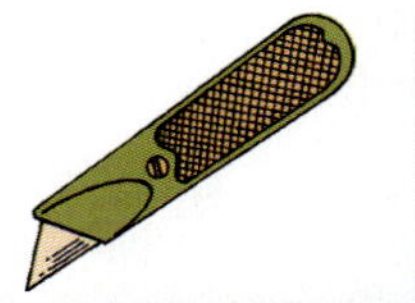
2

3
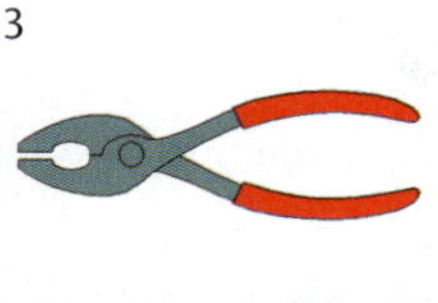
4
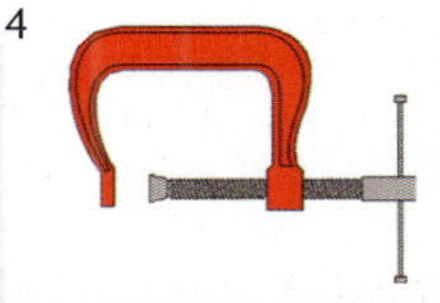
5

6

7

8

9

10

11

12

13
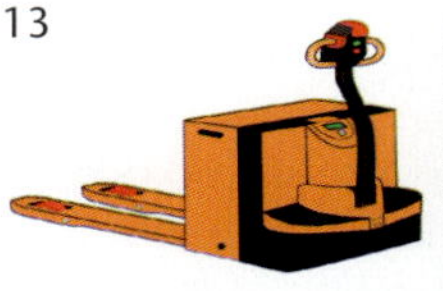
14

15

16
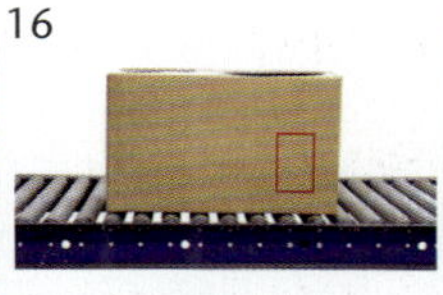

utility knife · clamp · electric drill · nails and screws · hammer · pallet · forklift truck · hand forklift truck · pallet truck · counting scale · adhesive tape · strapping tool · conveyor · folding ruler · pliers · nail gun

Task 9

What do you think: What is the difference between a tool and a piece of equipment?

Racking systems

Racking systems allow well arranged storing. They are also usable for non-stackable goods and can be adjusted to the goods which need to be stored.

The storing of goods can be static or dynamic.

1. Static storing means that the stored goods are not moved from the stock placement to the stock removal.
   - **pallet racks** – They are for the storage of palletised goods. They don't have shelf boards but supporting beams on which the pallets are placed. They are suitable for the storage of large quantities per article.
   - **drive-in pallet racks** – They have one open face side per aisle into which the forklift truck drives to insert or retrieve pallets. The pallets are placed one after the other on the supporting beams. The lifo-principle (last in – first out) applies here.
   - **modular racks** – They are for the storage of non-palletised goods. Primarily they are used as single- and multi-storey picking storage. The shelf board height can be varied.
   - **high-rise racks** – Goods can be stored space-savingly since they have a high utilisation of available floor space. The racks are separated from each other by aisles. Goods are stored mainly in lattice boxes and on flat pallets.
   - **comb racks** – Primarily long goods such as thread rod and pipes are stored on this rack. The long goods are inserted from the face side of the rack.
2. Dynamic storing means that goods are moved during their shelf life limit. The goods can be moved in the following stationary racking systems:
   - **push-back pallet racks** – Most palletised loading units are stored on roller conveyors with an up to 5% slope. The rack is loaded from one long side. Stored goods are pushed back when new goods are added. Therefore, the lifo-principle applies.
   - **continuous racks** – They have separate input and output of goods. Because of a slope goods move from the input to the output of the rack. Slopes higher than 8% require a braking system. The fifo-principle (first in – first out) is possible if the same articles are stored on the rack.
3. Or the stationary goods are moved with these racking systems:
   - **mobile racks** – With the help of a crank or a single motor the individual rack can be pushed sideways so that an aisle opens between two racks. The utilisation of the storage space is very good as just one single aisle is required for the rapid access to all stored goods.
   - **carousel/rotating racks** – The input and output of goods are at a fixed point. The racks move either horizontally or vertically. The picking system "goods to man" is realised.

Task 10

Explain which types of racks are shown in the picture and for which types of goods they are suitable.

Task 11

Find the English expressions out of the text for the following German terms.

Einfahrregal · Verschieberegal · Umlaufregal · Durchlaufregal · Palettenregal · Fachbodenregal · Hochregal · Wabenregal · Einschubregal

Task 12

Copy the questions on the text and answer them.

a. What kind of goods are stored in a modular rack?
b. Which of the given information for the continuous rack is correct?
   1. A single-item insertion is not wise.
   2. The fifo-principle is possible.
   3. The tilt angle of the ducts must be over 8°.
c. Why is the storage of e.g. folders in mobile racks much more space-saving than in fixed modular racks?
d. Explain the picking system "goods to man".
e. Which rack system realizes this picking system?
f. Which advantage does a high-rise rack have?
g. What is the difference between static and dynamic storage?

Listening

Different types of forklift trucks and their equipment

In the storage, Jan learns how to use modern machinery such as handtrucks and forklift trucks, which makes work easier. Jan's colleagues show him how to use the handtruck, but he is not allowed to operate the forklifter without a licence. Jan has to be patient until he has his own licence. He has to be of age. He also has to pass a theoretical and a practical test. He will need to learn about weights and measures, how to start the forklift, how fast it may be driven, how to turn it, how high it may be loaded and

other important and useful things. Jan has already learned how to use some tools to open, check and pack goods. For example, he uses a utility knife, a handscanner and stretch film.
But right now, he is eager to learn about the different types of forklift trucks and their attachments.

Audio

Task 13

**a. Listen to the descriptions of the forklift trucks.
Match the English expressions with the pictures.**

1

2

3

4

Reach-Stacker · man-carrying platform · Straddle Carrier · clamp

**b. Listen to the descriptions again.
Which information in the box belongs to which forklift truck?
Use an extra sheet to write them down.**

vehicle for use in ports only · can lift up to two full containers · also known as Gantry Lift, "Van Carrier" or "Portalhubwagen" · used to lift persons · has a spreader at the end of an arm · can move as fast as 30 km/h · used for carrying and storing goods without pallets · an alternative to gantry cranes · used for handling intermodal cargo containers in small terminals

Grammar

Simple Present or Simple Past

Task 14

Copy the sentences and fill in the right form of the verbs in the simple present or simple past.

a. Jan often ... (to use) a handtruck.
b. Yesterday Klaus ... (to drive) a forklift truck.
c. On Sundays he usually ... (not/to go) to work.
d. Last week Laura ... (to write) a complaint.
e. Her colleague ... (to learn) how to use the right equipment during his/her apprenticeship.
f. Another colleague ... (to have) an accident with the hoisting platform last year.
g. In 2011 the company ... (to buy) new shelf access equipment.
h. Jan often ... (to ask) Klaus to help him, when he ... (to have) a problem.
i. Continuous acting equipment generally ... (to save) a lot of time.
j. Klaus always ... (to store) the goods on the shelves.

For help see Skill Files Grammar pages 130f.

Activity

Accidents with the forklift truck

Task 15

Work with a partner. Choose one of the eight pictures and describe it. Your partner has to guess which one you have described. Then he/she has to give advice on how the accident or the wrong handling could have been avoided.
Take turns.

1

2

3

4

5

6

7

8

Task 16

What do you have to do before you start the engine of the forklift truck to guarantee a safe tour with it?

Vocabulary Trainer

Different racking systems

Task 17

Read the explanations and match them with correct racking system listed in the box below.

a. This rack uses a crane or motor to open an aisle between two racks. Many goods can be stored in a small storage space.
b. The rack is twelve metres and higher. Warehouses with this racking system often have a fully electronically regulated warehouse management system.
c. The racks are mainly for goods on pallets or in lattice boxes. The racks can be adjusted to the size of the palletised goods.
d. This rack is used for the space-saving storage of long goods. These are inserted from the face side.
e. The goods move on roller conveyors through the rack to the output. The fifo-principle is possible if the rack is loaded with the same articles.

comb rack · pallet rack · mobile rack · continuous rack · high-rise rack

Word Bank

floor (storage) · rack storage · third-party warehouse · own warehouse · commission warehouse · retail company · wholesale company · production company · crafts enterprise · spare-parts · handling and hoisting equipment · conveyor · continuous and sporadic acting · tool · racking system · rack access equipment · (drive-in) pallet rack · modular rack · high-rise rack · comb rack · push-back pallet rack · continuous rack · mobile rack · carousel/rotating rack · ground conveyor · reach stacker · straddle carrier · clamp · man-carrying platform

ORDER PICKING
Skills and Competencies

UNIT 5

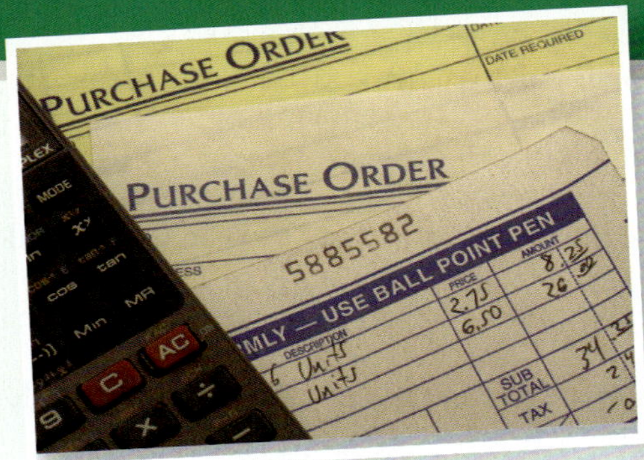

Dear student,

after working with this unit you will be able to ...

- describe four different picking methods.
- distinguish between static and dynamic allocation of items.
- name and specify five paperless picking methods.
- characterise various picking policies.
- use the passive voice.

At the end of this unit you will find a vocabulary training section which may help you to prepare for a class test.

Enjoy!

INDIVIDUAL TASK

Rory and Pjotr are having a break together. They both work in the picking department this month. It is their first day there and Pete Green, the chief storekeeper has just introduced the picking method of their company to them.

Rory: "I think this picking, using bar codes is pretty advanced. There seems to be no room for mistakes."

Pjotr: "Not while picking. When it comes to the packing, you're on your own again. I once read about some picking methods, where the warehouse operator stays in one place and robots get you to the right rack. In front of you is another rack with packages already chosen in the correct size. When a new rack arrives, lights indicate which goods have to be extracted and to be put into which package. Sounds cool, right? No more running."

Rory: "I don't know. It sounds like you need no brains to do it...so, why having a qualified warehouse operator at all?"
Pjotr: "Mmmh...you've got a point there."
Rory: "Have you ever thought about the future? I mean, the future of our job? Can you imagine working on a spaceship, storing and picking goods?"
Pjotr: "Who needs warehouse operators on a spaceship, Rory?"
Rory: "Think about it. If there aren't any replicators, who gets the spacemen their food, soap etc.?"
It would be like: "Captain Quork to Warehouse 1, Captain Quork to Warehouse 1. Are you reading Warehouse 1? We need more relays on the bridge to beam up Mr Kook." And I would be like:"Aye Captain, copy that.""
Pjotr: "Ok, but they would need the relays in the transporter room, not on the bridge, right?"
Rory: "Haha! My bad! But tell me: How would you pick all those things needed on a spaceship?"
Pjotr: "I think it would depend on the type of goods. Their size, weight, amount, how they need to be dealt with, sensitivity, transshipment and handling, investment costs..."
Rory: "Sounds as complicated in the future as it is in the present. Maybe I'll stick with the robots after all."

Have a look at the pictures on page 34.
After planning the warehouses for these goods, which picking methods would you choose?
Explain your decision based on the Pjotr's reasoning.

Order Picking

Order picking is one of a logistic warehouse's processes. It means picking and collecting articles in a specified quantity according to customers' orders.

It is a basic warehousing process and has an important influence on productivity. This makes order picking one of the most controlled logistic processes.

Orders can be sent in different ways – e.g. in writing, by a letter sent by post or fax or by e-mail.

Customers can also order parts by phone or by EDP (electronic data processing).

When the orders arrive in the company they are processed and picking lists are printed. Picking lists include a number of details, so that the order picker knows where to go and what to do, e.g. name, quantity and the storage location of the articles, information about dangerous goods and picking method.

Picking lists are either printed out immediately after the order is received, in "real time", or several orders are grouped into a series or "batch" and then all items for all orders are picked together.

There are different methods of order picking:

- ***Piece picking or picker to part method:*** One order picker moves to collect the products for one order.
- ***Zone picking method:*** Each order picker only picks goods in one specific zone for one specific order.
- ***Wave picking method:*** The order pickers collect the goods not only for one, but for several orders in their zone. After the items have been picked, they are sorted to the individual order.
- ***Pick to box method:*** Several order pickers use one picking list for one order split into picking zones. The pickers collect the goods from their zone and then they pass on the box to the next order picker.

The allocation of items can either be static or dynamic.

Sometimes, order pickers have to walk quite a distance when the items on the picking list are stored in different parts of the warehouse. When a person moves to collect the goods, this allocation of items is called ***man to goods***.

With ***goods to man*** no movement of the order pickers is necessary, as with dynamic racking systems the goods can be transported right to the place where they are needed.

Comprehension

Task 1

Find out the English expressions for the following German terms and write them on an extra sheet of paper.

auftragsorientierte serielle Kommissionierung mit Übergabestellen · Kommissionierung Mann zur Ware · auftragsorientierte parallele Kommissionierung · Ware zum Mann · serienorientierte parallele Kommissionierung · Kommissionierer · auftragsorientierte serielle Kommissionierung · Bereitstellung der Artikel

Task 2

Imagine you have to explain the picking methods to a German colleague. Sum up the meaning of each method in German.

Task 3

Which rackings fit to the static or dynamic allocation of goods? See Unit 4 for help. Make a list and explain which principle is realized: *goods to man* **or** *man to goods*.

Paperless picking methods

In order to avoid picking errors and increase picking efficiency, warehouses have introduced a number of paperless picking methods, e.g.

- order picking with mobile data terminals
- picking using bar code (or scan)
- picking using RFID
- pick to light
- voice picking or voice directed warehousing, and – most recently –
- pick by vision.

Order picking with mobile data terminals

A mobile data terminal can be attached to the vehicle used by the order picker. It shows him all necessary data concerning the customer order (e.g. order number, article name and number, amount and storage location of the article). When the order picker switches on the terminal and identifies himself, the display shows him the order and all relevant data. Then the picker moves to the location of the article and extracts the correct quantity of the article shown on the display. After that he confirms the extraction on the terminal. Then the display shows the next article or tells him that the order is completed.

Picking using bar code (or scan)

In his job, Klaus uses the *picking using bar code technology* because his company wants to minimize picking errors. This means, when Klaus picks orders he also uses a mobile terminal on his picking cart and special picking containers that are labelled with bar codes. When he gets a new picking order, the terminal shows him the name and location of the article and the quantity he has to pick. Then Klaus uses a scanner that reads the bar code of his (still empty) container and the order is linked to this container. When Klaus reaches the location of the article he scans the location and article number.

Picking using RFID

Pjotr's company has introduced the *RFID technology* in the warehouse. The picking procedure is similar to pick to bar code. RFID uses radio frequency technology, RFID tags and tag readers to identify objects. RFID tags are little chips and Pjotr has a tag reader that reads and describes the data on the chip. The chips are so small that they are easily fixed to boxes and can be read over long distances. One main advantage is that RFID tag data can be updated or changed very quickly.

Pick to light

Because Jan's company also has a storage area with a great number of picking locations for small parts and picking needs to be fast and accurate, they have installed a light-directed system. When Jan has to pick goods, he uses the *pick to light method.*

First he has to scan a bar-coded label on his picking container. This label represents the customer order. A digital display located at the racking in front of the storage location (or pick bin) informs Jan of the item and quantity that he needs to pick. After Jan has taken out the right quantity, he has to confirm the pick by pressing a lighted button next to the storage compartment. He knows the picking for the order is complete when no more lights are illuminated.

Companies that use *pick to light systems* report that they can expect over 450 picks to be made per hour by each worker. This is approximately ten times the number of picks made by a warehouse operator using a paper based system. The process is also very simple, so very little staff training is needed.

Voice picking or voice directed warehousing

In Laura's company the order pickers are guided simply and reliably through the picking process by a *voice picking system.*

Voice picking systems inform the employees of pick instructions through a headset. The order pickers can concentrate on the picking process without looking at paperwork and they have both hands free to perform the pick.

So Laura receives instructions about the order via her headset. The computer tells her where she has to go. When she reaches the storage location of the article, she confirms her position by speaking a check digit into her microphone. Next, the system tells her the quantity she has to pick. When she has taken out the right quantity, she confirms this and the system tells her where she has to go next.

Depending on the system configuration, the computer may ask her for a location check digit or a container check digit as well as a count-back.

Here is an example of a possible picking dialogue:

Computer: Go to building six.
Laura: *Ready.*
Computer: Go to aisle sixteen.
Laura: *Ready.*
Computer: Bay twenty-three.
Laura: *Ready.*
Computer: Pick four cases of c-screws.
Laura: *Ready.*
Computer: What are the check digits?
Laura: *One-Five-Two. (These might be from the pallet licence or location.)*
Computer: How many remain? *(Optional count-back – this increases accuracy, but reduces speed.)*
Laura: *Eight.*
Computer: Go to aisle six ...

...and so on, until the order is complete. The system then directs her to the location to put her picking container or pallet and then tells her to take a new container or pallet and start the next pick.

Before Laura could start picking orders in this way, the system had to be trained to recognize her voice.

Voice picking allows warehouse operators to move freely in the warehouse and not only in one location. There is no special light system needed and does not require any special modification to the racks and locations in the warehouse.
The latest development for order picking is another technology.

Pick by vision

The order picker has to wear special glasses and a headset. Through his glasses he can see the virtual warehouse and is shown the way to the location of the article. There he can see a picture of the right place and the quantity he has to pick. When he has made the pick, he has to confirm it and the process is repeated until the whole order is completed.
The enhanced or augmented reality the order picker sees through the glasses speeds up the picking process and the efficiency.

Task 4

Look at the pictures and match them with the English expressions.

mobile data terminal · picking list · pick by vision · pick to light · picking using RFID · picking using bar code · voice directed warehousing or voice picking

1

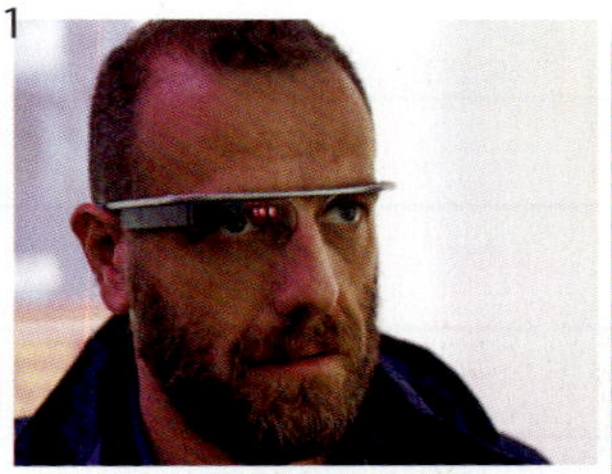

2

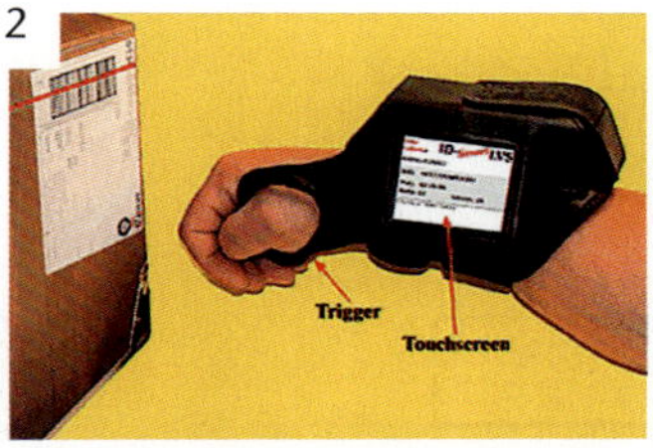

3

4

5

6

7

Task 5

a. Copy the chart.
b. Think of two different possibilities of passing on the picking order and write them down in the second layer.
c. Match the words in the box below to the corresponding possibilities.

voice directed warehousing or voice picking · mobile data terminal · picking list · pick by vision · packing list · pick to light · picking using bar code · delivery note · picking using RFID · packing slip

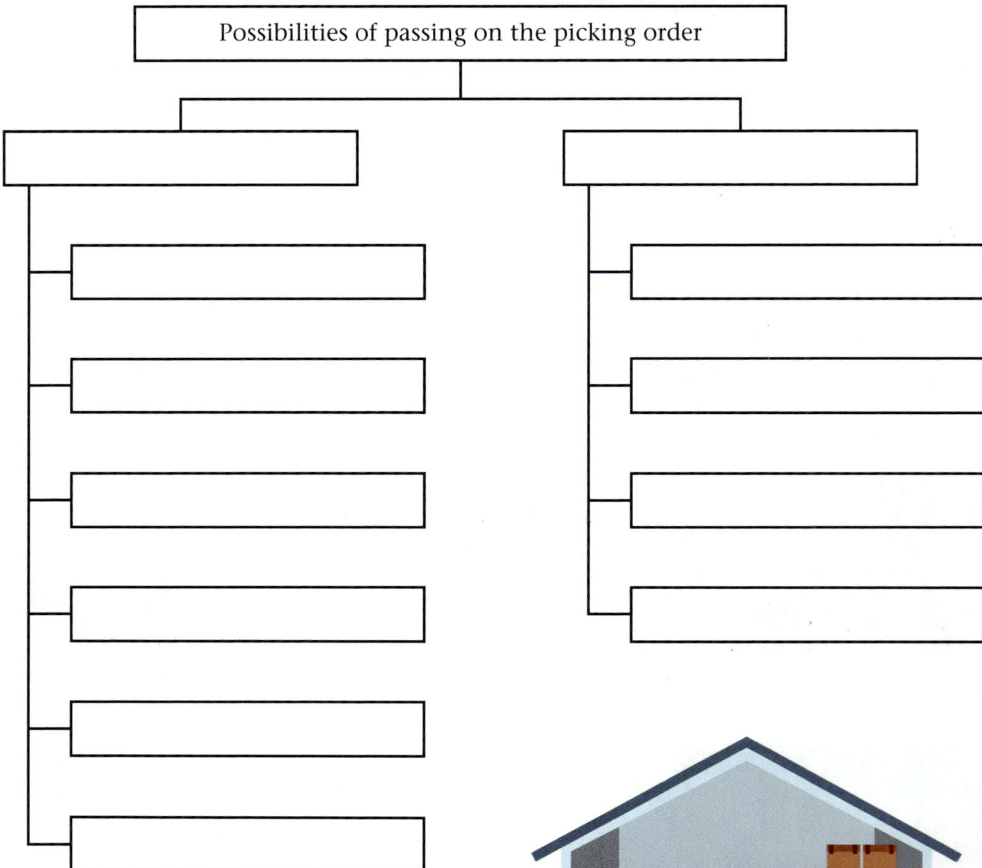

Listening

Pick to light

Task 6

Listen to the story of *The Colour Company Ltd.* and find out the following aspects:

a. How many employees does *The Colour Company Ltd.* have?
b. What is the name of one of its major customers?
c. How many stores does the customer have?
d. What does the customer want to change?
e. How does *The Colour Company Ltd.* change their picking process?

Grammar

Passive voice

Task 7

Copy the active sentences and put them into the passive voice.

Example:
active voice: *A conveyor connects the picking stations*
passive voice: *The picking stations are connected by a conveyor.*

a. The picker completes the order.
b. The company stores the goods in different parts of the warehouse.
c. You can attach a mobile data terminal to the vehicle.
d. The company can update or change RFID tag data very quickly.
e. A voice picking system guides the order pickers simply and reliably through the picking process.
f. You can send orders in different ways.
g. The system groups several orders into a series or "batch".
h. Dynamic racking systems can transport the goods right to the place where the workers need them.
i. You usually load lorries and container ships *last in – first out*.
j. With *HiFo*, the company sells the most expensive goods first.

For help see Skill Files Grammar pages 138f.

Activity

Task 8

Work in groups. Each group chooses one of the paperless picking methods.
Create a poster that explains the process of your picking method and its advantages and disadvantages. Then present your poster to the class.

Vocabulary Trainer

Picking Policy – *FiFo* and *LiFo*

There are different methods to store and pick goods: ***FiFo* and *LiFo***

FiFo means: ***First in – First out***: Goods that came into the warehouse first leave first. This is especially important for fresh articles with a shelf-life limit. The goods that came in first should be picked first.

LiFo means: ***Last in – First out***: Goods that came into the warehouse last, leave first. This method is suitable for goods with no fixed expiry date. When goods are stored in blocks on the ground, usually only *LiFo* is possible. Lorries and container ships are usually loaded *Last in – First out* as well. The last pallet – or container – will be the first one to be unloaded. Therefore it is important to load the goods in the right order, otherwise everything will have to be unpacked when the lorry reaches the first customer.

Valuation of inventories – *HiFo* and *LoFo*

There are also two other principles for valueing the stock in the warehouse according to the price of the goods. They are only important for the accounts department, e.g. when preparing the balance sheets for the company.

HiFo means: ***Highest in – First out***: Goods with the highest price leave first. When the most expensive goods are sold first, the value of the stock gets lower.

LoFo means: ***Lowest in – First out***: This is the opposite of *HiFo*. Goods with the lowest price leave first. This means that the cheapest goods are sold first and the value of the remaining stock gets higher. In Germany, this has never been accepted in accounting as the stock has to be valued at the lower of cost or market value.

Since 2010 only the *LiFo* and *FiFo* principles are acceptable for valuing the stock for accounting purposes in Germany.

Task 9

Copy the table and write down which goods are stored with the *FiFo* and which with the *LiFo* principle. Write down at least three examples for each principle.

FiFo	LiFo

Task 10

Make a list of racks that can store goods *FiFo* and *LiFo*.

Racks that can store goods …	
FiFo	LiFo

Task 11

Work with a partner and take turns. Describe the order picking system in your company and find out what this system is called.
Take notes and tell the class about the picking system in your partner's company.

Word Bank

order picking · picking list · piece picking/picker to part method · zone picking method · wave picking method · pick to box method · allocation of items · man to goods vs. goods to man · paperless picking · mobile data terminals · bar code · RFID · pick to light · voice picking/voice directed warehousing · to confirm · FiFo/LiFo

PACKING GOODS

Skills and Competencies

UNIT 6

Dear student,

after working with this unit you will be able to ...

- give reasons for packing goods.
- explain the difference between packaging and packing.
- name several packaging means and packaging aids.
- decide which packing is suitable for which good.
- find reasons for reducing the costs for packing.
- use the simple past and present perfect in the right way.

Of course, like in every unit you will find a vocabulary training section at the end of this unit which may help you to prepare for a class test.

Enjoy!

INDIVIDUAL TASK

Jan has received an instruction manual for new goods. They will arrive soon from Rory's company in England. The manual contains instructions how to handle, store and transport the goods. Jan asks the exchange student to explain the general content of the text.

Instruction Manual

Care of goods – motorcar spare parts

In the following you will find all the necessary instruction regarding the care of the goods owned by Waverider Inc., Dover, England. To guarantee mint condition the instructions must be followed.
Immediately inform your superior if you notice any faults on the goods or if the proper handling cannot be maintained.

Motorcar spare parts nos. 853-14; 853-15; 853-17
Goods with the numbers mentioned above need to be kept in cardboard cartons, which can be stacked. Maximum stacking limitation is six cartons. Secure them with special foil which is not see-through. Because of sensitivity to humidity the spare parts need to be kept in a dry place.

Motorcar spare parts no. 234-78
Goods with the number mentioned above are easily broken. They may only be stored individually, packed in polystyrene mould and cardboard carton. If they are each packed into metal boxes, you may stack them with a maximum stacking limitation of two boxes.

Motorcar spare parts no. 589-01
Goods with the number mentioned above are heavy. They need to be stored individually in racks. Keep them in a dry place. Once a month they need to be dusted and oiled if necessary.

Motorcar spare parts nos. 567-78; 457-58
Goods with the numbers mentioned above can be stacked in cardboard cartons. No stacking limitation. Use soft tissue for extra protection to reduce the risk of scratches on the surface.

Questions:

Which information is essential to know?
Where do the goods have to be stored?
How do they have to be packed to guarantee safe transport?

Sum up the most important aspects regarding the handling of the goods in German without translating the entire text.

Reasons for packing goods

Laura has been working in the packing station for several weeks. She has learned a lot about the correct packing of goods to ensure they are safe and secure. She discovered that there is a difference between packaging and packing. Packaging is the kind of package which is used for selling goods, while packing is less colourful and only used for transporting goods. As warehouse logistics operator she has to choose the right packing for all goods or each item. So, she had to get to know different types of packing and packaging aid. For example, she had to pack 2000 porcelain figures which came in a special packaging. For this she chose 10 suitable cardboard cartons and some wrapping paper for each packing, to make sure that they would not get damaged during transport. The cardboard cartons were closed with adhesive tape, stacked on a pallet and wrapped with stretch foil.
She also learned an interesting fact, namely that nowadays, 90% of all goods are packed for storage and transport, and sold in packaging. This happens for several reasons: protection, storage, transport, sales and information. Sometimes packaging and packing have proven to be quite handy.

Comprehension

Task 1

Read the text above.
Discuss the several reasons for packaging and packing:
What do you think lies behind the reasons "protection, storage, transport, sales and information"?
Explain why packaging and packing seem to be handy?

Different types of packing and packaging aids

Task 2

1. Copy the words and match the German expressions with the correct English ones.

Packgut	package, parcel
Packmittel	packaging aid
Packstoff	package contents
Packhilfsmittel	packaging means
Packstück	packaging material

2. Find the right term for each definition.

1. The goods that have to be packed are called … .
2. When everything is packed and labelled, you call it … .
3. A … fits to the goods and is used to transport or store them.
4. Packaging means consist of … .
5. To secure goods during transport, you use … .

Task 3

a. Copy and divide the expressions into the categories: packaging means and packaging aid.

b. Match the English with the German words.

carboy	Truhe, Kiste
seaworthy packing	Trommel
cask/ (metal or wooden) barrel	Ballen
foam	Lattenkiste, Holzverschlag
crate	Plastikbeutel
bubble envelope	Styroporform
big bag	Euro-Palette
lattice box	Dose
chest	Seidenpapier
drum	Klebeband
cardboard carton	Luftpolsterfolie
euro-pallet	(Stretch) Folie
parcel/package	Korbflasche
metal strapped wooden box	Container
reel	(Metall- oder Holz-) Fass
styrofoam / polystyrene mould	Dokumententasche
(hessian) sack	Holzwolle
bundle	Rolle, Spule
container	Wellpappe
adhesive tape	Verpackungschips
can	Luftpolstertasche
wrapping paper	stahlbandummantelte Holzkiste
plastic bag	Umreifungsband
bale	Seekiste

(stretch) foil	Gitterbox
wood wool	Paket
bubble wrap	Schaum(-stoff)
foam peanuts	Pappkarton/Schachtel
soft tissue	Bündel
shipping document pouch	Packpapier
strap	Big Bag
corrugated cardboard	(Jute-)Sack

Task 4

Which kinds of packing are shown in the illustrations below?

1

2

3

4

5

6

7

8

9

10

11

12
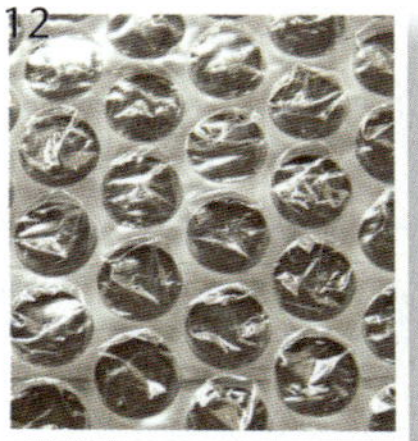
13

14

15

16
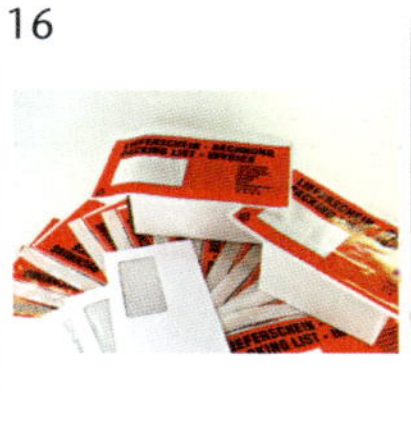

Suitable packings for goods

Task 5

Copy the table and find types of packing that are suitable for the following goods:

goods	packing
wine	
strawberries	
a TV-set	
a glass vase	
coffee beans	
motor oil	
a bunch of roses	
5 books	
100 cotton T-shirts	
car tyres	

Task 6

Copy and complete the text with the following words:

barrel · bulk · cardboard · cask · container · foam · fragile · liquid · salt

You pack … goods in a carton with … or polystyrene. You can store wine in a … or a … . Cartons are made of … . For the transport of … cargo you can use a tank …, for goods like sand or … you use a … container.

Task 7

Copy the table and find examples for each term.

term	examples
packaging means	
packaging material	
packaging aid	

Task 8

In each case, identify the package contents, the packaging means, packaging material, packaging aid and the package/parcel.

a. 50 screws are packed into little plastic boxes. 100 of these plastic boxes are packed into a cardboard carton. 24 cardboard cartons are stretched into foil on a euro-pallet.

b. Vases are put into polysterene moulds and packed into a cardboard carton. Delivery note and invoice are put into a shipping document pouch which is glued onto the case, which is finally closed with tape.

c. 100 TVs are shipped from Hamburg to Canada in seaworthy packing. The TVs are packed into plastic bags and polysterene moulds. Each TV is packed into a cardboard carton which is taped with adhesive tape. Then 100 packed TVs are packed into seaworthy packing and the wooden box is nailed closed.

Listening

True or false?

Task 9

Listen to the statements about packing and decide whether they are true or false.

Grammar

Simple Past or Present Perfect

Task 10

Simple Past or Present Perfect? Copy the sentences and choose the correct form.

a. Last year, we ... (to receive) a lot of barrels with liquids.
b. The number of containers with goods from China ... (to go) down since 2010.
c. During the last two years the use of packaging ... (to rise) dramatically.
d. But so far this year the costs for packaging material ... (to stay) constant.
e. We ... (to change) the supplier for our packaging material recently. It is a different company now.
f. In 2010 labelling of chemicals of different hazard classes ... (to change) according to the GHS-system.

Task 11

Copy the following sentences and translate them into English.

a. In den 80ern war Plastik als Verpackungsmaterial normal.
b. Seit Ende der 90er-Jahre benutzen immer mehr Fast-Food-Ketten Papier als Verpackungsmaterial.
c. Im Laufe dieses Jahres sind die Verkäufe gesunken.
d. Ich bin gestern zum Meeting gegangen.
e. Er ist immer noch im Büro. Er ist noch nicht gegangen.

For help see Skill Files Grammar pages 133f.

Activity

Reducing the costs for packing

The Head of the Packing Department in Laura's company wants to reduce the costs for packing.
He wants to discuss this with his everyday experts for packing.

Task 12

Assume the roles of the everyday experts for packing.
Divide into two groups:

a. One group should find reasons why packing is necessary and can't be reduced.
b. The other group should find reasons why it is essential to reduce packing. This group should think of environmental problems, too.
c. Write down your arguments.

When you have finished, every group sends two to three experts into the discussion. Choose one person who plays the part of the Head of the Packing Department. This person should lead the discussion.
After both sides have presented their arguments, they should find a way to reduce the costs for packing together.

Vocabulary Trainer

Odd one out!

Task 13

One word does not fit into the row. Sort the odd one out and explain why it does not fit.

Example:
barrel · vase · bottle · crate · drum
Solution: Crate does not fit because you cannot fill liquids in it.

a. polysterene mould · adhesive tape · cardboard carton · foil · foam
b. wool · cardboard · plastic · bubble wrap · paper
c. vase · can · glass bottle · window · porcelain figures
d. big bag · reel · drum · bundle · bubble wrap
e. lattice box · barrel · pallet · seaworthy packing · crate

Task 14

Build sentences with the following words.
You have to add words.
Use the simple past.

a. Klaus · (to) pack · cardboard carton · the day before yesterday
b. Laura · (to) check · lattice box · pallet · last time
c. Jan · foil · pallet · drum · yesterday
d. Pjotr · (to) unload · lorry · crate · foam · last Tuesday
e. Laura · (to) write · letter · broken cask · on Monday
f. Klaus · seaworthy packing · close · nails · last month
g. Jan · (to) send · sacks · by train · an hour ago
h. Pjotr · forklift truck · reel · this morning

Task 15

Work with a partner.
One chooses and describes a picture, the other one has to guess, which picture is described.

1

2

3

4

5

6

Word Bank

packaging · packing · packaging aid · packaging means · packaging material · cardboard carton · cask/barrel · foam · crate · big bag · drum · euro-pallet · polystyrene mould · bundle · adhesive tape · wrapping paper · bubble wrap · foam peanuts · soft tissue · to strap

LABELLING GOODS AND PACKINGS

Skills and Competencies

UNIT 7

Dear student,

after working with this unit you will be able to ...

- give reasons for labelling goods, packings and containers.
- find suitable labels for goods and packings.
- name different handling signs and label various goods with them.
- describe hazardous material labels.
- identify dangerous goods safety marks.
- use the will- and going to- future in the right way.

Just like in the other units, you will find a vocabulary training section at the end of this unit which may help you to prepare for a class test.

Enjoy!

INDIVIDUAL TASK

Klaus and Pjotr meet in the gym. Klaus wanted to unload containers more effective, so he asked Pjotr to go weight lifting with him.
After working out they take a shower. When Pjotr starts to use his deodorant, Klaus is concerned. He states that Pjotr's deodorant is full of toxic aluminium.

Pjotr: "Ah, that's what the sign means. I always wondered..."
Klaus: "The square red and black one on the back? No, that has nothing to do with the aluminium."
Pjotr: "What does it mean? Man, I have to know this stuff for my test. I want to be a dangerous goods safety advisor."
Klaus: "I don't know for sure. Jan told me something about hazardous goods and that they require special labels or something. Anyway, you should use deodorants without aluminium if you want to avoid severe damage to your nervous system and bone growth."

Questions:

What are those square signs on the back of deodorants, hairsprays etc.? Do you label containers and packages with them, too?

Task

a. Find out everything about the following labels and explain their general meaning and where they are used.
   1. handling signs
   2. hazardous material labels
   3. dangerous goods safety marks
b. Choose three goods and explain how they, their packings and their containers have to be labelled.

The correct label for all goods

Pjotr is really proud. He may participate in a training to become a dangerous goods safety adviser. That means he will be responsible for hazardous materials and dangerous goods at Y-Store.
Hazardous goods which are stored on a company's premises are called hazardous materials. When these goods are loaded and leave the premises they are called dangerous goods. It is important to label containers if they contain dangerous goods. Think about a tank-container transporting petrol. If it has an accident it is essential to know the kind of dangerous goods it is transporting, so that the fire brigade knows which protective measures they must use.
Therefore, it is important to label everything with suitable information, not only the containers and goods but also the packing. Besides the labels for dangerous goods and hazardous material, there are also labels for the correct handling of a package e.g. if the goods have to be protected from rain.
When Pjotr learns about the different labels, he will realize that he already knows some of the labels not only from his work experience, because in future, every morning when he shaves and does his hair, he will notice the square, orange labels on the cans. They warn you not to spray the substance into your eyes or to expose to an open flame. Pjotr will also learn that these labels are going to be substituted by others soon, as a new directive changed them in 2011. So, it's not only necessary to know these labels at home but it is essential to know them at work to avoid dangerous situations. So look out for hazardous material labels, dangerous goods safety marks and handling signs.

Comprehension

Task 1

Answer the following questions on the text.

a. What is the difference between hazardous materials and dangerous goods?
b. What does Pjotr's new position "dangerous goods safety adviser" mean in German?
c. What are the duties of a dangerous goods safety adviser?
d. Why do you have to label goods, packages and containers?
e. What are the labels: "hazardous material labels", "dangerous goods safety marks", and "handling signs" called in German?

Handling signs

Task 2

Copy the English expressions on the next page and find the corresponding signs. After that, translate them into German.

1

2

3

4

5
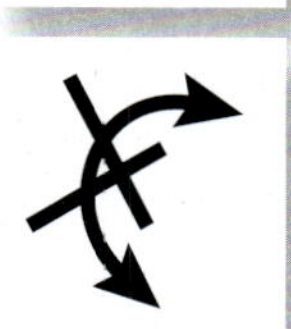
6

7

8

9

10

11

12

13

14
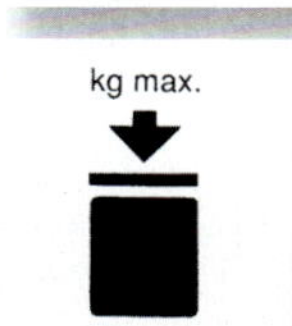

15

16
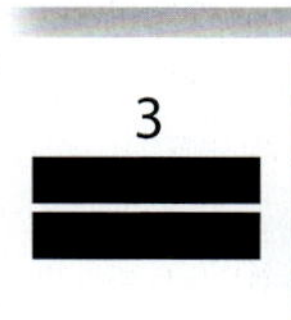

17

18

19

20

don't destroy barrier · stacking limitation in units · don't roll · centre of gravity · temperature limitation · flammable · this side up · clamp here · don't stack · fragile/handle with care · keep away from heat · electrostatic sensitive device · stacking limitation · use no hooks · sling here · keep away from frost · no handtruck here · tear off here · keep dry · no use of forklift truck here

Hazardous material labels

Hazard pictograms by Globally Harmonized System of Classification and Labelling and Packing of Chemicals (GHS)

Task 3

Find the right English descriptions of the pictures.

Physical hazards

1

2

3

4

5

Health hazards

6

7

8

9

Environmental hazards

10

environment · corrosion · flame · gas cylinder · exclamation mark · health hazard · bomb · skull & crossbones · flame over circle

Task 4

Nothing ventured, nothing gained. Who of you is the quickest and finds out more about the GHS hazard pictograms on the internet? Present your information to the class.

Dangerous goods safety marks

Transport pictograms by the European Agreement concerning the International Carriage of Dangerous Goods by Road (ADR)

Task 5

Find the right English expressions for the pictures.

1
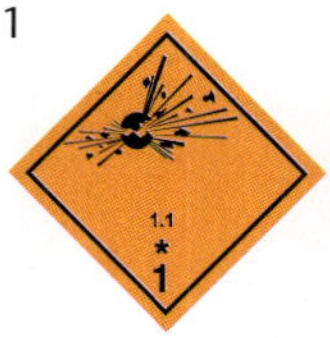

2

3

4

5

6

7

8

9

10

11

12

13

14
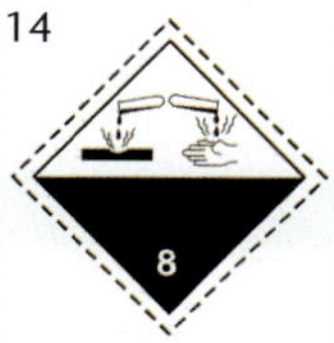

15

substances which in contact with water emit flammable gases · flammable gases · toxic gases · infectious substances · oxidizing substances · miscellaneous dangerous substances and articles · non-flammable non-toxic gases · flammable liquids · toxic substances · substances liable to spontaneous combustion · flammable solids self-reactive substances and solid desensitized explosives · radioactive material · organic peroxides · explosives · corrosive substances

Listening

Some story to tell ...

Task 6

Audio

Listen to the story of Pjotr and Jan and answer the following questions. Copy them on an extra sheet of paper to take notes while listening.

a. What happens in the story? Write a short summary.
b. What do you think: How will the story end? Write your own short ending before listening to it.

Grammar

Will- or Going to- Future

Task 7

Copy the sentences and put the verbs in brackets into the will- *('ll)* or the *going to-future*.

a. Look, it's raining. I think the goods ... (to get) wet.
b. The customer just called me. He ... (to send) the goods back.
c. It's Wednesday. The boss ... (to be) here at 9 a.m.
d. What is your plan? When ... (you, to start) work tomorrow?
e. Oh, there is a traffic jam. I think, I ... (to be) late for work.
f. Pjotr ... (to start) his training soon.
g. When he finishes it, he ... (to be) responsible for dangerous goods.
h. The company ... (to send) the containers by sea.
i. I have to check this first. I ... (to call) you back later.
j. We ... (to get) a new forklift truck next month. The boss ordered it yesterday.

For help see Skill Files Grammar page 135f.

Activity

How do you label packages?

Task 8

Work in groups and choose one of the situations below. In the situation you have to imagine you work for a company that has to send goods. You are responsible for packing the goods safely and correctly. Therefore, you have to choose handling signs which make sure that the package is handled in the right way.

a. Copy the drawing of the picture, decide on at least three signs and draw them on the package.
b. After that, present your work to your classmates by describing why you chose those signs.

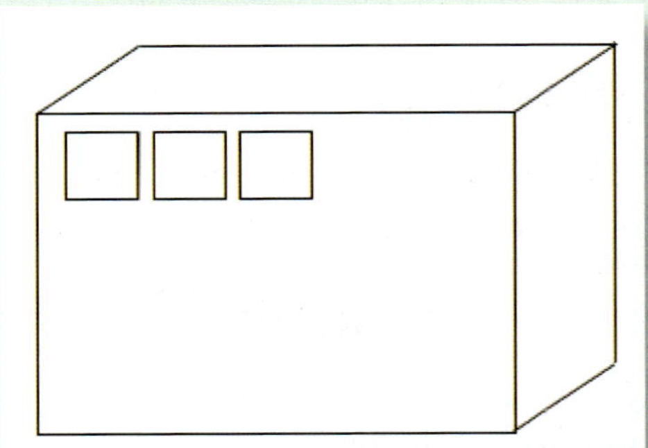

Situation 1
Your company has got the order to pack vases and send them from Hamburg to Poole, England.

Situation 2
Your company has got the order to pack personal computers and send them from Hamburg to Munich.

Situation 3
Your company has got the order to pack fireworks and send them from Hamburg to Bergen, Norway.

Situation 4
Your company has got the order to send a part of a machine weighing 25t to Abha, Saudi Arabia. The machine is packed in a seaworthy container. The centre of gravity is not in the middle.

Situation 5
Your company has got the order to send playground equipment to Wellington, New Zealand. You have to pack it into two seaworthy packings. One packing contains the part of equipment which weighs over 15t. The other contains more fragile parts, which are packed with a barrier. Both packings have to be transported in the same container.
Choose the signs for the first packing.

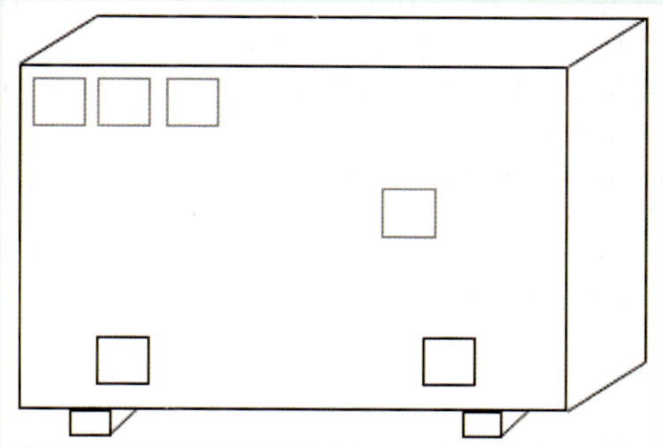

Situation 6
Your company has got the order to send playground equipment to Wellington, New Zealand. You have to pack it into two seaworthy packings. One packing contains the part of equipment which weighs over 15t. The other packing contains more fragile parts, which are packed with a barrier. Both packings have to be transported in the same container.
Choose the signs for the second packing.

Vocabulary Trainer

How to label goods, packings and containers

Task 9

Decide on the correct packings and labels for the following goods.

1

2

3

4

Task 10

Work in pairs.
Decide on a good.
Create a poster with the following information like in the example below.
You may add information or leave out any of the examples which are not suitable.

picture of good

description of good:

____
____
____
____

suitable packing:
packaging means: ______________________
packaging aid: ______________________

label on packing:

picture of label ______________________

picture of label ______________________

label on goods:

picture of label ______________________

picture of label ______________________

Word Bank

handling sign · stacking · limitation · hook · clamp · fragile · centre of gravity · environment · hazardous material (label) · hazard · dangerous goods safety mark · (non) flammable · (non) toxic · liquid · solid · substance · infectious · oxidizing · miscellaneous · radioactive · explosive · corrosive

CONTAINERS

Skills and Competencies

UNIT 8

Dear student,

after working with this unit you will be able to …

- distinguish various types of containers.
- find suitable containers for various cargo.
- name external and internal measurements of a container.
- explain how to secure the cargo inside a container.
- describe the pattern for safe loading of containers.
- decide when to use an adjective or adverb.
- ask questions in the right way.

Of course, like in every unit you will also find a vocabulary training section which may help you to prepare for a class test.

Enjoy!

INDIVIDUAL TASK

Pjotr likes to load and unload containers. It's like weight lifting at the gym, but for free. So he didn't have to think about it very long when his teacher asked him, if he would like to give a talk about the history of containers. He is free to add any information he likes.

Task

a. Give a brief overview of the history of containers.
   1. What led to their invention?
   2. Where are they used?

b. What information do you need to have about containers when working with them? Make a list.

c. Present your findings on a poster.

The story of containers

In 1937 a truck driver had the idea of using a container to transport goods. Today there are more than 21 million containers travelling around the world. Malcolm McLean (1913–2001) was tired of packing heavy cotton bags onto his truck, so he thought of packing them into boxes made of steel – containers. After he sold his forwarding agency, the "McLean Trucking Company", he founded a company called "Sea-Land" for shipping the containers by sea. In April 1956 his first ship "Ideal X" carrying 58 containers left Port Newark, New Jersey, for Houston, Texas. Container shipment became so popular that during the Vietnam War (1957/58–1975) containers were used to transport military equipment to South East Asia.

Today, the Danish shipping line Maersk, which took over McLean's company "Sea-Land" in 1999, has a fleet of the world's largest container ships. In 2006 the "Emma Maersk" was built, followed by seven more ships of the same size. These ships can transport up to 14,770 TEU (nominal 15,550 TEU), which means Twenty Foot Equivalent Unit – or the size of a 20′ container.

Even bigger container vessels called "Triple-E" were built by Maersk in 2013. They have a 18,000 TEU (twenty-foot container) capacity, 16 percent greater (2,500 containers) than the "Emma Maersk" and are four metres longer and three metres wider.

The biggest container ships nowadays belong to the shipping lines of CSCL and MSC. They have a capacity of more than 19,000 TEU. However, they can carry a full load of containers only if each container weighs less than its maximum gross weight.

Every year more than 4,000 container ships leave the port of Hamburg to carry more than 9 million containers (or TEU) around the world. Most cargo leaving Hamburg is transported in containers, even coffee, cocoa, grain, wood, waste paper and scrap iron. There are a number of different types of containers for different types of cargo.

The size of a container

In the middle of the 1960s the Russians, the Americans, the English and the French met in Paris to decide on the size of the container. After four days and a lot of whisky, they finally agreed on a standard size: 6.058 metres (20 feet) long, 2.438 metres (8 feet) wide and 2.591 metres (8 feet 6 inches) high for the 20-foot container.

Metre and foot

Metre and foot – that sounds quite complicated. Here's a short historical explanation: In Egypt the measure foot has existed for more than 4,000 years. It was the foot of a pharaoh and three feet were called a yard. But of course feet have a different length and a standard had to be fixed to avoid unfairness in trade. In the Middle Ages yard-sticks were made by governments and town councils and the English took this system with them when they colonialized Egypt and the other parts of the world. After Napoleon's initiative to measure the circumference of the earth, the Metre convention was signed on May 20th, 1875, in Paris. The revolutionary French National Assembly, however, had already decided in 1791 to set up a universal standard of length which did not refer to human body parts. So nowadays both systems still exist. We become aware of the older one with each of the 21 million containers travelling around the world: 1 meter is 3.2808399 feet or 3 feet 3⅜ inches.

Comprehension

Task 1

Copy the sentences and complete them with information from the text.

a. The container is ... years old.
b. In 1956 the first container ship transported ... containers from ... to ... .
c. The standard container is ... long, ... wide and ... high.
d. The shipping line "Sea-Land" was taken over by ... .
e. Today the biggest container ships can transport ... containers.
f. TEU means ... or the size of one ... .

Task 2

When talking about the size of containers, you can use the following expressions:
The length of a standard container is 20 feet, the width is eight feet and the height is 8 feet 6 inches.
Now copy the table and find the German translations and the English adjectives corresponding to the nouns.

English noun	German	English adjective	German
length			
width			
height			
weight			

Measurements

When loading goods into a container it is necessary to know the measurements and capacities of it by heart. For example, when Laura works in the truck dispatch, she needs to be 100 % sure about how much weight a container can be loaded with. Laura books a suitable container according to the weight and measurements of the cargo, the maximum capacity of the container as well as its internal measurements.
Klaus, Jan and Pjotr have to know how to stack the goods in the most appropriate way. Thus they have to take into consideration which types of goods have to be loaded and how the goods fit into the container so they won't create dead space. Last but not least they have to make sure everything is secured. That means they do not only have to know about the right lashing material and methods but also about gravity and centrifugal force.

Task 3

Copy the sentences and put in the missing words.

a. Machine parts wider than 2.438 m have to be transported with ... .
b. Coffee bags are transported with ... .
c. Loose small stones are transported with ... .
d. Machine parts higher than 2.591 m have to be transported with ... .
e. Meat has to be transported in ... .

Task 4

Answer the following questions about this container.
Copy the sentences and fill in the gaps with the following words:

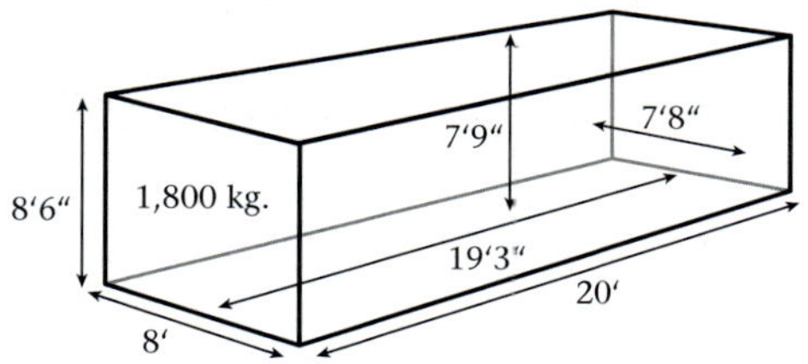

heavy · height · inches · length · high · weighs · wide · width · weight · feet · long

a. What are the container's external measurements?
The ... is 20 ... , the ... is 8 ... and its ... is 8 ... 6 ... .
b. What are its internal measurements?
It is 7 ... and 9 ... ... , it is 7 ... and 8 ... ... and it is 19 ... and 3 ... .
c. What is its tare weight?
It is 1,800 kgs ... , that means the ... is 1,800 kgs, or the container ... 1,800 kgs.
d. The goods weigh 24,900 kgs. What is the gross weight of the container?

Task 5

You can find the following and other abbreviations on a container.
What do these mean in English and German?

M.G.W.
NET
TARE
CU.CAP.

Task 6

Have a look at the container in the picture and answer the following questions in full sentences.

a. What is the maximum gross weight of the container?
b. What is the tare weight of the container?
c. What is the maximum net weight of the cargo for this container?
d. What is the cubic capacity of the container?

Listening

Load securing

Today Jan is working with Pjotr. They have to load and unload the incoming lorries and containers. Together with a contract worker they are a gang. Among other things, they are responsible for the technically correct loading and unloading of lorries and containers as well as inspecting the proper securing of the cargo.

Their loadmaster always says: "A proper vehicle and the observance of the load balancing are general basics for a safe transport". The reason for securing cargo is to prevent personal injuries as well as environmental and cargo damages. Many traffic accidents happen because of insufficient securing of cargo. While loading a vehicle it is therefore necessary to remember that forces have an influence on the cargo during transport.
Jan and Pjotr know that in the case of an accident caused by poor securing, they and their loadmaster are held responsible for it. In the worst case, when a person is injured or dies, it can mean fines or even imprisonment. Jan and Pjotr have also learnt that all people involved have to work together to guarantee the safety for transport and traffic.
While the three of them are unloading the second lorry, the first driver says that he is ready to go. Jan and Pjotr check the securing of the cargo. They come to the conclusion that the securing is well done. As verification they ask their loadmaster to give his opinion. He agrees and the lorry driver may leave the company's premises.

Task 7

Listen to the dialogue of Jan and Pjotr.
They are talking about different types of lashing material.
Look at the pictures and try to match them with the English expressions by Jan's and Pjotr's descriptions.

1

2

3

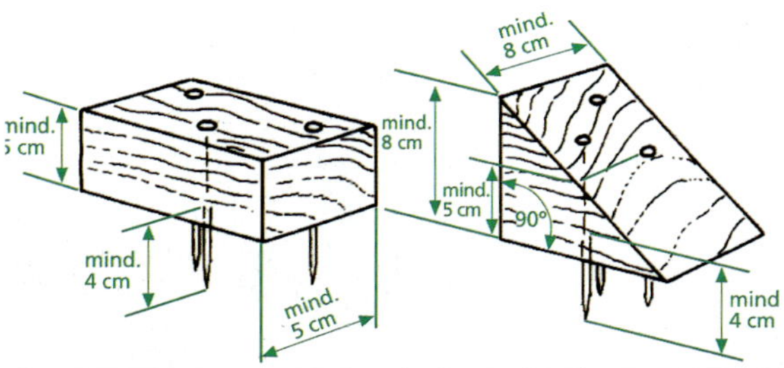

4

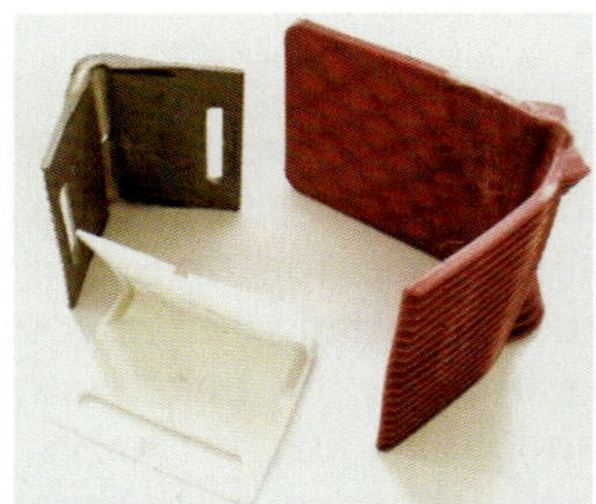

5

wooden wedge · lashing strap · edge protector · lashing point · anti-slip mat

Grammar

Adjective or Adverb – Asking questions

Task 8

Copy these sentences and use the words in brackets to fill in the gaps. Decide whether to use the adjective or the adverb.

a. Please let us know the shipment date … (immediate/immediately).
b. The transport in containers is … (safe/safely) and … (fast/fast).
c. The goods arrived … (late/late or lately) because of the dock workers' strike.
d. There is a … (regular/regularly) ferry service for the transport of the containers.
e. Some workers on the container ship do not understand German very … (good/well).
f. The … (new/newly) built container port is very important for Hamburg's economy.
g. The loading of the goods has not been … (complete/completely) finished.
h. These goods have to be transported … (quick/quickly).
i. We need these containers … (extreme/extremely) … (urgent/urgently).
j. Please be … (extreme/extremely) … (careful/carefully) with the goods when you load them into the container.

Task 9

Read the sentences and put them into questions, so that the underlined parts are the answer!

Example: The lorry transports <u>a container.</u>
Question: What does the lorry transport?
Answer: A container.

a. The warehouse logistics operator packs <u>a container.</u>
b. Malcolm McLean invented <u>the container.</u>
c. <u>Malcolm McLean</u> invented the container.
d. The "Ideal X" transported the first 58 containers <u>in 1956.</u>
e. The "Ideal X" transported <u>the first 58 containers</u> in 1956.
f. <u>The standard container is 20 feet long, 8 feet wide and 8 feet 6 inches high.</u>
g. The container weighs <u>1,800 kgs.</u>
h. The shipment costs <u>454 euros and 90 cents.</u>
i. The biggest container vessels can transport <u>up to 14,770 TEU.</u>
j. The customer paid for the transport. – Answer: <u>Yes.</u>

For help see Skill Files Grammar pages 141f.

Activity

Packing pattern

There are a lot of different ways to load a container. Most important is the secure and safe loading. But it is also necessary to avoid dead space, i.e. the container must contain as many goods as possible.
To find the ideal packing pattern, you must know some things by heart:

- measurements of a container
- maximum payload of a lorry
- measurements of a pallet
- net and loading weight of a pallet

And of course, you have to stack goods on the pallet in an efficient way.

Task 10

Copy the delivery note and fill it in correctly with the information given in the text and the packing list on the next page.

On 16th March 2013 Tortuga Limited Company orders 360 concrete stones from Alabaster Stones for Gardening (order number: 09/153217).

Alabaster Stones for Gardening (Fährhaus Straße 134 – 136, 47279 Duisburg) ships l-type concrete stones to Tortuga Limited Company in Kriusweg 184–186, 3012 GT Rotterdam, Netherlands; VAT-Number IT00325624831.

Because this is not only inland traffic, they cooperate with the forwarding agency 123 Express.

123 Express sends a lorry with the licence number: DU-FL 456.

Packing List

Customer:	Tortuga Ltd. Company
Order no.:	88268
Lot:	12/22/05
Amount:	360 concrete stones
Analysis:	Al 35 %
Material:	Al concrete, l-type, min 34 % Al approx 60 × 60 × 40, 72 kgs

Maybe you have noticed that you don't have all the necessary information. You have to first calculate the gross, the net weight and the number of pallets. Use an extra sheet of paper to do so.

Hint: Sometimes it helps to draw the pallet and the goods to get a better idea of the situation.

Shipping Dep.:

Delivery Note

Your order:
Our order-no.:
EX stock:
Lot:
Registration-no.:
to:

Weights in kgs gross net

Analysis:

Material:

Packing:

Your VAT-No.:

I have been informed that the material must definitely be transported in dry condition / ack. of receipt:

<u>Loading Affirmation:</u> *Recipient:*..
Date, signature, stamp

....

Vocabulary trainer

Different types of containers and their cargo

Picture	Type	Measures		
		length	height	width
	standard container, ventilated container, high-cube container	20′, 40′, 45′	8′6″, 9′6″	8′, pallet wide
	hard-top container	20′, 40′	8′6″, 9′6″	8′
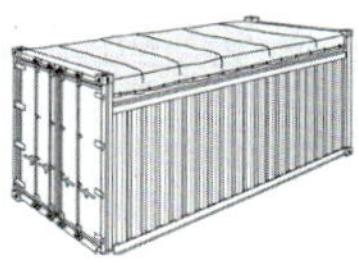	open-top container	20′, 40′	8′6″, 9′6″	8′
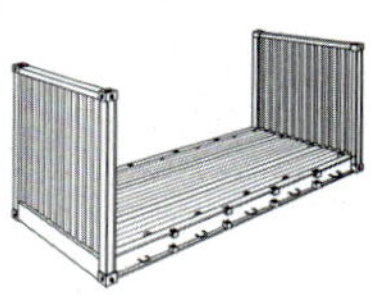	flatrack (flat)	20′, 40′	8′6″, 9′6″	8′
	platform (plat)	20′, 40′		8′
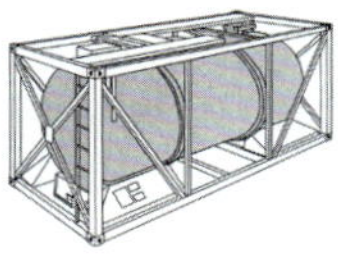	tank container	20′	4′3″, 8′6″	8′
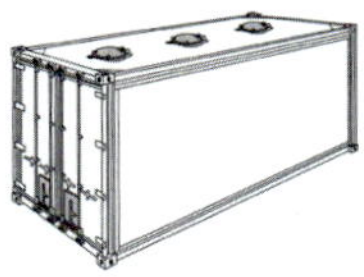	bulk container	20′, 30′, 40′	8′6″, 9′, 9′6″	8′
	insulated/refrigerated container	20′, 40′, 45′	8′6″, 9′6″	8′, pallet wide

Task 11

Form 8 groups.
Each group chooses one container from the table on the previous page.
Find out for which type of cargo "your" container is suitable.
Use the internet or your technical book as a source of information.
Design a poster with a picture of the container, its name, measurements and typical cargo.

Task 12

Your customer wants to know which types of containers he can use for his shipments. Discuss this matter in your group and make a decision for the following consignments. Report to the class and give reasons for your choice.

a. Frozen meat from Bremerhaven to Hongkong.
b. Machinery parts packed in wooden boxes; 12 pieces each measuring 2.50 × 1.10 × 0.80 m (l × w × h); each having a weight of 900 kgs; to be transported from Hamburg to Nigeria.
c. Onions packed in nets; 5 kgs each; total of 1,800 pieces; from Poland to Canada.
d. Removal goods (e.g. furniture, books) to South Africa; 8.4 tons with about 15 cbm.
e. Parts for a wind turbine, measuring 8.25 × 1.85 × 1.60 m (l × w × h); weight 36 tons; from Emden to Kobe / Japan.
f. Grain from Rotterdam to New York.

Word Bank

shipping line · measurement · length · height · width · weight · foot / feet · inch · cubic capacity · net · gross · tare · payload · refrigerated · bulk goods · pattern

MEANS AND MODES OF TRANSPORT
Skills and Competencies

UNIT 9

Dear student,

after working with this unit you will be able to …

- name the four modes of transport.
- list several means of transport for each mode.
- describe documents in domestic and international trade.
- find relevant information in transport documents.
- choose the right Incoterm for a contract.
- identify damages to a shipment.
- compare means and modes of transport according to different aspects using the right comparative and superlative forms of adjectives.

At the end of this unit you will find a vocabulary training section which may help you to prepare for a class test.

Enjoy!

INDIVIDUAL TASK

Jan's car is in need of new tyres for the summer. To save money, he wants to order them online. He finds an unbeatable offer on tyres_ex_works.com. He orders them and looks forward to his delivery. After two days he receives an email from the company in English. Jan is confused. He shows the email to Laura, who explains that the tyres Jan has ordered are not as cheap as he thinks. He actually has to organize the transport on his own, as the tyres are EXW, which is short for ex works. This means Jan has to either fetch them at the production company or he has to pay for transportation separately. As the company is in the USA, he has no desire to collect the tyres there.
Now Jan knows that he has a lot to learn when it comes to domestic and international transport. So, pay attention the next time you order something online.

Task

a. Explain which mode of transport you would choose when
   - you have to transport the goods over a long distance and it must be quick
   - you have a big quantity of goods and time is not an important aspect

b. Explain with which modes of transport a consignment can be sent from Hamburg to Copenhagen.
   Name at least 3 and explain in which situation you would choose them.

c. Explain the term "multimodal transport" in full sentences.

d. Explain the term TEU – what it means and where it comes from.

The best way to send goods

Goods can be transported by rail, road, sea or air. Trains, vehicles, aircraft and ships are used to transport goods all over the world. Everything should be delivered as quickly as possible. If this is too expensive, costs can be reduced by using a combination of different modes of transport, which is called multimodal transport. For example, you could combine transport by sea and rail. Using big cranes, containers can be loaded directly onto trains from container vessels. However, trains are not suitable for all types of goods. Lorries are better for short distances. In the evening they can return to their depots and the drivers may go home again. The distance between supplier and client may be closer. On the other hand, driving a lorry over long distances can be dangerous and it demands a lot of concentration on the part of the driver.

Comprehension

Means and modes of transport

Task 1

a. Look at the pictures on this page and identify the three modes of transport. How do you think the fourth mode of transport is called?

b. Copy the table on the next page and write down the four modes of transport.

mode:				
means:				

c. **List the following means of transport under the correct mode.**

truck · helicopter · vessel · aircraft · car · train · barge · lorry · ship · roadtrain

d. **Find more means of transport and put them under the corresponding modes.**

Task 2

a. **Which of the following adjectives fit to the different modes of transport? Complete the list of advantages and disadvantages of the modes of transport. Some words may fit to more than one mode of transport.**

reliable · punctual · expensive · environmentally (un)friendly · cheap · unreliable · slow · fast · risky · railbound

mode of transport	advantages	disadvantages
rail		
road		
sea		
air		

b. **Now explain why and when something is an advantage or disadvantage. Write full sentences.**
Example:
Transport by rail is cheap when you have to transport great amounts but it is railbound.

Documents in international trade

When you send goods abroad, you need different documents.
Waybills are used for transport by road or rail. When you transport goods by air, you have to fill in an Air Waybill.
For transport by sea the Bill of Lading (B/L) is the most important document. You also use it in combined transport, when the transportation involves transport by sea and other modes of transport. It is very valuable, because it is a document of title. This means that the lawful holder

of the B/L is the rightful owner of the goods. The owner of the B/L can sell the document for the same value as the value of the goods.
For goods from other countries, a Certificate of Origin shows the country of origin or where the goods were mainly produced. For goods produced in the EU, there is a common EU Certificate of Origin.
A Commercial Invoice tells the customer how much he has to pay for the goods that he ordered.

Task 3

What are the specific forwarding documents for the four modes of transport from task 1?

Task 4

Match the words in the table below.

In every document you find:		Auf jedem dieser Dokumente sind zu finden:	
1	the shipper	a	eine Unterschrift
2	the consignee	b	der Bestimmungsort
3	a description of the consignment	c	das Lieferdatum
4	the destination	d	das Gewicht der Ladung
5	the weight of the cargo	e	die Frachtkosten
6	the freight charges	f	der Versender
7	a signature	g	der Frachtführer
8	the date of delivery	h	eine Beschreibung der Sendung
9	the place of delivery	i	der Empfänger
10	the carrier	j	der Lieferort

Task 5

Read the following text and decide whether the descriptions on the next page are taken from a clean or dirty B/L.

A bill of lading is a negotiable document. When you have the signed original B/L in your hands, it means that you own the goods. Sellers need a clean bill of lading to get money from their buyer's bank. A dirty bill of lading means that something is wrong with the goods. The captain of the ship has to write that on the B/L, so that it is clear that the carrier is not responsible for the damage.

descriptions	clean	dirty
in apparently good order and condition		
fragile goods packed without foam		
six drums short shipped		
in external good order		
two barrels leaking		

Task 6

Give the German translation for:

a. negotiable document
b. non-negotiable document

Listening

Audio

Task 7

Listen to the situations and decide which problem is described.

a. Match the documents to their descriptions by listening to the explanation.
b. Then copy the table in the right order and give the German translation for the documents.

document		description	
a	Road Waybill	1	A title document issued by the carrier for sea-freight.
b	Insurance certificate	2	A short statement saying which insurance company covers what risks.
c	Commercial Invoice	3	A non-negotiable document issued by the airline.
d	Air Waybill	4	A standard consignment note for road transport.
e	Bill of Lading	5	A document which states in which country the goods were produced.
f	Certificate of origin	6	International rail carriers use this standard consignment note.
g	Rail Waybill	7	A copy of the standard invoice which usually contains an Incoterm.

Route Planning

Task 8

Listen to the dialogue where Klaus has to arrange a route planning.
Copy the questions on the dialogue below and answer them.

a. Why does Ole Hansen call Klaus Schmidt?
b. Which information does Klaus Schmidt need before he can tell Ole Hansen the mode of transport?
c. Which mode of transport does he choose?
d. How long will the shipment take from Denmark to Namibia? Why?

Grammar

Comparative or Superlative

Task 9

Copy the sentences and complete them with the adjectives in the right form.

Examples:
*It will take a lot **longer** if it's sent by ship.*
*Transport by air is **more expensive** than sea freight.*

a. In most cases, transport by road is ... than transport by air. (cheap)
b. Transport by sea is ... than transport by rail. (expensive)
c. Sending goods by plane is ... than sending them by truck. (fast)
d. Shipment by rail is ... than sending goods by road. (safe)
e. Transport by road is ... than transport by air. (risky)
f. If you transport consignments by air it is ... than transport by rail. (environmentally friendly)
g. Sending goods by plane is ... than sending them by lorry. (reliable)
h. Sea freight is ... than transport by rail. (slow)
i. Air freight is ... mode of transport. (choose a suitable adjective)

For help see Skill Files Grammar pages 141f.

Incoterms®

Activity

The Incoterms®[1] are a set of internationally accepted rules that define the most commonly used terms of delivery. They identify the tasks of seller and buyer and when the responsibility for the costs of and the risks during transport are passed from seller to buyer.
Incoterms® are issued by the International Chamber of Commerce in Paris and were last revised in 2010.
The 11 rules are grouped into two categories:
- rules for any mode or modes of transport : EXW, FCA, CPT, CIP, DAT, DAP and DDP
- rules for sea and inland waterway transport: FAS, FOB, CFR and CIF.

Task 10

Look at the picture and explain the following Incoterms®.

a. EXW
b. FAS
c. FOB
d. CIF
e. DDP

Task 11

Imagine you are an exporter of goods from a company in Buxtehude.
You send goods first to Hamburg docks, then by ship to Newark in the USA and finally to the buyer's company in Rochester.
The freight charges differ depending on the kind of shipping the customer wants. Copy the table below and calculate the following prices for your customer according to the list of freight charges.

These are the costs in the order:

goods	850,- €
packing	10,- €
carriage to Hamburg docks	20,- €
loading costs	5,- €
shipping costs	30,- €
insurance	40,- €
unloading costs in Newark	8,- €
carriage to the buyer's premises in Rochester	15,- €

[1] Die Incoterms® sind urheberrechtlich geschützt und einsehbar unter www.iccgermany.de/standards-regelwerke/incoterms

List of freight charges	
EXW price:	
FOB price:	
CIF price:	
DDP price:	

Task 12

Work with a partner and generate your own offer like in task 11. Switch your offer with another pair and calculate their prices.

Vocabulary trainer

Damages to a shipment

This morning Jan had to get up very early. His boss called to tell him that the lorry they were expecting this morning had had an accident last night. It had finally arrived with the shipment but the load had suffered a lot of damage.
What a mess! This damage needed to be described in detail. As the delivery came from England, Jan had to write the damage list in English. So he grabbed a draft, where he might choose the right description of the damage and then went to the lorry to start his work.
This is what the draft looked like:

List of damage	Moniturliste
deformed	
newly taped	
burst	
partly ripped	
open, full	
open, not full	
open, contents visible	
condensation	
container with hole	
slightly / heavily compressed	

List of damage	Moniturliste
mouldy	
slightly / severely bashed / dented	
not sortable	
not countable	
skid broken	
boards/planks broken	
pallet re-packed	
bags perforated	
contents (partly) leaking out	
package perforated	
package dirty	
package not transportable	

Task 13

Copy the table above and translate the list of damage.

Task 14

Look at the pictures and explain what kind of damage you see.

1

2

3

4

5

6

7

8

9

Task 15

Copy the sentences and translate them.

a. Der Kaffee ist schimmelig.
b. Die Verpackung ist stark ramponiert.
c. Die Kakaosäcke sind löchrig.
d. Die Schachtel ist stark verschmutzt.
e. Der Container ist voller Schwitzwasser.
f. Die Palette ist gebrochen.
g. Der Inhalt rieselt heraus.
h. Die Kolli sind aufgeplatzt.

Task 16

Be creative!
Imagine, you wanted to unload a container. When you opened it, you realized that there is something terribly wrong with the shipment.
Copy and fill out the damage report, describing what happened to the shipment and what it looks like.
Read out your result to the class. Who of you wrote the fanciest one?

Damage Report

Place of event: ______________________________

Date of event: ______________________________

Time of event: ______________________________

Witnesses: ______________________________

Description of damage:

____

____

____

Course of event:

____

____

____

____

____

____

____

Signature

Word Bank

mode of transport · means of transport · rail · road · sea · air · shipper · carrier · consignee · vessel · barge · aircraft · destination · freight charges · Waybill · Bill of Lading · Insurance certificate · Certificate of origin · Commercial Invoice · chamber of commerce · Incoterm

SKILL FILES BUSINESS COMMUNICATION

Skills and Competencies

Dear student,

after working with these skill files you will be able to …

- write a letter of application including a Curriculum Vitae.
- prepare for a job interview.
- order food and drinks in a restaurant.
- survive business small talk.
- understand facial expressions.
- handle commercial correspondence, e.g. e-mail, business letters, fax.
- answer the phone professionally.
- tell the way.

Enjoy!

Applying for an internship

Klaus and Laura share the same interest: they would both like to get some experience in a foreign country. Their school provides a partnership with companies in Dover in England, at the Port Franc de Barcelona in Spain and Riga in Latvia. So they both decide that they would like to take part in this project in the middle of their apprenticeship. As Laura began with her apprenticeship one year before Klaus, she is at the end of her second and he of his first year.
They choose the company in England, because it is at the port in Dover, which would be a new challenge for both of them, and because both speak neither Spanish nor Latvian. Rory McLake normally lives in Dover, too. As his exchange year ends when their year begins, they will already have a friend there. So Rory could show them around town in their free time.
To get the internship Laura and Klaus have to apply for it, so they write a Curriculum Vitae and a letter of application for the qualification for the internship.

Task 1

Write your own Curriculum Vitae (CV) using the example of Klaus Schmidt.

Writing a curriculum vitae

Curriculum Vitae

Name	Klaus Schmidt	
Address	Goetheallee 12 22567 Hamburg Telephone (evenings) (+49) 40 2345 Email k.schmidt@t-online.de	
Date of birth	26th of January 1994	
Place of birth	Hamburg, Germany	
School education[1]	2000–2004	Hatzper Grundschule (elementary school)[2]
	2004–2010	Pestalozzi Gymnasium, (higher secondary school)[2]
Professional Training	2010–2013	Berufsschule Hamburg (vocational school)[2]
Qualifications	2013	Warehouse operator
Experience	2010–2011	Trainee at Tokens, Hamburg
	2011–2013	Apprentice at Tokens, Hamburg
	2013–current	Employee Tokens, Hamburg
Hobbies	Handball (captain of Pestalozzi men's team) Trainer for the Pestalozzi Junior Boy Handball team	
Languages	German (native speaker), English (fluent)	
References[3]	Mr Kurt Schwartz Chief Storekeeper Tokens 22057 Hamburg	Mrs Nicola Ewert Berufsschule Hamburg Bachweg 51 22145 Hamburg
	Hamburg, August 20..	Klaus Schmidt

[1] *European CVs are written chronologically. North Americans write "résumés" which start with the points most relevant to the job applied for. These days, you can choose how to do it. Your CV is the document that decides if you get a job interview or not, so make it sound as positive as you can.*

[2] *Do not translate qualifications, names or titles into English: leave them in German with a short explanation, e.g. Gymnasium (higher secondary school)/Abitur (A-level equivalent)*

[3] *British and US applicants do not send open testimonials (Zeugnisse) with their CV. They give the names and addresses of people who have agreed to give the new employer relevant information.*

Writing letters

Letter of application

After they successfully wrote their CVs, Laura and Klaus have to write a letter of application. Therefore, they find out what an official business letter looks like in general.

Before writing her letter of application Laura talked to her friend Jan via a chat programme about her likes and fears concerning the internship.

Laura: Hi Jan, what's up?
Jan: Hey Laura. Fine. How r u?
Laura: I'm kinda ... at the moment
Jan: Why's that?
Laura: 'Cos of this internship in England. I really like ....
Jan: So what's your problem?
Laura: I'm not sure about ... or if ... . What if ... ?
Jan: Can't you come back early in that case?
Laura: Nah, I don't think so. Besides, I don't like to leave something unfinished.
Jan: Yeah, that's like leaving the theatre too soon and not knowing how the movie ended.
Laura: Exactly. Maybe I should just start with my letter. It's due tomorrow.
Jan: Get going. I think everything will work out just fine. See you at school tomorrow.
Laura: CU & thanx for your help.
Jan: U r welcome!

Task 2

Work with a partner.
Copy the dialogue and fill in the gaps with the following expressions:
Note: There are several possibilities which are all correct. Choose the ones which you like most. You may also add new expressions, if you like.

the idea of going abroad · meeting new people · having difficulties adjusting · having problems with the language · staying at a foreign home · learning new skills for work

Read the dialogue out loud to the class. One person takes the part of Laura, the other one the part of Jan.

Task 3

What do you like about the idea of going abroad?
What would your fears be?
Talk about it in class.

Writing a letter of application

Task 4

Laura e-mailed Klaus her letter of application but it got all mixed up.
Help Klaus to find the right order again and correct the writing.
Copy the text and generate a qualified business letter.
If you need help with the structure, go to pages 100f. and have a look at Jan's example.

From: laura.maertens@gmx.de
To: k.schmidt@t-online.de
Subject: My application

Naugels Logistics
For the attention of:
Alexander Williamson
12 Ballifeary Road
DOVER
PH10 8YR
GREAT BRITAIN

28th August 2016

Enc.:
CV

dear mr Williamson i would like to apply for the internship as warehouse logistics operator at the moment i'm working at Zig Zag Store in Hamburg where i worked in the incoming and outgoing goods, the picking and also the customer service department my duties include quality control, picking goods and customer correspondence i also have some experience with route planning of cargo transports therefore i would fit exactly to your company's profile in particular my language abilities in english and french are ideally suited to a position in an internationally operating company i would love to increase my abilities in business communication thank you for considering my application if you need any further information please write or call me yours sincerely laura märtens

Application for internship at your company

Laura Märtens
Heiligengeistbrücke 95
21039 Hamburg
GERMANY
E-Mail: laura.maertens@gmx.de

Job advertisements

We're looking for a

warehouse operator or warehouse logistics operator

We expect you to have completed an apprenticeship and achieved the following skills:

- quality check shipments
- picking customer's orders
- secure packing of goods

We offer payment above the general pay scale and 30 days holiday.

Please send your complete application to:

Runark Cargo Transport
to attn.
Peter Kappel
Brandenburgische Straße 22
12045 Berlin

Warehouse operator
Warehouse logistics operator

3 months internship with payment
later acquisition included
Field of activity:

- incoming goods
- outgoing goods
- loading and unloading containers

Please send application stating your qualifications to:

Enria Logistics Group
Heidi Suárez Romo
C/ Domingo Beltrán,
74 02320 Balazote
Spain

Looking for a new job opportunity?

We are a logistics company with focus on freight forwarding business.
We require employees with experience in the field of logistics. We prefer applicants with a completed apprenticeship as warehouse operator or warehouse logistics operator.

Send applications to:

CargoTen
Marek Nowicki
Pl. Zbawiciela 56
00-573 Warszawa
Poland

Quogreen Delivery

You are a warehouse operator or
warehouse logistics operator?
We want you!

Send applications with CV to

Tuomas Gardemeister
Ulimarinpolku 70
74250 NISSILÄ
Finnland

Experience in stock-keeping, route planning and correspondence welcome.

Task 5

Apply to one of the job advertisements given above.
Write an authentic letter of application.
Look at Jan's example of the structure of business letters for help.
If you need help on pages 100f. regarding the phrasing go to pages 110f. to have a look at useful sentences.

Writing a letter

Klaus asks Jan for some advice regarding the structure of business letters. Jan has already written some at work, so he lends his records to Klaus. Have a look at the example of how you might write a business letter.

1 Letterhead:
It tells you the company or organization the letter is from. Jan is the sender of the letter. So it must be his company's address.

2 Reference:
Your ref: and Our ref:

3 Inside address:
It shows who the letter is to.

4 Date:
6 August 2006 or 6th August 2006 without a comma (British English)
August 6, 2006 or August 6th, 2006 with a comma (American English)

5 Salutation:
Jan knows the surname of the person, so he can write "Dear Ms Miller". Otherwise he would have had to write the impersonal form: "Dear Sir or Madam".

6 Subject line:
In a few words you write what the letter is about. This line comes immediately after the salutation. In German letters it comes before the salutation. It has to be typed in bold letters.

7 Body of the letter:
This is the text of the letter. Use short paragraphs.

8 Complimentary close:
Jan finishes his letter with "Yours sincerely" because he starts with the name of the person he is writing to (Ms Miller). When he starts with "Dear Sir or Madam", he finishes with "Yours faithfully".

9 Signature block:
As Jan writes in Mr Sharp's name, he has to sign as follows: "Jan for Mr Sharp".

10 Copies:
The letters cc mean carbon copy. This shows to which other persons a copy of the letter has been sent or given.

11 Enclosures:
Under Enc: or plural Encs: you say that you have put something into the envelope together with the letter.

12 VAT-number

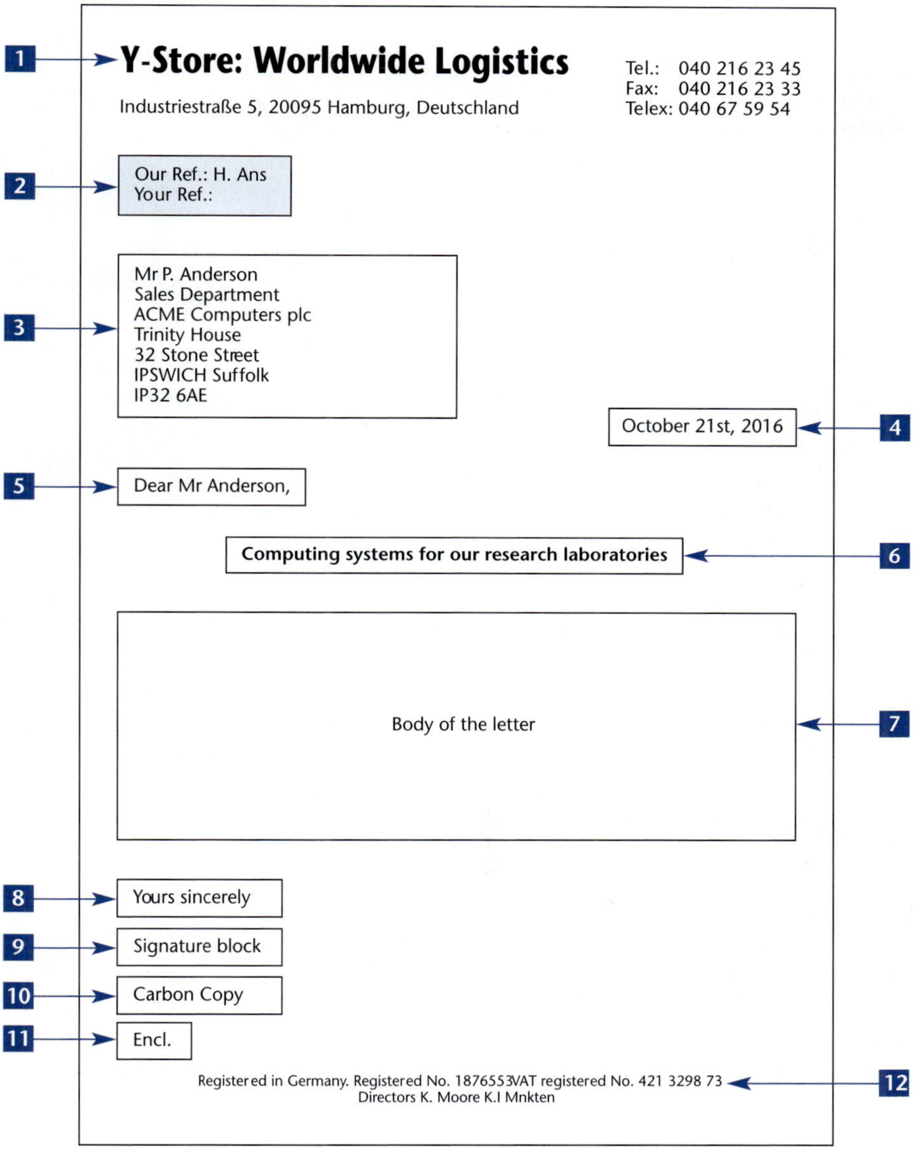

1 **Y-Store: Worldwide Logistics**

Industriestraße 5, 20095 Hamburg, Deutschland

Tel.: 040 216 23 45
Fax: 040 216 23 33
Telex: 040 67 59 54

2 Our Ref.: H. Ans
Your Ref.:

3 Mr P. Anderson
Sales Department
ACME Computers plc
Trinity House
32 Stone Street
IPSWICH Suffolk
IP32 6AE

October 21st, 2016 4

5 Dear Mr Anderson,

Computing systems for our research laboratories 6

Body of the letter 7

8 Yours sincerely

9 Signature block

10 Carbon Copy

11 Encl.

Registered in Germany. Registered No. 1876553VAT registered No. 421 3298 73 12
Directors K. Moore K.I Mnkten

The job interview

Klaus and Laura would like to prepare themselves for their first job interview. They are going to be interviewed by a representative of the company they would like to work for. So the interview will be held in English. They made a list of things, which seem to be important in a job interview.

1. It is very useful to find out as much as possible about the company you are applying at. It shows an interest in the company.
2. Making a list of possible questions would be good. So you are not unprepared when you are asked if you have any further questions.

   Good topics would be: the type of work, which department(s) you will work in, how much customer contact is involved or is there any further training to improve your working skills. If applying for a permanent position you may ask about starting salary as well.
3. Dress according to the situation. Don't go to an interview wearing jeans and t-shirt. Males at least wear a shirt, while females stick to a blouse. Both may wear trousers and of course, appearance should be neat and clean in general.

They also found some useful tips on the internet:

Five tips for a perfect interview

- **Be a good listener**
  Listen carefully when the interviewer is speaking and look interested.
  Never interrupt the interviewer.
- **Be honest**
  Never say things which are not true in an interview.
  The interviewer will probably know.
  If you don't understand a question, ask.
  If you don't know an answer, say so.
- **Don't talk too much**
  Answer the question, but then stop talking.
  Let the interviewer ask the next question.
- **Think about your body language**
  When you sit still, you look confident.
  If you fidget, you look nervous.
  Sit up straight. If you slump down, you look bored.
- **Always be positive**
  Don't criticise your colleagues, your teachers or your friends.
  If you are negative about them, then perhaps you will be negative about your company.

Task 6

Read the text above and decide which statements are true and which ones are false. Correct the false statements.

1. You should talk fast and endlessly to appear interested.
2. Sit comfortably. That demonstrates great self-confidence.
3. First of all, ask about the salary so you're not wasting your time.
4. Talk honestly about yourself.
5. A clean t-shirt is mandatory.
6. Prepare the questions that you have about the job.
7. It is not necessary to know much about the company you're applying at.
8. It is important not to seem nervous, so smoke a last cigarette and chew gum to cover the smell.

Task 7

Prepare yourself for a job interview. Imagine, you apply for the job you wrote the letter of application for in task 5. Copy and do the following tasks on an extra sheet of paper.

a. You completed your apprenticeship as ... (occupation) at ... (company).
b. List five tools or pieces of equipment you had to use.
c. List five occupational skills you have achieved.
d. List three things about your tutor or your boss.
e. List three things about your colleagues.
f. List three things about the company.
g. List three positive and three negative things about your apprenticeship.

Listening

Task 8

Audio

Listen to Laura's job interview.
Work with a partner and generate a role play where you have a job interview at the company you applied at in task 5. One of you is the interviewer and one the interviewee.
Take turns.

Meet & Greet

Laura and Klaus made it. They can both participate in the project at their schools and will work at Naugels Logistics in Dover, England.

On their first day they meet the other interns. There are two other girls and another boy. Carissa Ruiz Guevara comes from Ezcabarte in Spain; Sarah Hunt lives in Memphis, Tennessee, USA and Jurek Czarnecki was born in Kraków, Poland. They are all nearly the same age as Klaus and Laura, so they are between 17–20 years old.

Their tutor, Mrs Zoe Brennan, gives them all the necessary instructions regarding their internship at the companies, their Oyster Card for the underground along with a map and the address of their residence.

After the official part, they go to a pub to have some dinner.

Listening

At the restaurant

Task 9

Listen to the orders of the six people and have a look at the menu.
What are they ordering? Take notes on an extra sheet of paper.

Dover's Traditional

Starters

1 **White onion and Cider soup**
Thinly sliced onions, cooked with Cider

2 **Mini spicy fish cakes with chili**
Lightly fired until golden brown and served with red pepper and tomato dipping sauce

3 **Roast tomato soup**
Garden tomatoes, roasted then made to a creamy soup

Drinks

Red Wine
30 Merlot, France
31 Cabernet Sauvignon, Chile

White Wine
32 Sauvignon Blanc, France

Beer
40 Guinness
41 Cider
42 Light Ale
43 Black Sheep

Main Course

10 Steak, Guinness and mushroom pie
Steak in a sauce of mushrooms, tomatoes and Guinness, with chips
Please tell us if you like your steak English, medium or well done!

11 Lamb and apricot pie
Chopped lamp with apricots, mint and onion sauce and noodles

12 Creamy chicken and broccoli pie
Diced chicken with broccoli in a creamy white sauce and rice

13 English lamb steak
Leg of lamb steak with mashed potatoes and gravy

Desserts

20 Homemade caramelized pineapple carrot cake

21 Homemade white chocolate ice cream

22 Homemade vanilla ice cream topped with chocolate sauce and toasted nuts

Soft Drinks

50 Coke
51 Lemonade
52 Mineral Water
Sparkling or non-sparkling
53 Apple Juice
54 Orange Juice

60 Tea
Earl Grey, English Breakfast, peppermint
61 Hot chocolate with cream

70 Coffee
71 Café au lait
72 Latte macchiato
73 Cappuccino
74 Espresso

Small talk and facial expressions

When the young interns visit the company for their first day of work, they all make a different experience about how they were welcomed. In the evening they all meet again to talk about their day. Carissa only tells about a warm and friendly welcome while Sarah and Jurek both found their first day somewhat unwelcoming. Laura and Klaus both describe their first meeting with their colleagues in the incoming goods department differently. While Klaus liked the chief storekeeper very much, Laura describes him as a man who treats others rather roughly. She is glad that she will work in the administrative department from tomorrow. Klaus will work in the truck dispatch and in the storage department.

1

2

3

4

5

6

7

8

9

10

11

12

Task 10

Have a look at the pictures above. Which of these are friendly and make you feel welcome? What makes the unwelcoming persons seem unfriendly and unhelpful? Describe the pictures and explain your impressions.

Task 11

What impression do you try to make on the people you work with?
What impression do you try to avoid?
How do you do that?
Make a list on an extra sheet of paper.

Topics for small talk

When Klaus and Laura met the chief storekeeper, he showed them around the warehouse. While they walked around the premises, he talked about the goods they store, the storage system and the equipment they use. Sometimes, when he was not talking, there was an awkward silence, because Klaus and Laura both didn't know what to talk about. That would have been a great opportunity for some small talk, because this helps to get to know each other and makes one seem interested and friendly. But what should the two of them have talked about?

Task 12

What are proper topics for small talk and which ones should you better avoid? Work with a partner and make a mind map on an extra sheet of paper.

Task 13

Form groups of four or five.
Generate a role play where you meet each other for the first time in a restaurant like Klaus and Laura in the story.
You are all going to work for one of the companies you applied at in task 5.
Use the menu from task 9 and order something to eat and to drink before you start your small talk.
Present the results to your classmates.

Commercial correspondence

Writing an e-mail

As Laura is working in the administrative department she has to deal with a lot of commercial correspondence. There are many different ways to communicate with each other. They can be divided into oral and written communication.
First, Laura has to handle the written communication. She has to write an e-mail to a supplier asking if they would send her the new catalogue with warehouse equipment. This form is called an enquiry. Here is how the e-mail could look:

From: laura.maertens@naugels_logistics.co.uk

To: contact@warehouse-demand.com

Subject: Enquiry: Product catalogue 2016

1 Dear Sir or Madam

2 I'm writing on behalf of Naugels Logistics. We are very interested in your catalogue about warehouse equipment. Is it possible for you to send us the latest one?

I'm looking forward to your answer.

4 Yours faithfully
5 Laura Märtens

---

6 Naugels Logistics
12 Ballifeary Road
DOVER
PH10 8YR
GREAT BRITAIN

Telephone:	070 1450 2558
Fax:	070 1450 2559
E-mail:	contact@naugels_logistics.co.uk
Website:	www.naugels_logistics.co.uk

1 Salutation

2 Body of the email topic of the email

4 Complimentary close
5 Full name

6 Address and further contact information

Note: The subject line is in the head of the e-mail.
You should not write the date, because this is automatically added by the e-mail programme!

Mr Matthew Chandler of Warehouse Demand is answering Laura's e-mail. He calls and asks her if there is anything in particular she is interested in. Her head of department told her that they are looking for a new distribution system. Therefore, they are interested in a system where little robots help to enable the goods-to-man principle. With this system the workers do not move but the goods are brought to them by moving the whole shelf. Naugels wants to establish a new department for one specific customer and therefore, has the opportunity to test the new system.
Mr Chandler asks for more details, which Laura's head of department provides after a quick consultation with the future chief storekeeper of the new storage department. After that Mr Chandler sends Laura an offer via e-mail.

From: matthew.chandler@warehouse-demand.com

To: laura.maertens@naugels_logistics.co.uk

Subject: Offer No. 2013-7-458 regarding automated distribution system

Dear Ms Maertens

Referring to our telephone conversation of 2nd July 2016, we are pleased to inform you that we can provide you with the following:

Quantity	Description	Unit Price USD	Total USD
9000	Automated shelves 160x60x60	30.-	270,000.-
10	Distribution robot "Retriever"	20,000.-	200,000.-
1	Restock station	10,000.-	10,000.-
1	Picking station	15,000.-	15,000.-
1	Packing station	5,000.-	5,000.-
	Total incl. installation		500,000.-
	3% discount on net cash 30 days	15,000.-	485,000,-
	Freight charges & insurance		128,420.-
		Total:	**613,420.-**

We ensure delivery within four weeks from receipt of order, CIF Dover.
Payment accepted within 30 days from receipt of invoice, net cash.

We're looking forward to receiving your order.

Sincerely yours,
Matthew Chandler

Warehouse Demand
181 Snider Street
Colorado Springs, CO 80903
USA
Telephone: 719-884-7726/27
Fax: 719-884-7728

Task 14

Have a look at the offer. What does Laura have to consider regarding the price? Make a route plan from the premises of the seller to the premises of the buyer. Write down the best route and calculate the total price for Naugels Logistics on your own sheet of paper.

	USD
goods	485,000.-
carriage to docks in USA	64,360.-
loading costs	50.-
shipping costs	24,000.-
insurance	40,000.-
	GBP
unloading costs in Dover	50.-
carriage to the buyer's premises in Dover	100.-

After Laura showed her chief storekeeper the offer from Warehouse Demand, she has to write an order.

Helpful phrases for writing a business letter

Task 15

Now write Laura's order.
Use the sentences below or the structure of a business letter on pages 100f. for help. You may not exactly know how to write a business letter, so here are some helpful phrases.

Salutation
- Dear Sir or Madam,
- Dear Mr …,/Dear Mrs …,

Purpose of the letter
- We are writing/I am writing...
  - to confirm...
  - to let you know...
  - to ask...

Stating a reference
- Thank you for your letter of 26th July.
- We/I refer to your order for ...
- I have received your inquiry regarding...
- Further to our telephone conversation today,...
- Referring to your job ad in...

Good news
- I am delighted to tell you that...
- You will be pleased to hear that...

Bad news

- We regret to inform you that...
- I am afraid that...
- The material is damaged, I'll send it back.
- The quantity is not correct.
- The quality does not correspond to the one ordered.
- You have sent us the wrong article.
- The document is missing.
- The documents are (in)complete.

Making a request
- Please could you...
- I would appreciate it if you could...
- Please let us know ... .
- Please write your address clearly on the fax.
- Please fill in these documents. (BrE)
- Please fill out these documents. (AmE)
- Could you please send us written information about the required part?
- Could you please tell me when we can expect shipment?

Offering help
- Would you like us to...?
- Do you need copies? / Do you need any documents as a copy?

Giving information
- We wish to inform you that...
- The consignment is not subject to duty.
- Customs documents aren't necessary.
- I'm having problems/trouble with the local customs.
- We need the customs documents (urgently).
- We handed the consignment/shipment over to the forwarding agency on (date).
- The freight charges amount to/are USD120.
- The consignment/shipment was taken to the aircraft/ship directly.
- We/You need to start a search at the forwarding department, to find out what happened to the consignment/shipment and where to find it.
- We keep records of all transactions.

Enclosing documents
- I am enclosing...
- Please find attached ... (e-mail attachment/paper fixed to letter with a clip etc.)

Thanking
- Thank you for sending me...
- Thank you very much for your cooperation.

Background
- After leaving primary school, I attended secondary school (name)...
- At present I'm attending...

Apologizing

- I am sorry about the delay in replying.
- We were sorry to hear about the problem.
- We regret that this has happened.
- We apologize for any inconvenience caused.

Setting deadlines/Insisting/Threatening
- Please ensure that the goods reach us by (+ deadline).
- We must insist on payment by (+ deadline) at the latest.
- If the goods do not reach us by (+ deadline), we will ... (+ threat)

Assuring
- Please rest assured that we will do our utmost.
- You can count on us to ensure smooth delivery in future.

Making concessions
- We agree to reduce the price by (percentage/sum of money)
- We are happy to grant you a discount of 3 % on the goods.

Closing
- If you have any questions, please do not hesitate to call me/us on (+ tel.no.)
- Should you require further details, please contact us again.
- If we can help in any way, we would be happy to be of assistance.

Future contact
- I look forward to hearing from you soon.
- I am looking forward to receiving your order.
- I hope to receive your payment by ....
- I'm available for an interview any day of the week.

Complimentary close
- BE: Yours sincerely ..., AE: Sincerely yours, ...
- BE: Yours faithfully ..., AE: Yours truly, ...
- Regards ...

Writing a fax (facsimile messages)

30 days after Laura ordered the distribution robots, the goods arrive at Naugels Logistics. The new system is installed in an extra department in order to test it. Laura compares the invoice which came with the shipment with the offer. She finds some differences and immediately writes a complaint. Klaus, who helped to unload the twelve containers and check the shipment, also informs her that one robot is malfunctioning. To save time, she sends a fax to Warehouse Demand. As there are no established layouts for faxes, she designs it as she likes.

This is how Laura's fax looks:

1 **Naugels Logistics**
12 Ballifeary Road
DOVER
PH10 8YR
GREAT BRITAIN

Telephone: 070 1450 2558
Fax: 070 1450 2559
Website: www.naugels_logistics.co.uk

2 **To:** Warehouse Demand
181 Snider Street
Colorado Springs, CO 80903
USA

Attn: Matthew Chandler
Fax: 719-884-7728

From: Laura Märtens, Administrative Dept.

3 **Date:** 1st Sept 2016 4 **Pages:** (incl. this one) 2

5 **Subject:** Complaint about our order from 15th July 2016
and your invoice no. 2016-07-1859

Dear Mr Chandler

I'm writing to inform you that the invoice with the number 2016-07-1859 you sent us is incorrect. We ordered according to the conditions given in your offer of 3rd July 2016, so I request a new invoice for our documentation.
Please find the incorrect invoice attached.
Furthermore, I regret to inform you that one of the distribution robots "Retriever" you delivered is malfunctioning.
Please inform us how you are going to fix the robot.

I look forward to hearing from you soon.

Regards
Laura Märtens
Laura Märtens

1 + 2
Names, addresses, telephone and fax numbers of both consignor and consignee should be displayed on the fax.

3 + 4
As a fax transmission is easily interrupted, it is necessary to show a date and the number of pages.

5
An appropriate subject line is essential

Task 16

Have a look at the attached invoice and compare it with the offer on page 109. Name the incorrect parts.

WAREHOUSE DEMAND
181 Snider Street
Colorado Springs, CO 80903
USA

Telephone: 719-884-7726 /27
Fax: 719-884-7728

Naugels Logistics
12 Ballifeary Road
DOVER
PH10 8YR
GREAT BRITAIN

Invoice
Order from 15th July 2016 Order no. DVR-GB-54 Invoice no. 2016-07-1859
Date: 30th July 2016

Quantity	Description	Unit Price USD	Total USD
8500	Automated shelves 160x60x60	30.-	270,000.-
10	Distribution robot "Retriever"	20,000.-	400,000.-
1	Restock station	10,000.-	10,000.-
1	Packing station	15,000.-	15,000.-
1	Packing station	5,000.-	5,000.-
	Total excl. installation		500,000.-
	3% discount on net cash 14 days	15,000.-	485,000,-
	Freight charges & insurance		138,420.-
		Total:	**613,425.-**

Warehouse Demand immediately sends a new invoice with the corrections. They also inform Laura that Naugels should send the defective robot back to Warehouse Demand so that they can mend or replace it. Laura passes the information on to the chief storekeeper who checks the invoice again and sends it to the accounts department. Ten days later she receives a reminder via fax.

Task 17

Imagine you work at Warehouse Demand and received Laura's fax. You reply by fax to Naugel's Logistics. Remind them that they have to send back the malfunctioning robot, so that you can repair or replace it, if necessary.

Telephone Training

As Laura is working in the administrative department, she is doing a lot of commercial correspondence. She also has to answer the telephone. When she wrote an enquiry to Warehouse Demand, she received a phone call from Mr Chandler, who wanted to ask her if Naugels Logistics was interested in anything in particular.

Answering the phone

Task 18

Spelling names, addresses and numbers

Listen to the dialogue between Laura and Mr Chandler and focus on the spelling.

Task 19

Have a look at the international aviation alphabet and the name code in the Skill Files Phonetics on page 151.

a. Spell the names in three different ways:
   - English spelling
   - Name code
   - International aviation alphabet

b. Spell the street names

c. Spell the e-mail addresses

d. Spell the numbers

Spelling names
Note that **ä, ö, ü** are spelt *a-e, o-e, u-e* or a *Umlaut, o Umlaut, u Umlaut* and **ß** as *double s*.

Saying telephone numbers
Say the individual numbers of the telephone numbers one after the other.
When two or three numbers are the same, you can say double or triple ..., e.g. double-four triple-eight for 44 888.

Saying e-mail and website addresses
In **e-mail addresses** say **at** for the symbol @ and **dot** for (.).
Say letters one after the other.
Note that we often leave out *http://* when saying website addresses.

If you need more help for the correct English spelling, see the Skill Files Phonetics on page 151 for the phonetic alphabet.
For help with the numbers, have a look at page 147f. in the Grammar Skill Files.

Names and addresses

Staweczewski	Müller	Kogner
Speicherstraße 22 55436 Münster	556, Hyde Park Street London, SE6 5AJ	Münchener Straße 1 45896 Bad Seege
note64@gmail.com	cww@muellernet.de	c.k.gerklein@gmx.de

Numbers

0201 – 737669	0049 – 060 – 885933	040 – 9955661
0208 – 17765555	0035 – 169 – 5553672	0209 – 15496373
020 – 44398	0018 – 2317 – 554	060 – 17787737

Helpful phrases for talking on the phone

Task 20

Now it's your turn to practise telephone calls.
Look at the situations below and choose one to generate a telephone call.
Work with a partner and use the sentences below for help.

Generate a situation where...
- something isn't in stock.
- you have to put someone through.
- someone has dialed the wrong number.
- the goods you've received are damaged.
- you received a wrong number of goods.
- you received goods you've never ordered.
- you have to order goods.
- someone orders goods.

Here are some helpful sentences when someone calls you in English.

Phoning somebody
- My name is ... . Can I speak to ... , please?
- Could I speak to somebody who is responsible for ... , please?

Answering the phone
- Good morning/afternoon. This is Mr/Mrs/Ms.... How can I help you?
- Who is calling, please?

Putting a caller through
- Can you hold the line, please? I'll put you through to ...
- Just one moment, please.
- Try asking ..., please.

Saying somebody or something is not available
- I'm sorry, but ... is not available at the moment.
- I'm afraid we do not have it in stock at the moment.
- We can't deliver the goods before ...
- I'm afraid we don't have enough room/space for the goods at the moment.
- I cannot get hold of the shipping department.
- I'm (still) waiting for a part from the manufacturer.

Offering help
- Would you like to call back or should we call you back?
- Would you like to have a similar article?
- I'll check that for you.
- Let me just check, please.
- May I help you?
- No problem.
- Don't worry!

Giving information
- Your consignment/shipment is ..., and it will probably arrive here on ... at ... o' clock.
- We were told that the consignment/ shipment will be in ... at ... o' clock on ...

Asking for information

- What was the name again, please?
- Could you spell that for me, please?
- Could you please spell your name?
- Could you give me your number, please?
- When are you able to deliver the goods?
- When should we deliver the goods?
- Could you please send us written information about the required part?
- Which flight is the part on?
- Could you please tell me which container it was, give me the (air) waybill number, and tell me when you sent the part, and which company you are using?
- Could you please give me your cost centre?
- Could you please give me the material number, serial number, quantity and weight of the part?
- When did you send the consignment/shipment?
- When will the consignment/shipment arrive?
- Could you tell me what the contents of the consignment/shipment are?
- Which is the department responsible?/Which department deals with this?
- What is your fax address?/Could you please give me your fax address?
- Who is the sender?
- How did you send the consignment/shipment?
- What is the flight number?
- How should I request the material?
- Where is the part located?
- Where shall I put the material?

Getting out of trouble
- I'm sorry, I did not get that. Could you repeat that, please?
- Could you speak more slowly, please?
- I'm sorry, I cannot help you, please speak to ...
- I'm sorry, I cannot help you. You could try calling the manufacturer for further information.
- I am sorry, but I cannot understand you.
- I'll have to ask the carrier.
- I'll have to make inquiries first. I'll contact you as soon as possible.
- I'll make out an invoice for you.
- I am (not) familiar with this procedure.

- You can borrow a part from ...
- If you need the part urgently, I can refer you to the ... team.
- Pardon me?

Closing
- Thank you very much for your help./Thanks a lot for your help.
- You're welcome.
- Thank you for your call. Goodbye.
- Goodbye and thanks a lot for your help.
- Have a nice day!

Telling the way

During their internship at Naugels Logistics, all interns visit other companies. Today they are visiting Blooming, which trades in bulk and other cargoes. They were divided into groups. Carissa and Sarah were in the first group together with their mentor Zoe and have already visited the company. Klaus, Jurek and Laura are in the second group and haven't seen the company yet. They meet each other at the roundabout and ask for the way to the canteen, where they are supposed to meet their guide for the tour.

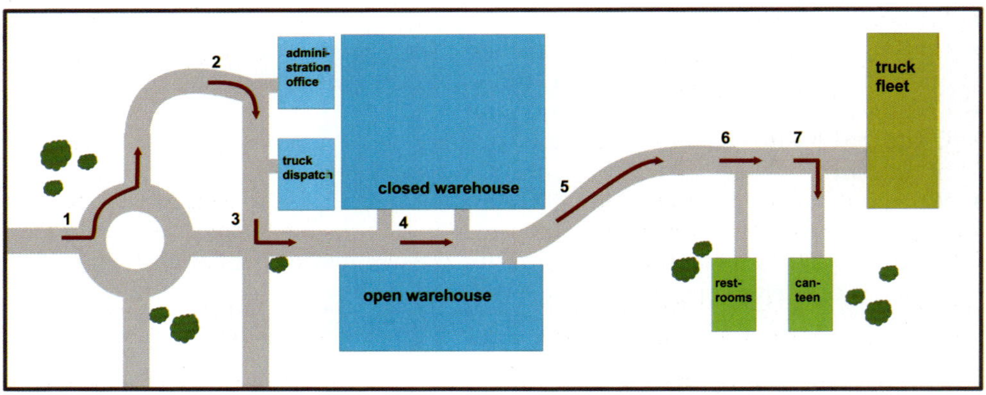

Listening

Task 21

Listen to the conversation between Carissa, Sarah, Jurek, Zoe, Klaus and Laura. Copy the numbers next to the arrows on the plan of the company and write down what the arrows stand for.

Telling the way in the warehouse

Klaus is working in the storage of Naugels Logistics. As he already had some experience with the forklift truck the chief storekeeper lets him transport some goods to different warehouse areas.

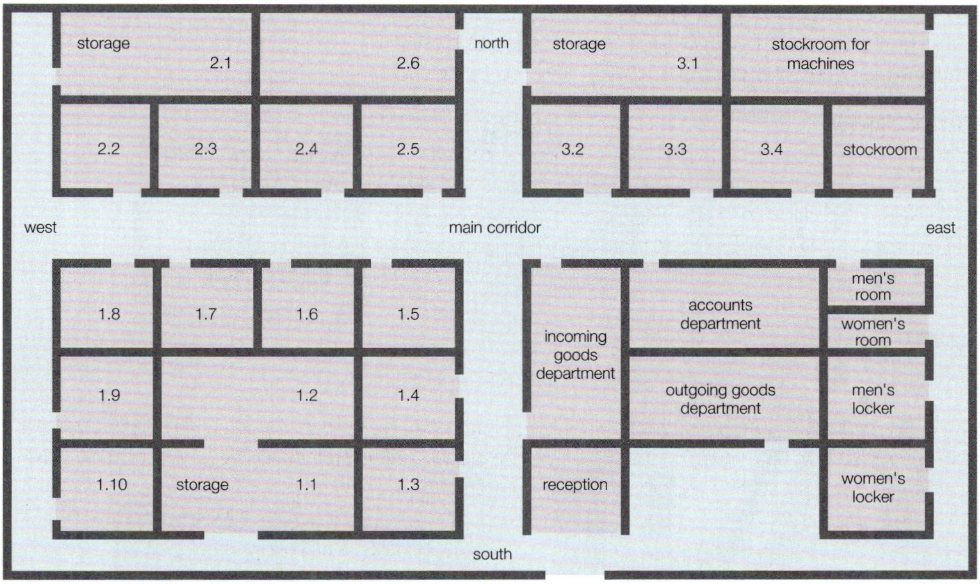

Task 22

Klaus starts at the south entrance and has to fetch the goods from the incoming goods department first. Describe the way.

Task 23

Klaus has to move the goods he fetched from the incoming goods department to storage 2.1. He asks a colleague in the incoming goods department where storage 2.1 is.

Generate a conversation where you have to describe the way to storage 2.1. Work with a partner and present your result to your classmates.

Klaus: Can you tell me the way to storage 2.1, please? It's my first day here with the forklift truck.

You: ...

Task 24

When Klaus arrives at storage 2.1 he finds out that the goods he is transporting do not belong there. He has to move them to storage 1.1. What a pity that he does not know the way. Can you help him?

Generate a dialogue (in spoken English) between Klaus and yourself by looking at the following aspects:

Klaus sagt, dass er hier im Lager 2.1 falsch ist. Er muss zu Lager 1.1 und fragt deshalb nach dem Weg.

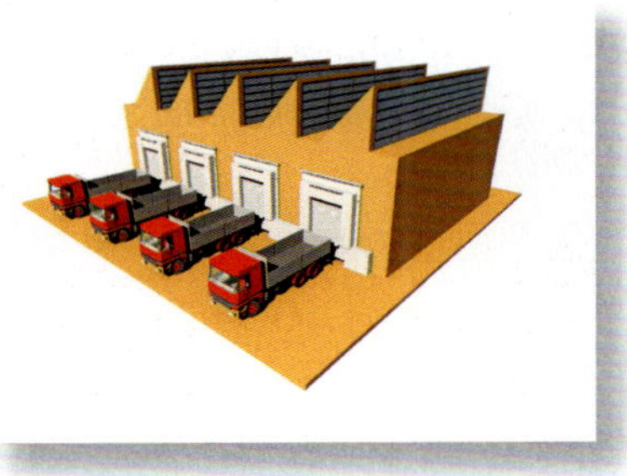

Du erklärst ihm den Weg von Lager 2.1 zu Lager 1.1.
Klaus bedankt sich höflich und verabschiedet sich.
Du verabschiedest dich freundlich.

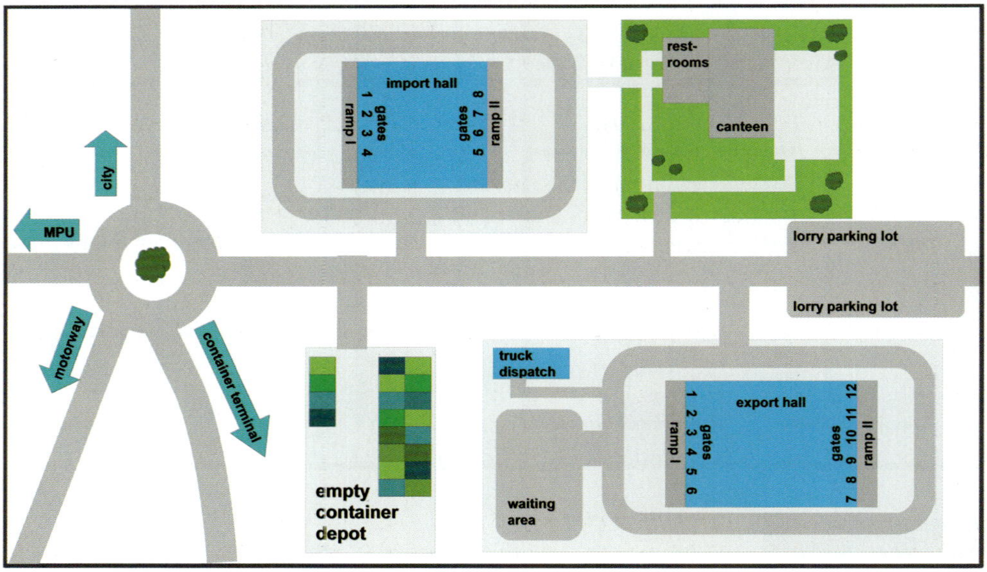

Task 25

Form groups of five and choose one situation.
Generate the conversations where a lorry driver asks his way around Naugels Logistics.
Present your results to your classmates.

Situation 1

Ein LKW-Fahrer fragt Sarah am Kreisverkehr nach dem Weg zur Hebestelle des Betriebes Naugels Logistics.
Sarah erklärt ihm den Weg zum Vorstau, weil der LKW-Fahrer dort zunächst parken muss. Zudem weist Sarah ihn darauf hin, welche Sicherheitskleidung zu tragen ist, solange er sich auf dem Betriebsgelände aufhält.
Dort angekommen, schickt ihn Klaus, der heute in der Hebestelle arbeitet, zur Rampe 1, Tor 3 der Exporthalle.
Der LKW-Fahrer möchte danach noch die Kantine besuchen und fragt den in der Exporthalle arbeitenden Jurek nach dem Weg. Dieser teilt ihm mit, dass er das Kantinengelände nur zu Fuß betreten darf und deshalb seinen LKW auf den dafür vorgesehenen Parkplätzen abzustellen hat.
In der Kantine erkundigt sich der LKW-Fahrer bei Carissa nach dem Weg zu seiner Firma MPU & Co.

Situation 2

Ein LKW-Fahrer fragt Sarah am Kreisverkehr nach dem Weg zur Hebestelle des Betriebes Naugels Logistics.

Sarah erklärt ihm den Weg zum Vorstau, weil der LKW-Fahrer dort zunächst parken muss. Zudem weist Sarah ihn darauf hin, welche Sicherheitskleidung zu tragen ist, solange er sich auf dem Betriebsgelände aufhält.

Dort angekommen, schickt ihn Klaus, der heute in der Hebestelle arbeitet, zur Rampe 2, Tor 11 der Exporthalle.

Der LKW-Fahrer möchte danach noch die Sanitäranlage besuchen und fragt den in der Exporthalle arbeitenden Jurek nach dem Weg. Dieser teilt ihm mit, dass er das Gelände nur zu Fuß betreten darf und deshalb seinen LKW auf den dafür vorgesehenen Parkplätzen abzustellen hat.

In der Kantine erkundigt sich der LKW-Fahrer bei Carissa nach dem Weg zur Autobahn.

Situation 3

Ein LKW-Fahrer fragt Sarah am Kreisverkehr nach dem Weg zur Hebestelle des Betriebes Naugels Logistics.

Sarah erklärt ihm den Weg zum Vorstau, weil der LKW-Fahrer dort zunächst parken muss. Zudem weist Sarah ihn darauf hin, welche Sicherheitskleidung zu tragen ist, solange er sich auf dem Betriebsgelände aufhält.

Dort angekommen schickt ihn Klaus, der heute in der Hebestelle arbeitet, zur Rampe 1, Tor 4 der Importhalle.

Während der LKW beladen wird, möchte der Fahrer die Sanitäranlagen aufsuchen und fragt den Lagerarbeiter in der Importhalle nach dem Weg. Dieser erklärt ihm den Weg.

In der Kantine erkundigt sich der LKW-Fahrer bei Carissa nach dem Weg zum Containerterminal.

Situation 4

Ein LKW-Fahrer fragt Sarah am Kreisverkehr nach dem Weg zur Hebestelle des Betriebes Naugels Logistics.

Sarah erklärt ihm den Weg zum Vorstau, weil der LKW-Fahrer dort zunächst parken muss. Zudem weist Sarah ihn darauf hin, welche Sicherheitskleidung zu tragen ist, solange er sich auf dem Betriebsgelände aufhält.

Dort angekommen schickt ihn der Zuständige von der Hebestelle zur Rampe 2, Tor 6 der Importhalle.

Der LKW-Fahrer möchte danach noch die Kantine besuchen und fragt den Lagerarbeiter in der Importhalle nach dem Weg. Dieser teilt ihm mit, dass er das Kantinengelände nur zu Fuß betreten darf und deshalb seinen LKW auf den dafür vorgesehenen Parkplätzen abzustellen hat.

In der Kantine erkundigt sich der LKW-Fahrer bei Carissa nach dem Weg in die Stadt.

SKILL FILES WORKING WITH LITERATURE

Skills and Competencies

Dear student,

after working with these skill files you will be able to …

- work with a text and analyse it.
- divide a text into different units of meaning.
- summarize the general thoughts of a text.
- name the main topic of a text.
- extract information out of a text by searching for keywords in the text.
- compare your everyday work with that of a non-fictional character in literature.

Enjoy!

Teacher Man by Frank McCourt

Frank McCourt was born 1930 in Manhattan, New York, but he grew up in Ireland. He emigrated to the United States when he was 19. Before he became an award-winning writer, he worked as a teacher in several secondary schools in New York.
In "Teacher Man" Frank McCourt describes his life as a teacher at a Vocational and Technical High School in New York. In Chapter 4 he tells his students what he did before he became a teacher.

Chapter 4

Hey, Mr. McCourt, did you ever do real work, not teaching, but, you know, real work?
Are you joking? What do you call teaching? Look around this room and ask yourself if you'd like to get up here and face you every day. You. Teaching is harder than working on docks and warehouses. How many of you have relatives working along the waterfront?
Half the class, mostly Italian, a few Irish.
Before I came to this school I worked on Manhattan, Hoboken and Brooklyn piers, I said. One boy said his father knew me from Hoboken.
I told them, After College I passed the exams for the teacher's license but I didn't think I was cut out for the life of a teacher. I knew nothing about American teenagers. Wouldn't know what to say to you. Dockside work was easier. Trucks backed in. We swung our hooks. Haul, hoist, pull, push. Stack on pallets. Forklift slides in, lift the load, reverses, stacks the load in the warehouse, and back to the platform. You worked with your body and your brain had a day off. You worked eight to noon, had a foot-long sandwich and a quart of beer for lunch, sweated it off from one to five, headed home, hungry for dinner, ready for a movie and a few beers in a Third Avenue bar.

Once you got the hang of it you moved like a robot. You kept up with the strongest man on the platform and size didn't matter. You used your knees to save your back. If you forgot, platform men would bark, Chrissakes, you got a rubber spine or sumpin'?
You learned to use the hook in different ways with different loads: boxes, sacks, crates, furniture, great chunks of greasy machinery. A sack of beans or peppers has a mind of its own. It can change shape one way or another and you have to go with it. You looked at the size, shape and weight of an item and you knew in a second how to lift and swing it. You learned the ways of truckers and their helpers. Independent truckers were easy. They worked for themselves, set their own pace. Corporation truckers prodded you to hurry up, man, lift the damn load, let's go, I wanna get outaheah. Truckers' helpers were surly no matter who they worked for. They played little games to test you and throw you off, especially if they thought you were just off the boat. If you worked close to the edge of pier or platform they'd suddenly drop their side of the sack or crate hard enough to pull an arm from its socket and you learned to stay away from the edge of anything. Then they'd laugh and say, Faith an' begorrah, Paddy, or Top o' the mornin' with a fake Irish accent. You'd never complain to a boss about any of this. He'd say, Whassa matter, kid? Can't you take a little joke? Complaining only made matters worse. The word might get to a trucker or a helper and he might accidentally bump you off the platform or even the pier. [...]

I told my classes, I was so uncertain about teaching I thought of simply spending my life at Port Warehouses, big fish, small pond. My bosses would be so impressed with my college degree they'd hire me as checker and promote me to an office job where I'd surely rise in the world. I might become boss of all checkers. I know how it was with warehouse office workers or office workers anywhere. They pushed papers around, yawned, looked out the window at us slaving away on the platform. [...]
What I missed about the piers was the way people spoke their minds and didn't give a shit. Not like the college professors who would tell you, On the one hand, yes, on the other hand, no, and you didn't know what to think. It was important to know what professors thought so you could give it back to them at exam time. In the warehouses everyone insulted everyone else in a joking way till someone stepped over the line and the hooks came out. It was remarkable when that happened. You could see from the way the laughs faded and the smiles got tighter that some bigmouth was getting too close to the bone and you knew the next thing was the hook or the fist. [...]

Source: Frank Mc Court, Teacher Man. Scribner: New York (2005)

Annotations

line 11: to be cut out for sth. - für etw. geeignet sein
line 32: Paddy – nickname for an Irish person

Task 1

Step 1 - Extensive Reading
Read the whole text carefully.

Task 2

Step 2 - Dealing with Background Information
a) Make a list with the words you don't know.
b) Compare your list with your neighbor.
c) Find the translations together.

Task 3

Step 3 - Summing up the general thoughts
a) Divide the text into different units of meaning. Write down the lines for each unit.
b) Then describe what is happening in each unit by summing up the meaning in keywords. Write them down.

Task 4

Step 4 – Expressing the main topic
Have a look at your keywords.
What is the main topic of the text? What is the text about in general?
Write down two to three sentences that describe the main idea of the text.

Task 5

Step 5 – Answering questions
Read the questions below.
Answer each question by having a look at all paragraphs searching for keywords.
Example:
If the question is: "How was his work at dockside?" then you look for the keyword "dockside".

Write down the information on an extra sheet of paper before answering the question. Note! Always search the complete text even if you think you've already found the answer.

a) Where did Frank McCourt work before he became a teacher?
b) What does he mean by "You worked with your body and your brain had a day off." ?
c) What was a typical "Dockside" working day like? Describe the routine.
d) What happened if you did not use "your knees to save your back"? Why?
e) How does he describe the office workers in comparison to the warehouse workers?
f) Compare your work to the work at the docks that Frank McCourt describes.

Therefore copy the table and list all the activities at the port.

activities	Frank McCourt's description	my work
stack pallets	*X*	

- Do you do other things at work? Add them to the list.
- Tick the activities you do at work and the activities in Frank Mc Court's text.
- Now compare your works by stating the similarities and differences.

SKILL FILES GRAMMAR

Skills and Competencies

Dear student,

these skill files help you to do the grammar tasks in each unit.
They are also designed to give you orientation in the wide world of grammar.
You will find explanations in German and several examples in English for every grammatical situation.

Please see the content on page 7 for details.

Nouns (Nomen/Hauptwörter)

Zunächst gilt, dass alle Hauptwörter im Englischen **klein**geschrieben werden.

The worker is not in the warehouse.

Ausnahme sind alle Eigennamen, d. h. bestimmte einzelne Personen, Länder, Orte, Tage und Monate.

On Monday Paul is in the incoming goods department.
These goods are delivered by an Austrian forwarding agency.

Die **Mehrzahl**/derPlural wird durch das Anfügen von *-s* gebildet.

One warehouse operator is ill today, the other three warehouse operators are checking the deliveries.

Bei Zischlauten ist die Endung der Mehrzahl *-es*.

He hasn't got one box, he has got two boxes.

Bei bestimmten Hauptwörtern ändert sich die Rechtschreibung, z. B. bei einer Einzahlendung von Konsonant plus *-y* wird die Mehrzahlendung zu *-ies*.

The coffee comes from one country. The bananas come from different countries.

Es gibt auch **Ausnahmen**, bei denen sich die Mehrzahlform völlig verändert. Die wichtigsten sind hier aufgeführt:

Einzahl/Singular	Mehrzahl/Plural
child	*children*
man	*men*
woman	*women*
foot	*feet*
tooth	*teeth*

Es gibt auch Einzahlformen, die in der Mehrzahlform gleich aussehen und trotzdem zählbar sind.

Einzahl/Singular	Mehrzahl/Plural
fish	*fish*
sheep	*sheep*
aircraft	*aircraft*
Chinese	*Chinese*
Swiss	*Swiss*

Es gibt auch Hauptwörter, die nicht zählbar sind und/oder nicht in der Mehrzahl stehen dürfen.

Englisch	Deutsch
information	*Information/en*
furniture	*Möbel*
food	*Essen*
bread	*Brot*
tea	*Tee*
water	*Wasser*
damage	*Schaden/Schäden*
evidence	*Beweis/e*
advice	*Ratschlag/Ratschläge*

Um nicht zählbare Wörter zählbar zu machen, muss man Fügungen wie *a piece of* (ein Stück), *a bit of* (ein bisschen), *a packet of* (ein Paket), *a bottle of* (eine Flasche), *a slice of* (eine Scheibe), *a cup of* (eine Tasse) oder *an item of* (ein Artikel) davor setzen.

There are two packets of food.
She drinks four cups of coffee every morning. He eats two slices of bread for breakfast.
In each package are six bottles of water.

Achtung! Die Mehrzahl von *person* heißt *people*. *People* (Leute) und *police* (Polizei) gibt es nur in der Mehrzahl.

There is one person at the information desk, there are three people in the forwarding department.
Many people in our company don't like the new warehouse.
The police were not interested in our complaint.

Der sogenannte **s-Genitiv** wird bei Personen und häufig auch bei Tieren gebraucht, um eine Zugehörigkeit, einen Besitz oder eine Urheberschaft auszudrücken. Er kann aber auch im Zusammenhang mit Staaten, Städten und Institutionen benutzt werden.

Jan's hammer and nails are on the table.
London's harbour isn't the biggest in Europe.

The company's goods are stored in pallet racks.
Germany's economy depends on the export.

Die **of-Fügung** wird verwendet, wenn Personen und Tiere keine Rolle spielen.
These orders came from the University of Cambridge.
The material of the racks is made in Portugal.

Articles (Artikel)

Im Englischen gibt es keine Unterscheidung nach Geschlechtern für die Artikel. Der **bestimmte Artikel** in der deutschen Sprache kann „der", „die" oder „das" sein, in der englischen Sprache gibt es nur einen bestimmten Artikel: *the*. Ein bestimmter Artikel wird benutzt, wenn etwas näher beschrieben bzw. bestimmt wird.
The box over there is the one with the fragile goods.
Can you give me the hammer on the table?

Beginnt das Wort, das auf den Artikel folgt, mit einem Vokal (a,e,i,o,u), dann wird das *e* in *the* nicht wie ein kurzes „e", sondern wie ein langes „i" ausgesprochen:
The enquiry that you are looking for is on the desk.
Sorry, this is not the amount we ordered.

Der **unbestimmte Artikel** ist in der deutschen Sprache „ein" oder „eine", je nach dem Geschlecht. Im Englischen gibt es *a* oder *an*. Er wird nur in der Einzahl von zählbaren Begriffen verwendet, die einzeln und nicht näher bestimmt sind.
This is a new airway bill.
Peter wants to become a warehouse operator.

Beginnt das Wort, das auf den Artikel folgt, mit einem Vokal, dann wird *a* zu *an*.
This bag has got an average weight of one kilo.
This is an insulated container.

Achtung! Wird das *u* wie „ju" ausgesprochen – z.B. bei *useful* – dann wird nicht *an* benutzt.
A forklift truck is a useful vehicle in the warehouse.

Der unbestimmte Artikel wird bei nachgestellten Zeit-, Maß- und Mengenangaben verwendet und kann dann mit „pro" übersetzt werden.
My company delivers six containers a day.
The lorry does 80 miles an hour.

Pronouns (Pronomen)

Das **Personalpronomen** ersetzt ein Hauptwort in der Subjektform (Antwort auf die Frage: Wer oder Was?) oder in der Objektform (Antwort auf die Fragen: Wen oder Was?/ Wem oder Was?).

Subjektform:

	Englisch	Deutsch
Einzahl 1. Person 2. Person 3. Person	 *I* *you* *he* *she* *it*	 ich du/Sie er sie es
Mehrzahl 1. Person 2. Person 3. Person	 *we* *you* *they*	 wir ihr sie

Achtung! *I* (ich) wird immer großgeschrieben, auch in der Satzmitte!

Objektform:

	Englisch	Deutsch
Einzahl 1. Person 2. Person 3. Person	 *me* *you* *him* *her* *it*	 mich/mir dich/dir/ Sie/Ihnen ihn/ihm sie/ihr es/ihm
Mehrzahl 1. Person 2. Person 3. Person	 *us* *you* *them*	 uns euch sie/ihnen

I saw him yesterday.
Can you give me the picking list, please?

Im Englischen gibt es keine eigene Höflichkeitsform. *You* kann sowohl „du" als auch „Sie" heißen.

Mr Smith, could you please help me with the airway bill?
Paul, you are a nice colleague.

Possessivpronomen beschreiben eine Zugehörigkeit bzw. einen Besitz. Sie können zusammen mit einem Hauptwort stehen. Dann werden sie adjektivisch genannt:

	Englisch	Deutsch
Einzahl 1. Person 2. Person 3. Person	 *my* *your* *his* *her* *its*	 mein/e dein/e, Ihr/e sein/e ihr/e sein/e, ihr/e

	Englisch	Deutsch
Mehrzahl 1. Person 2. Person 3. Person	 *our* *your* *their*	 unser/e euer/eure ihr/e

These are my new safety boots.
I did not receive your last order.

Wenn Possessivpronomen ein Hauptwort ersetzen können, nennt man sie substantivisch:

	Englisch	Deutsch
Einzahl 1. Person 2. Person 3. Person	 *mine* *yours* *his* *hers* *its*	 meins/meine deins/deine, Ihres/Ihre seins/seine ihres/ihre ihres/ihre, seins/seine
Mehrzahl 1. Person 2. Person 3. Person	 *ours* *yours* *theirs*	 unsers/unsere euers/eure ihres/ihre

This is not my pair of goggles. Mine are in the drawer.
This is my desk. Hers is in the next room.

Verbs (Verben)

Das Verb *to be* (= sein) ist eine große Ausnahme bei den Verben. Es kann sowohl Vollverb als auch Hilfsverb sein. Als Vollverb hat *to be* folgende Formen im ***Simple Present***:

Bejahter Satz (Lang-/Kurzform)	Verneinter Satz (Lang-/Kurzform)	Frage
I am from England./I'm from England.	*I am not from England./ I'm not from England.*	*Am I from England?*
You are from England./You're from England.	*You are not from England./ You aren't from England.*	*Are you from England?*
He/She/It is from England./ He's/She's/It's from England.	*He/She/It is not from England./ He/She/It isn't from England.*	*Is he/she/it from England?*
We are from England./We're from England.	*We are not from England./ We aren't from England.*	*Are we from England?*
You are from England./You're from England.	*You are not from England./ You aren't from England.*	*Are you from England?*
They are from England./They're from England.	*They are not from England./ They aren't from England.*	*Are they from England?*

Im ***Simple Past*** hat *to be* die Formen ***was*** (bei *I, he, she it*) und ***were*** (bei *you, we, they*).

Bejahter Satz	Verneinter Satz (Lang-/Kurzform)	Frage
I was here.	*I was not here./ I wasn't here.*	*Was I here?*
You were here.	*You were not here./ You weren't here.*	*Were you here?*
He/She/It was here.	*He/She/It was not here./ He/She/It wasn't here.*	*Was he/she/it here?*
We were here.	*We were not here./ We weren't here.*	*Were we here?*
You were here.	*You were not here./ You weren't here.*	*Were you here?*
They were here.	*They were not here./ They weren't here.*	*Were they here?*

Für alle anderen Verben gelten folgende Regeln für die Bildung der Zeiten:

Simple Present (einfache Gegenwart)

Die Bildung des *Simple Present*
Das *Simple Present* wird gebildet aus dem Infinitiv (der Stammform) des Verbs. Bei der 3. Person Singular (*he, she, it* oder ein Name) wird an den Infinitiv ein *-s* angehängt.

Verneinte Sätze
Da man im Englischen ein Vollverb nicht direkt verneinen kann (außer ein paar besondere Verben, wie z. B. *to be*, siehe oben), steht das Hilfsverb *do*. In der 3. Person Singular (*he, she, it*) wird *does* verwendet.

Fragen
Auch bei Fragen im *Simple Present* benutzt man das Hilfsverb *do*. In der 3. Person Singular *(he, she, it)* wird *does* verwendet.

Bejahter Satz	Verneinter Satz (Lang-/Kurzform)	Frage
I work.	*I do not work./ I don't work.*	*Do I work?*
You work.	*You do not work./ You don't work.*	*Do you work?*
He/She/It works.	*He/She/It does not work./ He/She/It doesn't work.*	*Does he/she/it work?*
We work.	*We do not work./ We don't work.*	*Do we work?*
You work.	*You do not work./ You don't work.*	*Do you work?*
They work.	*They do not work./ They don't work.*	*Do they work?*

Achtung: Das Verb *to do* fungiert im *Simple Present* bei verneinten Sätzen und Fragen als Hilfsverb. Es gibt es aber natürlich auch als Vollverb (*to do* = tun, machen).

Beispiele:

I do my homework.	(Ich mache meine Hausaufgaben.)
Tim doesn't do his homework.	(Tim macht seine Hausaufgaben nicht.)
Do you do your homework?	(Machst du deine Hausaufgaben?)

Das Verb *to have* (haben) kann auch Vollverb und Hilfsverb sein.

Beispiele:

Vollverb:

I have a nice boss.	(Ich habe einen netten Chef.)
Jan doesn't have a nice flat.	(Jan hat keine schöne Wohnung.)
Do you have a nice job?	(Hast du eine gute Arbeit?)

Hilfsverb:

I have to work tomorrow.	(Ich muss morgen arbeiten.)
Tom hasn't packed the boxes yet.	(Tom hat die Kisten noch nicht gepackt.)
Have you had a good apprenticeship?	(Hast du eine gute Ausbildung gehabt?)

Wenn man ausdrücken möchte, dass man etwas besitzt oder es um Verwandte geht, so kann man entweder das Vollverb *have* benutzen oder die Form *have got* (hauptsächlich im britischen Englisch verbreitet).

Die Sätze (insbesondere Verneinungen und Fragen) werden dann unterschiedlich gebildet:

Bejahter Satz	Verneinter Satz (Lang-/Kurzform)	Frage
to have		
I have a job.	*I do not have a job./ I don't have a job.*	*Do I have a job?*
have got		
I have got a job. I've got a job.	*I have not got a job./ I haven't got a job.*	*Have I got a job?*

Das *Simple Present* wird benutzt für:
- wiederkehrende Ereignisse
- wiederholte Handlungen (regelmäßig, immer, jeden Tag, oft, manchmal oder nie)
- allgemeingültige Aussagen
- feststehende Handlungen (auch in der Zukunft, z. B. Fahrpläne)

Die Signalwörter im *Simple Present*

Signalwörter für das *Simple Present* sind Wörter, die eine wiederholte Handlung ausdrücken. Das sind zum Beispiel:

always (immer), *often* (oft), *usually* (gewöhnlich), *sometimes* (manchmal), *seldom* (selten), *never* (nie)

Auch andere Zeitangaben sind möglich, wie z. B. folgende Verbindungen:

every day/week/year etc. (jeden Tag/jede Woche/jedes Jahr usw.) *on Mondays* (montags), *after work* (nach der Arbeit)

Present Progressive/Present Continuous (Verlaufsform der Gegenwart)

Diese Verlaufsform der Gegenwart wird hauptsächlich verwendet, um einen Vorgang in der Gegenwart zu beschreiben, der noch nicht beendet ist.

Die Bildung des *Present Progressive*
Das *Present Progressive* wird gebildet aus einer Form von *to be (am, are* oder *is)* dem Infinitiv (der Stammform) des Verbs und der Endung *–ing*.

Bejahter Satz (Lang-/Kurzform)	Verneinter Satz (Lang-/Kurzform)	Frage
I am working./ I'm working.	*I am not working./ I'm not working.*	*Am I working?*
You are working./ You're working.	*You are not working./ You aren't working.*	*Are you working?*
He/She/It is working./ He's/She's/It's working.	*He/She/It is not working./ He/She/It isn't working.*	*Is he/she/it working?*
We are working./ We're working.	*We are not working./ We aren't working.*	*Are we working?*
You are working./ You're working.	*You are not working./ You aren't working.*	*Are you working?*
They are working./ They're working.	*They are not working./ They aren't working.*	*Are they working?*

Das *Present Progressive* wird benutzt
- bei Handlungen, die im Moment des Sprechens geschehen, z. B.
  Peter is reading a book now. (Peter liest jetzt gerade ein Buch.)
- bei Handlungen, die nur vorübergehend stattfinden, z. B.
  Klaus is working in London this month. (Klaus arbeitet diesen Monat in London.)
- bei Handlungen, die jetzt gerade geschehen (jedoch nicht unbedingt im Moment des Sprechens), z. B.
  My friend is preparing for his exam. (Mein Freund bereitet sich auf seine Prüfung vor.)
- bei bereits feststehenden Plänen für die Zukunft, z. B.
  She is going to Hamburg on Saturday. (Sie fährt am Samstag nach Hamburg.)
- bei Veränderungen, Trends, z. B.
  More and more people are using their computers to listen to music. (Immer mehr Menschen benutzen ihre Computer, um Musik zu hören)

Die Signalwörter im *Present Progressive*
Signalwörter für das *Present Progressive* sind Wörter, die ausdrücken, dass etwas jetzt, im Moment des Sprechens, geschieht. Zum Beispiel sind dies:

now (jetzt gerade), *at the moment* (in diesem Moment), *Look!* (Sieh mal!), *Listen!* (Hör mal!)

Verben, die normalerweise nicht im *Progressive* verwendet werden (diese Verben drücken Zustände, Gefühle, Besitz o. Ä. aus):
be, believe, belong, forget, hate, hear, like, love, mean, need, prefer, remain, realize, see, seem, smell, think, understand, want, wish

I understand English. (Ich verstehe Englisch.)
He doesn't like fish. (Er mag keinen Fisch.)

Gegenüberstellung *Simple Present/Present Progressive*

Simple Present	*Present Progressive*
wiederkehrende Handlungen, z. B. *Peter works as a warehouse operator.*	Handlungen, die im Moment des Sprechens geschehen, z. B. *Peter is working in the office at the moment.*
feststehende Handungen, z. B. *The train leaves at 4 p.m.*	feststehende Pläne für die Zukunft, z. B. *We are leaving for Amsterdam next week.*
allgemeingültige Aussagen, z. B. *A lot of tourists go to Spain on holiday.*	Handlungen, die nur vorübergehend stattfinden, z. B. *My car is broken, so I am going to work by bus this week.*

Simple Past (Einfache Vergangenheit)

Die Bildung des *Simple Past*

Das *Simple Past* wird gebildet:
- bei regelmäßigen Verben: Infinitiv + *-ed*
- bei unregelmäßigen Verben: 2. Spalte der Tabelle der unregelmäßigen Verben

Verneinte Sätze

Da man im Englischen ein Vollverb nicht direkt verneinen kann (außer ein paar besondere Verben, wie z. B. *to be)*, steht im *Simple Past* das Hilfsverb *did* (*Simple Past* von *do*).

Fragen

Bei Fragen im *Simple Past* wird *did* + Infinitiv verwendet.

Bejahter Satz	Verneinter Satz (Lang-/Kurzform)	Frage
I worked.	*I did not work./* *I didn't work.*	*Did I work?*
You worked.	*You did not work./* *You didn't work.*	*Did you work?*
He/She/It worked.	*He/She/It did not work./* *He/She/It didn't work.*	*Did he/she/it work?*
We worked.	*We did not work./* *We didn't work.*	*Did we work?*
You worked.	*You did not work./* *You didn't work.*	*Did you work?*
They worked.	*They did not work./* *They didn't work.*	*Did they work?*

Das *Simple Past* wird benutzt
- für Handlungen (einmalig oder wiederholt), die in der Vergangenheit abgeschlossen sind.
- für aufeinanderfolgende Handlungen in der Vergangenheit.

Achtung:
Das Verb *to do* fungiert auch hier bei verneinten Sätzen und Fragen als Hilfsverb. Es gibt es aber natürlich auch als Vollverb (*to do* = tun, machen).

Beispiel:

I did my tasks.	(Ich machte meine Aufgaben.)
I didn't do my tasks.	(Ich machte meine Aufgaben nicht.)
Did you do your homework?	(Machtest du deine Aufgaben?)

Die Signalwörter im *Simple Past*
Signalwörter für das *Simple Past* sind Zeitangaben, die etwas Vergangenes ausdrücken, unter anderem:

yesterday (gestern), *last week* (letzte Woche), *a month ago* (vor einem Monat), *in 2010* (2010)

Present Perfect (das Perfekt)

Die Bildung des *Present Perfect*
Das *Present Perfect* wird gebildet aus einer Form des Hilfsverbes *have* und dem *Past Participle* (regelmäßige Verben: Infinitiv + *-ed;* unregelmäßige Verben: 3. Spalte)

have/has + Past Participle

has: bei der 3. Person Singular (*he, she, it*)
have: bei allen anderen Formen

Past Participle:
- bei regelmäßigen Verben: Infinitiv + *-ed*
- bei unregelmäßigen Verben: 3. Spalte der Tabelle der unregelmäßigen Verben

Bejahter Satz (Lang-/Kurzform)	Verneinter Satz (Lang-/Kurzform)	Frage
I have worked./ I've worked.	*I have not worked./ I haven't worked.*	*Have I worked?*
You have worked./ You've worked.	*You have not worked./ You haven't worked.*	*Have you worked?*
He/She/It has worked./ He's/She's/It's worked.	*He/She/It has not worked./ He/She/It hasn't worked.*	*Has he/she/it worked?*
We have worked./ We've worked.	*We have not worked./ We haven't worked.*	*Have we worked?*
You have worked./ You've worked.	*You have not worked./ You haven't worked.*	*Have you worked?*
They have worked./ They've worked.	*They have not worked./ They haven't worked.*	*Have they worked?*

Das *Present Perfect* ist eine Art Mischform aus Vergangenheit und Gegenwart und wird hauptsächlich verwendet, wenn Vergangenes mit der Gegenwart in Verbindung gebracht wird – anders als das Perfekt im Deutschen, das viel öfter auch als Vergangenheit verwendet wird.

Es wird benutzt bei

- Handlungen, deren Resultat in der Gegenwart wichtig ist (dabei ist nicht wichtig, wann genau diese Handlungen geschahen; sobald eine genaue Zeitangabe – z. B. *yesterday* – vorhanden ist, wird das *Simple Past* verwendet), z. B.
  I have unloaded the container. (Ich habe den Container entladen. – Er ist jetzt leer.)
- Handlungen, die gerade abgeschlossen wurden, z. B.
  The boss has just arrived. (Der Chef ist gerade angekommen. – Jetzt ist er ansprechbar.)
- Zuständen, die in der Vergangenheit begannen und bis in die Gegenwart andauern mit *since* (Zeitpunkt) oder *for* (Zeitraum/Zeitspanne), z. B.
  We have worked in this company since 2006. (Wir arbeiten seit 2006 in dieser Firma. – Wir arbeiten jetzt immer noch hier)
- häufig zusammen mit *lately*, *recently*, *yet*, z. B.
  He has not written the e-mail yet. (Er hat die E-Mail noch nicht geschrieben – bis jetzt noch nicht.)

Die Signalwörter im *Present Perfect*

Signalwörter für das *Present Perfect* sind z. B. folgende Wörter:
just (gerade eben), *yet* (bis jetzt), *never* (noch nie), *already* (schon – in Aussagesätzen), *ever* (schon – in Fragen), *so far* (bis jetzt), *up to now* (bis jetzt), *recently* (kürzlich), *since* (seit einem Zeitpunkt, z. B. 2009), *for* (seit – bezogen auf einen Zeitraum, z. B. *three years*)

Gegenüberstellung *Present Perfect/Simple Past*

Present Perfect	*Simple Past*
Resultat von Handlungen ist in der Gegenwart wichtig, z. B.: *I have packed this box. Now it can be shipped.*	Handlungen sind in der Vergangenheit abgeschlossen (einmalig oder wiederholt), z. B.: *Yesterday, I packed 30 boxes.*
Handlungen, die gerade abgeschlossen wurden, z. B. *I have just talked to the customer. (Now he is informed.)*	Aufeinander folgende Handlungen in der Vergangenheit, z. B. *This morning I talked to my boss and then I went to the office.*
Vorgänge begannen in der Vergangenheit und dauern bis in die Gegenwart an, z. B.: *Peter has worked as a warehouse operator for the last 2 years.*	In Verbindung mit dem *Past Progressive* – Das *Simple Past* unterbrach eine Handlung, die sich in der Vergangenheit im Verlauf befand, z. B. *I was picking an order when my boss called me.*

The Future (die Zukunft)

Im Englischen gibt es mehrere Möglichkeiten, die Zukunft auszudrücken. Die beiden häufigsten sind *Will-Future* und *Going to-Future.*

Beide Zeitformen finden in der Zukunft statt.
Das *Will-Future* wird bei Vorhersagen, Vermutungen, Versprechen und bei spontanen Entscheidungen verwendet.
Das *Going to-Future* wird bei Handlungen verwendet, die geplant sind.

Die Bildung des *Will-Future*

Das *Will-Future* wird gebildet aus dem Hilfsverb *will* und dem Infinitiv (der Stammform) des Verbes.

Hinweis: Es wird in allen Formen *will* + Infinitiv (auch bei *he, she* oder *it)* verwendet.

Bejahter Satz (Lang-/Kurzform)	Verneinter Satz (Lang-/Kurzform)	Frage
I will work./ I'll work.	*I will not work./ I won't work.*	*Will I work?*
You will work./ You'll work.	*You will not work./ You won't work.*	*Will you work?*
He/She/It will work./ He'll/She'll/It'll work.	*He/She/It will not work./ He/She/It won't work.*	*Will he/she/it work?*
We will work./ We'll work.	*We will not work./ We won't work.*	*Will we work?*
You will work./ You'll work.	*You will not work./ You won't work.*	*Will you work?*
They will work./ They'll work.	*They will not work./ They won't work.*	*Will they work?*

Das *Will-Future* wird verwendet bei:

- zukünftigen Geschehen, die nicht von persönlichen Entscheidungen abhängig sind (Geburtstag, Wetter usw.)
  The sun will shine tomorrow. (Morgen wird die Sonne scheinen.)
  Peter will be 18 next Tuesday. (Peter wird nächste Woche 18.)
- Vorhersagen, Vermutungen (*I think, I hope, I'm sure, I'm afraid*)
  I think the shipment will arrive tomorrow around 3 pm. (Ich denke, dass die Sendung morgen gegen 15 Uhr ankommen wird.)
- spontanen Entschlüssen (Handlung ist nicht geplant)
  Hang on! I'll put you through. (Warten Sie. Ich werde Sie weiterleiten (am Telefon).)

Die Bildung des *Going to-Future*

Das *Going to-Future* wird gebildet aus einer Form von *to be (am, are* oder *is) going to* und dem Infinitiv (der Stammform) des Verbes.

to be (am, are, is) + *going to* + Infinitiv

Bejahter Satz (Lang-/Kurzform)	Verneinter Satz (Lang-/Kurzform)	Frage
I am going to work./ I'm going to work.	*I am not going to work./ I'm not going to work.*	*Am I going to work?*
You are going to work./ You're going to work.	*You are not going to work./ You're not going to work.*	*Are you going to work?*

Bejahter Satz (Lang-/Kurzform)	Verneinter Satz (Lang-/Kurzform)	Frage
He/She/It is going to work./ He/She/It's going to work.	*He/She/It is not going to work./ He/She/It isn't going to work.*	*Is he/she/it going to work?*
We are going to work./ We're going to work.	*We are not going to work./ We aren't going to work.*	*Are we going to work?*
You are going to work./ You're going to work.	*You are not going to work./ You aren't going to work.*	*Are you going to work?*
They are going to work./ They're going to work.	*They are not going to work./ They aren't going to work.*	*Are they going to work?*

Das *Going to-Future* wird verwendet bei:

- geplanten, zukünftigen Entscheidungen
  We are going to give the customer a discount. (Wir werden dem Kunden Rabatt gewähren.)
  They are going to fly to South Africa. (Sie werden nach Südafrika fliegen.)
- logischen Schlussfolgerungen für die Zukunft (man sieht etwas kommen)
  Look at that sky! It is going to rain. (Sieh mal in den Himmel! Es wird bald regnen.)

Außerdem gibt es noch weitere Möglichkeiten, die Zukunft auszudrücken, die in folgender Tabelle dargestellt werden:

Present Progressive	*Going to-Future*	*Will-Future*	*Future Progressive*	*Simple Present*
I am going to a meeting tonight.	*We are going to fly to Chicago in summer.*	*He will call you later.*	*They will be playing football on Sunday afternoon.*	*The train leaves at 6.45.*
feststehender Plan in der nahen Zukunft	Plan in der Zukunft; logische Konsequenz (man sieht etwas kommen)	Vorhersage, Vermutung; spontaner Entschluss	Handlung gilt in der Zukunft als sicher	zukünftige Handlung ist festgeschrieben (z. B. Fahrplan, Stundenplan)

Die Unterschiede zwischen den einzelnen Zeitformen sind zum Teil sehr gering und oft sprecherabhängig. Deswegen kann man öfters mehrere Zeitformen verwenden. Es kommt auch darauf an, ob die Sätze geschrieben oder gesprochen werden und ob man sich z. B. in England oder den USA aufhält.

In Zeitungen wird z. B. oft das *Will-Future* benutzt, wenn man sonst das *Going to-Future* nehmen würde.

Zeitung:
The company will close the old warehouse.
mündlich:
The company is going to close the old warehouse.

Imperative (Imperativ)

Im Englischen hat der Imperativ (Befehlsform) immer dieselbe Form wie der Infinitiv.

Bejahter Satz	Verneinter Satz
Come here. (Komm/Kommt her!)	*Don't come now.* (Komm/Kommt jetzt nicht her!)
Clean the warehouse. (Mach/Macht das Lager sauber!)	*Don't clean the office.* (Mach/Macht das Büro nicht sauber!)
Help your colleague. (Hilf deinen/Helft eurem Kollegen!)	*Don't smoke near the chemicals.* (Rauche/Raucht nicht in der Nähe der Chemikalien!)

Das Ausrufezeichen wird im Englischen nur dann benutzt, wenn man tatsächlich einen Ausruf macht, z. B. *Stop! Help!*

Außerdem gibt es noch den Imperativ mit *let's*.

Bejahter Satz	Verneinter Satz
Let's ask the teacher. (Lass uns den Lehrer fragen!)	*Let's not ask the teacher.* (Lass uns den Lehrer nicht fragen!)

The Passive Voice (das Passiv)

Das Passiv wird benutzt, wenn wir ein Objekt hervorheben wollen oder wenn wir gar nicht wissen, wer die Handlung ausgeführt hat.

A lot of goods are produced in China. (Viele Waren werden in China hergestellt).

Wir können aus einem Aktivsatz nur dann einen Passivsatz bilden, wenn im Aktivsatz ein Objekt vorhanden ist.

Das Passiv wird mit einer Form von *to be* in der jeweiligen Zeit und der 3. Form des Verbs *(Past Participle)* gebildet.

Die 3. Form bei regelmäßigen Verben – z. B. *to transport* – wird mit *-ed* gebildet

The box is transported. (Einzahl)
The boxes are transported. (Mehrzahl)

Soll aus einem Aktivsatz ein Passivsatz gebildet werden, dann gilt folgende Regel:
- Objekt des Aktivsatzes wird Subjekt des Passivsatzes
- Subjekt des Aktivsatzes wird Objekt des Passivsatzes (fällt sehr oft weg)

Hier ein Beispiel im *Simple Present*:

Aktivsatz	Passivsatz
The shipper packs the goods. (Der Versender verpackt die Waren.) Im Aktivsatz führt das Subjekt *(the shipper)* die Handlung aus.	*The goods are packed by the shipper.* (Die Waren werden vom Versender verpackt.) Im Passivsatz wird mit dem Subjekt (*the goods*) etwas getan. Wer das tut, wird durch den Zusatz *by* angegeben.

Im *Simple Past* heißt es dann:
Aktivsatz: *Yesterday, the shipper **packed** the goods.*
Passivsatz: *Yesterday, the goods **were packed** by the shipper.*

Modals/Defective Auxiliaries (Modale/Unvollständige Hilfsverben)

Unvollständige Hilfsverben sind z. B. *can, must, may* und *need.*
Sie besitzen nur eine bzw. zwei Verbformen (*Simple Present/Simple Past*). Fehlende Formen werden bei einigen durch Ersatzverben gebildet. Anders als im Deutschen können die unvollständigen Hilfsverben – außer *need* – nicht als Vollverben benutzt werden.

Beispiel:
Er kann Englisch. *He can speak English.*

can (können)
Für *can* benutzt man häufig die Ersatzformen *to be able to* oder *to be allowed to.* Das liegt daran, dass man von *can* nur das *Simple Past* bilden kann (*could*). Möchte man einen Satz in anderen Zeitformen bilden, dann nimmt man die Ersatzformen.

Der englische Satz: *I can drive the forklift truck.* – hat verschiedene Bedeutungen:

1. Ich kann den Gabelstapler fahren. oder
2. Ich darf den Gabelstapler fahren.

Für das Können (die Fähigkeit, etwas zu tun) steht die Ersatzform *to be able to,* für das Dürfen (Erlaubnis, etwas tun zu dürfen) steht die Ersatzform *to be allowed to.*

Bejahte Sätze:

Zeitform	Modalverb	Ersatzform
Simple Present	*I can speak English.*	*I am able to speak English.* *I am allowed to speak English.*
Simple Past	*I could speak English.*	*I was able to speak English.* *I was allowed to speak English.*
Will-Future	Das Modalverb *can* kann nicht im *Will-Future* verwendet werden.	*I will be able to speak English.* *I will be allowed to speak English.*

Verneinte Sätze:

Zeitform	Modalverb	Ersatzform
Simple Present	*I cannot speak English.*	*I am not able to speak English.* *I am not allowed to speak English.*
Simple Past	*I could not speak English.*	*I was not able to speak English.* *I was not allowed to speak English.*
Will-Future	Das Modalverb *can* kann nicht im *Will-Future* verwendet werden.	*I will not be able to speak English.* *I will not be allowed to speak English.*

must **(müssen)/*must not* (nicht dürfen)**
Für *must* benutzt man meistens die Ersatzform *to have to.*

Bejahte Sätze:

Zeitform	Modalverb	Ersatzform
Simple Present	*I must go to work.*	*I have to go to work.*
Simple Past	Das Modalverb *must* kann nicht im *Simple Past* verwendet werden.	*I had to go to work.*
Will-Future	Das Modalverb *must* kann nicht im *Will-Future* verwendet werden.	*I will have to go to work.*

Achtung:
Wenn man von *must* die Verneinung *must not (mustn't)* bildet, dann ändert sich die Bedeutung des Satzes. Man sagt dann aus, dass man etwas **nicht darf**.
Die Ersatzform ist dann *not to be allowed to.*

Verneinte Sätze:

Zeitform	Modalverb	Ersatzform
Simple Present	*I must not smoke here.*	*I am not allowed to smoke here.*
Simple Past	Das Modalverb *must* kann nicht im *Simple Past* verwendet werden.	*I was not allowed to smoke here.*
Will-Future	Das Modalverb *must* kann nicht im *Will-Future* verwendet werden.	*I will not be allowed to smoke here.*

may **(dürfen)**
Für *may* benutzt man die Ersatzform *to be allowed to.* Außer im *Simple Present* kann *may* in keiner anderen Zeitform verwendet werden.

need **(brauchen)**
Need kann als Vollverb, vollständiges Hilfsverb und unvollständiges Hilfsverb (nur im *Simple Present*) benutzt werden:
Vollverb: *I need a new car.*
Vollständiges Hilfsverb: *Do I need to help you with the container?*
Unvollständiges Hilfsverb:

Als unvollständiges Hilfsverb benutzt man *need*

- in Fragen, wenn eine verneinte Antwort erwartet wird: *Need I come?*
- in verneinten Sätzen im *Simple Present* in der Bedeutung „nicht brauchen, nötig haben, müssen". Hier kann auch die Ersatzform *not to have to* benutzt werden:
  You need not help me.
  You do not have to help me.

Adjectives (Adjektive)

Adjektive beschreiben, wie etwas ist und stehen meist vor einem Hauptwort oder nach einer Form von *to be.*

This is an explosive good.
She is very happy.

Kurze, einsilbige Adjektive werden mit *-er* und *-est* gesteigert. Beispiele sind:

big groß	*bigger* größer	*biggest* größte/r
quick schnell	*quicker* schneller	*quickest* schnellste/r

Bitte folgende **Ausnahmen** merken:

good gut	*better* besser	*best* beste/r
bad schlecht	*worse* schlechter	*worst* schlechteste/r

Zweisilbige Adjektive, die auf *-y* enden, werden mit *-ier* und *-iest* gesteigert. Beispiele sind:

heavy schwer	*heavier* schwerer	*heaviest* schwerste/r
bulky sperrig	*bulkier* sperriger	*bulkiest* sperrigste/r

Andere **mehrsilbige Adjektive** werden mit *more* und *most* gesteigert. Beispiele sind:

explosive explosiv	*more explosive* explosiver	*most explosive* explosivste/r
interesting interessant	*more interesting* interessanter	*most interesting* interessanteste/r

Die wichtigsten Formulierungen für **Vergleiche** sind:

*This delivery is **as** heavy **as** the other one.*
(Diese Lieferung ist **genauso** schwer **wie** die andere)
*This order was delivered fast**er** **than** the other.*
(Diese Bestellung wurde schnell**er** geliefert **als** die andere)
*This piece of information is **more** interesting **than** the other.*
(Diese Information ist interessant**er** **als** die andere)

Adverbs (Adverbien)

Adverbien bestimmen Verben (1), Adjektive (2), Adverbien (3) oder ganze Sätze (4) näher. Die Bildung von Adverbien erfolgt meist durch das Anhängen von *-ly* an das Adjektiv. **Ausnahme:** das Adverb zu *good* ist *well.*

(1) *You have to treat the goods carefully.*
(2) *This is an extremely explosive substance.*
(3) *She packed the goods surprisingly well.*
(4) *Unfortunately, the new bag is very heavy.*

Es gibt auch Adverbien, die die gleiche Form wie das entsprechende Adjektiv haben. Beispiele sind: *fast, early, little, long, low, straight, daily, weekly, yearly.*

Don't drive so fast. It's dangerous.
The shelves have to be cleaned daily.

Es gibt auch Adverbien mit **zwei Formen**, die sich allerdings in ihrer Bedeutung unterscheiden. Hier einige Beispiele:

Adverbien ohne *-ly*	Adverbien mit *–ly*
hard (schwer/hart) *high* (hoch) *late* (spät) *most* (am meisten) *near* (nahe heran) *just* (nur)	*hardly* (kaum) *highly* (höchst) *lately* (in letzter Zeit) *mostly* (meistens) *nearly* (fast/beinahe) *justly* (gerecht)

Don't come near!
(Komm nicht nah heran!)
She nearly had an accident.
(Sie hatte fast einen Unfall.)

Einsilbige Adverbien werden mit *-er* und *-est* gesteigert. Beispiele sind:

fast schnell	*faster* schneller	*fastest* schnellste/r
high hoch	*higher* höher	*highest* höchste/r

Ausnahme: *well – better – best.*

Mehrsilbige Adverbien bilden die Steigerungsformen mit *more* und *most.* Beispiele sind:

carefully vorsichtig	*more carefully* vorsichtiger	*most carefully* vorsichtigste/r
nervously nervös	*more nervously* nervöser	*most nervously* nervöseste/r

Ausnahme: *badly – worse – worst.*

Quantifiers (Mengenbezeichnungen)

some/any

In Aussagesätzen (1) wird *some* verwendet, in Fragesätzen nur bei einer Bitte oder einem Angebot (2). In Fragen (3) und verneinten Sätzen (4) wird *any* benutzt.

(1) *I have some new picking lists for you.*
(2) *Would you like to have some coffee?*
(3) *Is there any new delivery note for me?*
(4) *There is not anyone here.*

a lot of, many/much, a few, a little

A lot of (eine Menge, viele) kann bei zählbaren und bei nicht zählbaren Begriffen stehen.

There are a lot of carboys. (zählbar)
I have not got a lot of time. (nicht zählbar)

Many (viele) und *a few* (einige, ein paar) werden nur bei zählbaren Begriffen verwendet.

There are many containers to load.
She has got a few ideas to help you.

Much (viel) und *a little* (ein wenig, ein bisschen, etwas) stehen nur bei nicht zählbaren Begriffen.

There is not much food.
There is only a little coffee in the bag.

Question Words (Fragewörter)

Who (wer), *whose* (wessen) und *whom* (wen/wem) fragen nach Personen.
What (was, wie) fragt nach Dingen.

Who is the new operator?
Whose box is this?
Whom could we ask?
What did you answer in the letter?
What is your telephone number?

What (welche – ganz allgemein/was für ein) wird bei einer nicht begrenzten Auswahl oder bei der Frage nach der Eigenschaft oder Beschaffenheit verwendet. *Which* (welche – ganz speziell) wird bei einer begrenzten Anzahl verwendet.

What countries do you deliver to?
Which country would you like to deliver to?
Which product do they order most?

How much (wie viel) steht bei nicht zählbaren Begriffen und *how many* (wie viele) steht nur bei zählbaren Begriffen.

How much time do you have?
How much is it?
How many sacks are in the container?

Andere Fragewörter:
When (wann)
Where (wo)
Where … from (woher)

Why (wieso, warum)
How (wie – Art und Weise)
How long (wie lange)

When did the delivery arrive at the incoming goods department?
Where is the forklift truck?
Where is the cargo from?
Why did you come late?
How is this cargo packed properly?
How long does it take to transport the goods by train?

Achtung! Für Deutsche ist besonders schwierig: *Who* ist „wer“ und *where* ist „wo“.

Word Order (Wortstellung)

Die Satzordnung ist in der englischen Sprache anders als in der deutschen Sprache nicht sehr flexibel. Die Grundordnung ist immer **SPO**: Subjekt – Prädikat (Verb) – Objekt. In deutschen Sätzen steht das Verb häufig am Ende eines Satzes. Daher bitte nicht Wort für Wort vom Deutschen ins Englische übersetzen!

She can speak English very well. (Sie kann gut Englisch sprechen.)
This rack has not got a suitable board. (Dieses Regal hat kein geeignetes Brett.)

Bei **Fragesätzen** stehen meist die Fragewörter und danach die Hilfsverben (1 und 2) oder nur die Hilfsverben (3 und 4) bzw. *to be* als Vollverb (5) an erster Stelle, anschließend wird wieder SPO eingehalten.

(1) *When do you come back?*
(2) *How long have you been waiting?*
(3) *Can you help the new apprentice?*
(4) *Do you like your work?*
(5) *Are you from here?*

Achtung! Beim Fragewort *who* werden keine Hilfsverben gebraucht.

Who takes the bus to work?
Who worked in the company in 2001?

Adverbien können verschiedene Stellungen im Satz einnehmen:

Am **Satzanfang** stehen meist die Adverbien, die sich auf den ganzen Satz beziehen oder einen Ort bzw. eine Zeit beschreiben.

Suddenly the boxes fell down.
Yesterday the delivery did not arrive in time.

In der **Satzmitte** stehen die Adverbien der unbestimmten Häufigkeit, z.B. *always* (immer), *never* (niemals), *ever* (jemals), *often* (oft), *sometimes* (manchmal), *usually* (gewöhnlich). Sie stehen vor dem Verb (1) oder aber nach dem ersten Hilfsverb (2).

(1) *The goods usually arrive late.*
(2) *He would never have had an accident, if he had been careful.*

Am **Satzende** können Adverbien des Ortes und der Zeit (1 und 2) – Ort geht dabei vor Zeit (3) –, aber auch die Adverbien der Art und Weise (4 und 5) stehen.

(1) *The boxes could be over there.*
(2) *The delivery will arrive tomorrow.*
(3) *The container arrived in town yesterday.*
(4) *He didn't speak clearly.*
(5) *The forklift truck was driven quickly.*

Prepositions (Präpositionen)

Bei der Übersetzung von Präpositionen kommt es immer auf den Zusammenhang an, in dem sie stehen. Am besten lernt man sie mit dem Ausdruck zusammen.

Präpositionen für Zeitausdrücke:

Englisch	Deutsch
on Monday *on Wednesday evening* *on the 12th of June* *on time*	am Montag am Mittwochabend am 12. Juni pünktlich
in the morning *in a minute* *in January*	am Morgen in einer Minute im Januar
at 12 o'clock *at midday* *at the weekend* *at a quarter to ten* *at Easter* *at night* *at the moment* *at once*	um 12 Uhr am Mittag am Wochenende um Viertel vor zehn zu Ostern bei Nacht im Moment sofort

Präpositionen, die die Position oder die Richtung angeben:

Englisch	Deutsch
in the USA *in the office* *in the street* *in the picture*	in den USA im Büro auf der Straße auf dem Bild
on the wall *on the table* *on the left* *on board* *on the train*	an der Wand auf dem Tisch auf der linken Seite an Bord im Zug
at the corner *at work* *at home* *at school*	an der Ecke bei der Arbeit zu Hause in der Schule
next to the door	neben der Tür
under the shelf	unter dem Regal
between two racks	zwischen zwei Regalen (zwei)
among the people	zwischen den Leuten (mehrere)
over the table *over there* *all over the world*	über dem Tisch da drüben in der ganzen Welt
through a tunnel	durch einen Tunnel

Englisch	Deutsch
to New York *to a friend* *to bed*	nach New York an einen Freund ins Bett
opposite the factory	gegenüber der Fabrik
into the fire	in das Feuer hinein
onto the lorry	auf den LKW hinauf

Verben und Präpositionen
Auch hier kann sich durch eine (andere) Präposition die Bedeutung des Verbs völlig verändern. Beim Nachschlagen in Wörterbüchern daher bitte auf die nachfolgende Präposition achten! Hier einige Beispiele:

Englisch	Deutsch
to give in *to give up*	nachgeben aufgeben
to carry *to carry on* *to carry out*	tragen weitermachen durchführen
to look after *to look at* *to look for* *to look up* *to look forward to*	sich kümmern um anschauen suchen nachschlagen sich freuen auf
to work for *to work on* *to work out*	arbeiten bei arbeiten an ausrechnen, verstehen

False Friends (zum Verwechseln ähnliche Wörter)

False friends (falsche Freunde) sind Wörter, die im Deutschen und Englischen gleich oder ähnlich geschrieben werden, aber nicht das Gleiche bedeuten.

Englisch	Deutsch
sensible *sensitive*	vernünftig empfindlich, sensibel
to become *to get*	werden bekommen
chef *boss*	Chefkoch Chef
photograph *photographer*	Fotografie, Bild Fotograf

Englisch	Deutsch
gymnasium (gym) *grammar school*	Turnhalle Gymnasium
high school (USA) *university, college*	Oberschule Hochschule, Universität
brave *good, well-behaved*	mutig brav
start *take-off*	Anfang Start
note *grade (AE), mark (BE)*	Schein (BE), Notiz (Schul)note
action *campaign*	Handlung, Tat Aktion
murder *murderer*	Mord Mörder

Numbers (Zahlen)

Cardinal numbers Kardinalzahlen		*Ordinal numbers* Ordnungszahlen		
1	*one*	1. = 1st	*first*	**Die ersten drei Ordnungszahlen sind unregelmäßig. Alle anderen enden auf *-th.***
2	*two*	2. = 2nd	*second*	
3	*three*	3. = 3rd	*third*	
4	*four*	4. = 4th	*fourth*	
5	*five*	5. = 5th	*fifth*	
6	*six*	6. = 6th	*sixth*	
7	*seven*	7. = 7th	*seventh*	
8	*eight*	8. = 8th	*eighth*	**Beachte die besondere Schreibweise von**
9	*nine*	9. = 9th	*ninth*	
10	*ten*	10. = 10th	*tenth*	
11	*eleven*	11. = 11th	*eleventh*	• ***fifth***
12	*twelve*	12. = 12th	*twelfth*	• ***eighth***
13	*thirteen*	13. = 13th	*thirteenth*	• ***ninth***
14	*fourteen*	14. = 14th	*fourteenth*	• ***twelfth***
15	*fifteen*	15. = 15th	*fifteenth*	• ***fortieth***
...	...	...	...	
20	*twenty*	20. = 20th	*twentieth*	
21	*twenty-one*	21. = 21st	*twenty-first*	
...	...	...	...	
30	*thirty*	30. = 30th	*thirtieth*	
...	...	...	...	
40	*forty*	40. = 40th	*fortieth*	
...	...	...	...	
50	*fifty*	50. = 50th	*fiftieth*	
....	...	...	...	
60	*sixty*	60. = 60th	*sixtieth*	
...	...	...	...	
70	*seventy*	70.= 70th	*seventieth*	
...	...	...	...	

Cardinal numbers Kardinalzahlen		*Ordinal numbers* Ordnungszahlen		
80 ... 90 ... 100 ... 1,000	*eighty* ... *ninety* ... *one hundred* ... *one thousand*	80. = 80th ... 90. = 90th ... 100. = 100th ... 1,000. = 1,000th	*eightieth* ... *ninetieth* ... *one hundredth* ... *one thousandth*	

Achtung! Eine Million ist im Englischen *one milion*, eine Miliarde ist *one billion*.

The months of the year (Monate)

Spring	*Summer*	*Autumn*	*Winter*
March *April* *May*	*June* *July* *August*	*September* *October* *November*	*December* *January* *February*

Dates (Daten)

Problematisch bei Datumsangaben ist, dass man sie anders schreibt als ausspricht. Außerdem wird im amerikanischen Englisch zuerst der Monat geschrieben, während im britischen Englisch, wie in ganz Europa, zuerst der Tag geschrieben wird. Damit es nicht zu Verwechslungen kommt, sollte der Monat stets ausgeschrieben werden.

geschrieben	gesprochen
British English:	
4 January	
4th January	*the fourth of January*
21 May	
21st May	*the twenty-first of May*
American English:	
January, 4	
January, 4th	*January, the fourth*
May, 21	
May, 21st	*May, the twenty-first*
1998 – nineteen ninety-eight	
2002 – two thousand and two	
2016 – two thousand and sixteen / twenty-sixteen	
2nd March 2016 – It is the second of March two thousand and sixteen / twenty-sixteen.	

Telling the time (Uhrzeiten)

o'clock benutzt man für ganze Stunden.
It's five o'clock. (Es ist fünf Uhr.)

a.m. (aus dem Lateinischen 'ante meridiem') = morgens bzw. nach Mitternacht
p.m. (aus dem Lateinischen 'post meridiem') = nachmittags, abends oder vor Mitternacht

Benutzt man ***a.m.*** oder ***p.m.***, wird nicht ***o'clock*** gebraucht.
It is nine a.m. (Es ist neun Uhr morgens)
It is six p.m. (Es ist sechs Uhr abends.)

Häufig gebraucht werden:
half past = 30 Minuten nach
(a) quarter to = viertel vor
(a) quarter past = viertel nach

Es gibt oft mehrere Möglichkeiten, Uhrzeiten auszudrücken:

6:30	*It is six thirty.*	oder	*It is half past six.*	oder	*It is half six.*
4:45	*It is four forty-five*	oder	*It is (a) quarter to five.*		
9:15	*It is nine fifteen.*	oder	*It is (a) quarter past nine.*		
8:05	*It is five past eight.*	oder	*It is five minutes past eight.*		
7:50	*It is ten to eight.*	oder	*It is ten minutes to eight.*		

Achtung:
Im Deutschen bedeutet **halb fünf** eine halbe Stunde **vor** fünf, also 16:30.
Im Englischen bedeutet ***half (past) five*** eine halbe Stunde **nach** fünf, also 17:30.

Decimals (Dezimalzahlen)

Im Englischen wird – im Gegensatz zum Deutschen – ein Punkt statt eines Kommas als Dezimaltrennzeichen gesetzt – und *point* ausgesprochen.
Wo im Deutschen hingegen ein Punkt steht, wie bei Tausendertrennzeichen, steht im Englischen ein Komma.

	Dezimaltrennzeichen	Tausendertrennzeichen
Deutsch	Komma 1,5 Liter, 10,95 Euro	Punkt 80.200 Einwohner
Englisch	*Point* *1.5 litres, 10.95 euros*	*Comma* *80,200 inhabitants*

Beispiele:

geschrieben	gesprochen
25.2	*twenty-five point two*
300.247	*three hundred point two four seven*
12,670	*twelve thousand and six hundred seventy*

Measurements (Maße)

In den englischsprachigen Ländern wird häufig nicht das metrische System (*metric system*) mit Maßeinheiten wie Meter und Zentimeter benutzt, sondern das sogenannte *imperial system* mit Maßeinheiten wie Fuß (*foot/feet*) und Zoll (*inch/inches*).

one foot = 30.48 cms
one inch = 2.54 cms
one foot (1ft/1′) = twelve inches (12 ins/12″)

Bei der Beschreibung von Containern wird die Maßeinheit *foot* oft als Attribut gebraucht, z. B.: *a 20-foot container*

Für die unterschiedlichen Dimensionen Länge, Breite und Höhe kann man im Englischen die folgenden Ausdrücke verwenden:

The container is 20 feet long./Its length is 20 feet.
The box is two feet wide./Its width is two feet.
It is one foot ten inches high./Its height is one foot ten.

Das Gewicht (*weight*) wird in Kilo (*kilos*), Pfund (*pounds*) oder Tonnen (*tons*) gemessen.

Achtung:
Ein *Imperial Pound* ist weniger als ein metrisches Pfund:
one pound/1 lb = 0.4536 kilograms

SKILL FILES PHONETICS

Skills and Competencies

Dear student,

this skill file shows you how to read the phonetic code in the vocabulary section. Furthermore you will find examples for spelling, e.g. the name code and the international aviation alphabet. These two are very helpful when it comes to spelling names and addresses.

Enjoy!

International Phonetics Alphabet

Vowels		Consonants	
ʌ	result, bubble	b	bag, bay
ɑː	armature, article	d	delivery, valid
æ	stack, application	f	floorspace, efficiency
e	deadline, elevator	g	cargo, goggles
ə	barrel, apprentice	h	wholesaler, headset
ɜː^r	turn, courtesy	j	duty, yard
ɪ	heavy, demand	k	conveyor, sack
iː	consignee, trainee	l	bill, label
ɒ	stock, document	m	measure, room
ɔː	store, fault	n	sign, complain
ʊ	courier, hook	ŋ	sign, extinguisher
uː	goods, rule	p	plastic, clamp
aɪ	identity, aisle	r	wrap, rack
aʊ	now, out	s	capacity, lattice
eɪ	waybill, freight	ʃ	shelf, lash
əʊ	mould, foam	t	tax, transport
ɔɪ	hoist, employer	tʃ	check, pouch
eə^r	warehouse, air	θ	seaworthy, health

English Spelling

Letter	Phonetic Code	Name Code (British English)	International Aviation Alphabet
A	[eɪ]	Andrew	Alpha
B	[biː]	Benjamin	Bravo
C	[siː]	Charlie	Charlie
D	[diː]	David	Delta
E	[iː]	Edward	Echo
F	[ef]	Freddie	Foxtrot
G	[dʒiː]	George	Golf
H	[eɪtʃ]	Harry	Hotel
I	[aɪ]	Isabel	India
J	[dʒeɪ]	Jack	Juliett
K	[keɪ]	Katie	Kilo
L	[el]	Lucy	Lima
M	[em]	Mary	Mike
N	[en]	Nellie	November
O	[əʊ]	Oliver	Oscar
P	[piː]	Peter	Papa

Vowels		Consonants	
ɪəʳ	barrier, near	ð	this, further
ʊəʳ	tourist, manual	v	invoice, vessel
		w	wage, equipment
		z	zone, enterprise
		ʒ	vision, agency
		dʒ	just, barge

Letter	Phonetic Code	Name Code (British English)	International Aviation Alphabet
Q	[kju:]	Queenie	Quebec
R	[ɑ:]	Richard	Romeo
S	[es]	Susan	Sierra
T	[ti:]	Thomas	Tango
U	[ju:]	Ursula	Uniform
V	[vi:]	Victor	Victor
W	[dʌblju:]	William	Whiskey
X	[eks]	X-ray	X-Ray
Y	[waɪ]	Young	Yankee
Z	[zed]	Zoë	Zulu

Unit based Vocabulary

Unit 1

Introducing yourself

answer (v)	['ɑːnsə]	beantworten
apprenticeship (n)	[ə'prentɪsʃɪp]	die Ausbildung
box (n)	[bɒks]	die Schachtel
company (n)	['kʌmpəni]	die Firma
container (n)	[kən'teɪnə]	der Container
experience (n)	[ɪk'spɪəriəns]	die Erfahrung
load (v)	[ləʊd]	beladen
pack (v)	[pæk]	packen
warehouse (n)	['weəhaʊs]	das Lager, die Lagerhalle
warehouse logistics operator (n)	['weəhaʊs lə'dʒɪstɪks 'ɒpəreɪtə]	die Fachkraft für Lagerlogistik
warehouse operator (n)	['weəhaʊs 'ɒpəreɪtə]	der Fachlagerist

Getting started in a new job

apprentice (n)	[ə'prentɪs]	der Auszubildende
arrival (n)	[ə'raɪvəl]	die Ankunft
arrive (v)	[ə'raɪv]	ankommen
assistance (n)	[ə'sɪstəns]	die Unterstützung, die Hilfe
call (v)	[kɔːl]	anrufen, nennen
check (v)	[tʃek]	kontrollieren, -überprüfen
chief storekeeper (n)	['tʃiːf ˌstɔːkiːpə]	der Lagermeister
colleague (n)	['kɒliːg]	der Arbeitskollege
desperate to do something (adj)	['despərət tu duː ˌsʌmθɪŋ]	etwas unbedingt tun wollen
document (n)	['dɒkjəmənt]	das Dokument
fetch something/someone (v)	['fetʃ ˌsʌmθɪŋ/ˌsʌmwʌn]	etwas/jemanden abholen
further (adj)	['fɜːðə]	anderweitig, zusätzlich
gesture (v)	['dʒestʃə]	eine Handbewegung machen, gestikulieren
goods (n)	[gʊdz]	die Güter, die Ware
industrial estate (n)	[ɪn'dʌstriəl ɪ'steɪt]	das Industriegebiet
informal (adj)	[ɪn'fɔːməl]	formlos, informell, ungezwungen
initial medical examination (n)	[ɪ'nɪʃəl 'medɪkəl ɪgˌzæmɪ'neɪʃən]	die Erstuntersuchung
language (n)	['læŋgwɪdʒ]	die Sprache
lorry (n)	['lɒri]	der LKW
office (n)	['ɒfɪs]	das Büro
overcome (v)	[ˌəʊvə'kʌm]	überwinden
pick up (v)	[ˌpɪk 'ʌp]	abheben, aufnehmen, abholen
profession (n)	[prə'feʃən]	der Beruf
ramp (n)	[ræmp]	die Rampe
read (v)	[riːd]	lesen
receive (v)	[rɪ'siːv]	erhalten
result (n)	[rɪ'zʌlt]	das Ergebnis
social insurance identity card (n)	['səʊʃəl ɪn'ʃʊərəns aɪ'dentɪti ˌkɑːd]	der Sozialversicherungsausweis
store (v)	[stɔː]	einlagern
store superintendent (n)	['stɔː ˌsuːpərɪn'tendənt]	der Lagermeister
successful (adj)	[sək'sesfʊl]	erfolgreich
task (n)	[tɑːsk]	die Aufgabe
tax identification number (n)	['tæks aɪˌdentɪfɪ'keɪʃən 'nʌmbə]	die Steuer-Identifikationsnummer

trade (v)	[treɪd]	handeln, tauschen
trading company (n)	['treɪdɪŋ 'kʌmpəni]	die Großhandelsfirma
train (v)	[treɪn]	anlernen, einweisen, trainieren
transport (v)	[træn'spɔːt]	befördern, transportieren
unload (v)	[ʌn'ləʊd]	entladen
vehicle (n)	['vɪəkl]	das Fahrzeug
weariness (n)	['wɪərinəs]	die Müdigkeit

Job descriptions

accept (v)	[ək'sept]	akzeptieren, annehmen
according to (prep)	[ə'kɔːdɪŋ tu]	entsprechend, gemäß
achieve (v)	[ə'tʃiːv]	erlangen, erreichen, erzielen
cargo tours (n)	['kɑːgəʊ ˌtʊəz]	die Frachtrouten
correspondence (n)	[ˌkɒrɪ'spɒndəns]	Korrespondenz, Schriftverkehr
delivery (n)	[dɪ'lɪvəri]	die Lieferung
duration (n)	[djʊə'reɪʃən]	die Dauer
efficient (adj)	[ɪ'fɪʃənt]	effizient, leistungsfähig, wirtschaftlich
field of activity (n)	['fiːld ɒf ək'tɪvəti]	das Arbeitsgebiet, der Tätigkeitsbereich
foreign language terminology (n)	['fɒrɪn 'læŋgwɪdʒ ˌtɜːmɪ'nɒlədʒi]	die fremdsprachlichen Fachausdrücke
forklift truck (n)	['fɔːklɪft ˌtrʌk]	der Gabelstapler
forwarding company (n)	['fɔːwədɪŋ 'kʌmpəni]	die Spedition
forwarding document (n)	['fɔːwədɪŋ 'dɒkjəmənt]	das Frachtpapier
handle (v)	['hændl]	abfertigen, bearbeiten, handhaben
industrial company (n)	[ɪn'dʌstriəl 'kʌmpəni]	der Industriebetrieb
keyword (n)	['kiːwɜːd]	das Stichwort
occupational skills (n)	[ˌɒkjə'peɪʃənəl ˌskɪlz]	die beruflichen Fähigkeiten
organise (v)	['ɔːgənaɪz]	organisieren
part-time (adj)	[ˌpɑːt'taɪm]	teilzeitlich
pick (v)	[ˌpɪk]	kommissionieren, zusammen-stellen
place (v)	[pleɪs]	legen, setzen, stellen, unterbringen
plan (v)	[plæn]	planen
service company (n)	['sɜːvɪs 'kʌmpəni]	die Dienstleistungsfirma
sort (v)	[sɔːt]	ordnen, sortieren
storage (n)	['stɔːrɪdʒ]	das Lager, die Lagerhalle
storage document (n)	['stɔːrɪdʒ 'dɒkjəmənt]	die Bestandsdokumentation, die Lagerdokumentation
storage equipment (n)	['stɔːrɪdʒ ɪ'kwɪpmənt]	die Lagerausrüstung
unpack (v)	[ʌn'pæk]	entpacken
vocational school (n)	[vəʊ'keɪʃənəl 'skuːl]	die Berufsschule
warehouse system (n)	['weəhaʊs 'sɪstəm]	das Lagerverwaltungssystem

My daily routine

daily routine (n)	['deɪli ruː'tiːn]	der Tagesablauf
customer service department (n)	['kʌstəmə 'sɜːvɪs dɪ'pɑːtmənt]	der Kundendienst, die Kundendienstabteilung
extract (v)	[ɪk'strækt]	entnehmen, extrahieren
incoming (adj)	['ɪnkʌmɪŋ]	eingehend, hereinkommend
label (v)	['leɪbəl]	etikettieren, kennzeichnen, markieren

label (n)	['leɪbəl]	die Beschriftung, das Etikett
order (v)	['ɔːdə]	bestellen
sometimes (adv)	['sʌmtaɪmz]	manchmal, mitunter
stock records (n)	['stɒk ˌrekɔːdz]	der Lagerbestand, der Warenbestand
usually (adj)	['juːʒuəli]	gewöhnlich, normalerweise

Grammar Simple Present and Present Progressive

a.m. (ante meridiem) (abbr)	[eɪ æm], [ˌæntɪmə'rɪdiəm]	vor dem Mittag
conference (n)	['kɒnfərəns]	die Konferenz, die Sitzung
cover (v)	['kʌvə]	abdecken, bedecken
driver's license (n)	['draɪvəz ˌlaɪsəns]	der Führerschein
intern (n)	['ɪntɜːn]	der Praktikant
internship (n)	['ɪntɜːnʃɪp]	das Praktikum
meeting room (n)	['miːtɪŋ ˌrʊm]	das Besprechungszimmer, der Konferenzraum
normally (adv)	['nɔːməli]	normalerweise, üblicherweise
p.m. (post meridiem) (abbr)	[piː em], [ˌpəʊstmə'rɪdiəm]	nach dem Mittag
personnel department (n)	[ˌpɜːsə'nel dɪ'pɑːtmənt]	die Personalabteilung
practise (v)	['præktɪs]	trainieren, üben

Unit 2

A new delivery

accountant (n)	[ə'kaʊntənt]	der Buchhalter
accounts department (n)	[ə'kaʊntɪŋ dɪ'pɑːtmənt]	die Buchhaltung
add (v)	[æd]	addieren
amount (n)	[ə'maʊnt]	die Anzahl, die Menge
apparently (adv)	[ə'pærəntli]	anscheinend, offensichtlich
article number (n)	['ɑːtɪkl 'nʌmbə]	die Artikelnummer
aspect (n)	['æspekt]	der Aspekt
compare (v)	[kəm'peə]	vergleichen
comparison (n)	[kəm'pærɪsən]	der Vergleich
condition (n)	[kən'dɪʃən]	die Beschaffenheit
contents (n)	['kɒntents]	der Inhalt
correspond to (v)	[ˌkɒrɪ'spɒnd tu]	entsprechen
damage (n)	['dæmɪdʒ]	der Schaden
deliver (v)	[dɪ'lɪvə]	liefern
delivery note (n)	[dɪ'lɪvəri ˌnəʊt]	der Lieferschein
department (n)	[dɪ'pɑːtmənt]	die Abteilung
describe (v)	[dɪ'skraɪb]	beschreiben, darstellen, wiedergeben
difference (n)	['dɪfərəns]	der Unterschied
divide (v)	[dɪ'vaɪd]	aufgliedern, dividieren, unterteilen
feature (n)	['fiːtʃə]	der Bestandteil, die Eigenschaft, das Merkmal
fortnight (n)	['fɔːtnaɪt]	14 Tage
forwarding agency (n)	['fɔːwədɪŋ 'eɪdʒənsi]	die Spedition
harm (v)	[hɑːm]	schädigen, verletzen
identity (n)	[aɪ'dentətɪ]	die Identität
immediate (adj)	[ɪ'miːdiət]	direkt, sofortig, unverzüglich
incoming goods department (n)	['ɪnkʌmɪŋ 'gʊdz dɪ'pɑːtmənt]	der Wareneingang
invoice (n)	['ɪnvɔɪs]	die Rechnung
involve (v)	[ɪn'vɒlv]	beteiligen, involvieren
item (n)	['aɪtəm]	der Artikel, der Gegenstand

meaning (n)	['miːnɪŋ]	die Bedeutung
mention (v)	['menʃən]	erwähnen, vermerken
non-occupied (adj)	[ˌnɒn'ɒkjəpaɪd]	frei, nicht besetzt
occur (v)	[ə'kɜː]	auftreten, geschehen, passieren
offer (n)	['ɒfə]	das Angebot
order (n)	['ɔːdə]	die Bestellung
otherwise (adv)	['ʌðəwaɪz]	andernfalls, ansonsten
over-delivery (n)	[ˌəʊvə dɪ'lɪvəri]	die Mehrlieferung
package (n)	['pækɪdʒ]	das Packstück, das Paket
packing list (n)	['pækɪŋ ˌlɪst]	die Packliste
part (n)	[pɑːt]	das Teil
perform (v)	[pə'fɔːm]	ausführen, durchführen
pick out (v)	[ˌpɪk 'aʊt]	herausgreifen, heraussuchen
price (n)	[praɪs]	der Preis
product testing (n)	['prɒdʌkt 'testɪŋ]	Warenprüfung
quality (n)	['kwɒləti]	die Qualität
quality control department (n)	['kwɒləti kən'trəʊl dɪ'pɑːtmənt]	die Qualitätskontrolle
quantity (n)	['kwɒntəti]	die Quantität
random sampling (n)	['rændəm ˌsɑːmplɪŋ]	die Stichprobe
receipt of goods (n)	[rɪ'siːt ɒf gʊdz]	die Warenannahme
shelf (n)	[ʃelf]	das Regal
shelves (n)	[ʃelvz]	die Regale
ship (v)	[ʃɪp]	liefern, senden, verschiffen
shipment (n)	['ʃɪpmənt]	die Lieferung, die Sendung
short delivery (n)	['ʃɔːt dɪˌlɪvəri]	die Minderlieferung
sign (v)	[saɪn]	unterschreiben
stamp (v)	[stæmp]	abstempeln
stock list (n)	['stɒk ˌlɪst]	die Lagerliste, die Warenbestandsliste
sum up (v)	[ˌsʌm 'ʌp]	zusammenfassen
supplier (n)	[sə'plaɪə]	der Lieferant
truck dispatch (n)	['trʌk dɪˌspætʃ]	die Hebestelle
visual check (n)	[ˌvɪʒuəl 'tʃek]	die Sichtkontrolle

Flow of goods – departments in the warehouse

customer (n)	['kʌstəmə]	der Kunde
flow of goods (n)	[fləʊ ɒf gʊdz]	der Warenfluss
inventory	[ɪn'ventəri]	der Bestand, das Inventar, der Vorrat
located (adj)	[ləʊ'keɪtɪd]	angesiedelt, ansässig, lokalisiert
outgoing goods department (n)	['aʊtgəʊɪŋ 'gʊdz dɪ'pɑːtmənt]	der Warenausgang
picking department (n)	['pɪkɪŋ dɪ'pɑːtmənt]	die Kommissionierabteilung

The accounts department

complaint (n)	[kəm'pleɪnt]	die Beschwerde
financial accounting (n)	[faɪ'nænʃəl ə'kaʊntɪŋ]	die Finanzbuchhaltung
inventory department (n)	[ɪn'ventəri dɪ'pɑːtmənt]	die Bestandsabteilung
manage (v)	['mænɪdʒ]	erledigen, verwalten
reminder (n)	[rɪ'maɪndə]	die Erinnerung, der Mahnbrief, die Mahnung
subsection (n)	['sʌbˌsekʃən]	die Unterabteilung
wage (n)	[weɪdʒ]	der Lohn
wage accounting (n)	['weɪdʒ əˌkaʊntɪŋ]	die Lohnbuchhaltung

Grammar: Simple Past

enter (v)	['entə]	eingeben, hereinkommen
pallet (n)	['pælɪt]	die Palette
declare (v)	[dɪ'kleə]	angeben, anmelden, deklarieren
horizontal (adj)	[ˌhɒrɪ'zɒntəl]	horizontal, waagerecht
vertical (adj)	['vɜːtɪkəl]	senkrecht, vertikal

Unit 3

Safety First

advice (n)	[əd'vaɪs]	die Empfehlung, der Hinweis, der Ratschlag
avoid (v)	[ə'vɔɪd]	verhindern, vermeiden
error analysis (n)	['erə ə'næləsɪs]	die Fehleranalyse
formulate (v)	['fɔːmjəleɪt]	abfassen, formulieren
miserable (adj)	['mɪzərəbl]	elendig, jämmerlich
mistake (n)	[mɪs'teɪk]	der Fehler
suggest (v)	[sə'dʒest]	empfehlen, vorschlagen

Safety Signs

accident (n)	['æksɪdənt]	der Unfall
background (n)	['bækgraʊnd]	der Hintergrund
border (n)	['bɔːdə]	der Rahmen, der Rand
can (n)	[kæn]	die Dose, der Kanister, die Kanne
cardiac pacemaker (n)	['kɑːdiæk 'peɪsmeɪkə]	der Herzschrittmacher
carelessness (n)	['keələsnəs]	die Nachlässigkeit, die Unachtsamkeit
crossbar (n)	['krɒsbɑː]	der Querbalken
emergency call (n)	[ɪ'mɜːdʒənsi ˌkɔːl]	der Notruf
emergency sign (n)	[ɪ'mɜːdʒənsi ˌsaɪn]	das Rettungszeichen
equipment (n)	[ɪ'kwɪpmənt]	die Ausrüstung
explosive (n)	[ɪk'spləʊsɪv]	der Explosivstoff, der Sprengstoff
eye shower (n)	['aɪ ˌʃaʊə]	die Augendusche
fire alarm (n)	['faɪər əˌlɑːm]	der Feueralarm, der Feuermelder
fire extinguisher (n)	['faɪər ɪkˌstɪŋgwɪʃə]	der Feuerlöscher
fire fighting equipment (n)	['faɪə faɪtɪŋ ɪˌkwɪpmənt]	die Brandschutzausrüstung, das Feuerlöschgerät
fire hose (n)	['faɪə ˌhəʊz]	der Feuerlöschschlauch
fire safety sign (n)	['faɪə ˌseɪfti 'saɪn]	das Brandschutzzeichen
first-aid kit (n)	[ˌfɜːst 'eɪd ˌkɪt]	der Erste-Hilfe-Kasten
floating (adj)	['fləʊtɪŋ]	schwebend, schwimmend
forbid (v)	[fə'bɪd]	untersagen, verbieten, verhindern
gathering point (n)	['gæðərɪŋ ˌpɔɪnt]	der Frost
goggles	['gɒglz]	die Schutzbrille
hard hat (n)	['hɑːd ˌhæt]	der Schutzhelm, der Sicherheitshelm
heart defibrillator (n)	['hɑːt ˌdiː'fɪbrɪleɪtə]	der Defibrillator
high voltage (n)	[ˌhaɪ 'vəʊltɪdʒ]	die Hochspannung
ignore (v)	[ɪg'nɔː]	ignorieren, übergehen, vernachlässigen
indicate (v)	['ɪndɪkeɪt]	angeben, hinweisen, zeigen

industrial truck (n)	[ɪn'dʌstriəl 'trʌk]	das Flurförderzeug
instruction (n)	[ɪn'strʌkʃən]	die Anweisung, die Instruktion
lacking (adj)	['lækɪŋ]	fehlend, mangelnd
mandatory sign (n)	['mændətəri ˌsaɪn]	das Gebotszeichen
necessary (adj)	['nesəsəri]	erforderlich. notwendig
nevertheless (adv)	[ˌnevəðə'les]	dennoch, trotzdem
pedestrian (n)	[pɪ'destriən]	der Fußgänger
prohibition sign (n)	[prəʊhɪ'bɪʃən ˌsaɪn]	das Verbotszeichen
protect (v)	[prə'tekt]	schützen, sichern
protection (n)	[prə'tekʃən]	der Schutz
rectangular (adj)	[rek'tæŋgjələ]	rechteckig
result (v)	[rɪ'zʌlt]	entstehen, ergeben, resultieren
safety belt (n)	['seɪfti ˌbelt]	der Sicherheitsgurt
safety boot (n)	['seɪfti ˌbuːt]	der Sicherheitsstiefel
safety glove (n)	['seɪfti ˌglʌv]	der Sicherheitshandschuh
safety sign (n)	['seɪfti ˌsaɪn]	das Sicherheitszeichen
slippery (adj)	['slɪpəri]	glatt, rutschig
square (adj)	[skweə]	quadratisch
stack (v)	[stæk]	schichten, stapeln
triangular (adj)	[traɪ'æŋgjələ]	dreieckig
warn (v)	[wɔːn]	warnen
warning sign (n)	['wɔːnɪŋ ˌsaɪn]	das Warnzeichen

Grammar: Giving instructions with modal verbs
How to behave in case of an accident

bleeding (n)	['bliːdɪŋ]	das Bluten, die Blutung
broken (adj)	['brəʊkən]	beschädigt, gebrochen, kaputt
call the emergency (v)	['kɔːl ði ɪ'mɜːdʒənsi]	den Notruf anrufen
circumstance (n)	['sɜːkəmstəns]	der Umstand, die Sachlage
fast armature (n)	[ˌfɑːst 'ɑːmətʃə]	der Schnellläufer
first-aid (n)	[ˌfɜːst 'eɪd]	Erste Hilfe
generate (v)	['dʒenəreɪt]	entwickeln, erstellen, generieren
injure (v)	['ɪndʒə]	beschädigen, verletzen
learn by heart (v)	[lɜːn baɪ hɑːt]	etwas auswendig lernen
liquid (n)	['lɪkwɪd]	die Flüssigkeit
mobile phone (n)	['məʊbaɪl ˌfəʊn]	das Funktelefon, das Mobiltelefon
obey (v)	[ə'beɪ]	ausführen, befolgen, gehorchen
operator (n)	['ɒpəreɪtə]	der Bediener, der Betreiber, der Telefonist
pour out (v)	[ˌpɔːr 'aʊt]	ausgießen, ausschütten
require (v)	[rɪ'kwaɪə]	benötigen, brauchen, erfordern
rule (n)	[ruːl]	die Regel, die Richtlinie, die Vorschrift
seem (v)	[siːm]	erscheinen, scheinen, wirken
skip (v)	[skɪp]	auslassen, hüpfen, springen
slip (v)	[slɪp]	entgleiten, rutschen
stretch foil (n)	['stretʃ ˌfɔɪl]	die Stretchfolie
suddenly (adj)	['sʌdənli]	abrupt, plötzlich, unvermittelt
tissue (n)	['tɪʃuː]	das Gewebe, das Taschentuch

unconscious (adj)	[ʌn'kɒnʃəs]	bewusstlos, ohnmächtig
weigh (v)	[weɪ]	wiegen
witness (n)	['wɪtnəs]	der Zeuge

Vocabulary Trainer: Accident report

accident report (n)	['æksɪdənt rɪˌpɔːt]	der Unfallbericht
course of events (n)	['kɔːs ɒf ɪ'vents]	der Gang der Ereignisse, der Hergang
hand forklift truck (n)	['hænd ˌfɔːklɪft 'trʌk]	der Handhubwagen
health insurance (n)	['helθ ɪnˌʃʊərəns]	die Krankenversicherung
insurance (n)	[ɪn'ʃʊərəns]	die Versicherung
job title (n)	['dʒɔːb ˌtaɪtl]	die Berufsbezeichnung
signature (n)	['sɪgnətʃə]	die Unterschrift

Unit 4

Different types of warehouses

airhall store (n)	['eəhɔːl ˌstɔː]	Traglufthallenlager
bunker/silo/tank store (n)	['bʌŋkə], ['saɪləʊ], [tæŋk ˌstɔː]	Bunker-/Silo-/Tanklager
central (adj)	['sentrəl]	zentral
cheap (adj)	[tʃiːp]	billig, kostengünstig, preiswert
commission agent (n)	[kə'mɪʃən ˌeɪdʒənt]	der Kommissionär
commission warehouse (n)	[kə'mɪʃən 'weəhaʊs]	das Kommissionslager
connect (v)	[kə'nekt]	verbinden
consignment warehouse (n)	[kən'saɪnmənt 'weəhaʊs]	das Konsignationslager
crafts enterprise (n)	['krɑːfts ˌentəpraɪz]	der Handwerksbetrieb
decentralized (adj)	[diː'sentrəlaɪzd]	dezentral
dispatch warehouse (n)	[dɪ'spætʃ ˌweəhaʊs]	das Absatzlager
distributing warehouse (n)	[dɪ'strɪbjətɪŋ 'weəhaʊs]	das Versandlager, das Auslieferungslager
due to (sth.) (prep)	['djuː tu]	wegen, aufgrund
finished goods warehouse (n)	[ˌfɪnɪʃt 'gʊdz ˌweəhaʊs]	das Fertigwaren-/ Erzeugnislager
flat store (n)	['flæt ˌstɔː]	das Flachlager
floor storage (n)	['flɔː ˌstɔːrɪdʒ]	die Bodenlagerung
floor store (n)	['flɔː ˌstɔː]	das Etagenlager
goods receiving warehouse (n)	['gʊdz rɪ'siːvɪŋ ˌweəhaʊs]	das Wareneingangslager
hazardous (adj)	['hæzədəs]	gefährlich
highrise rack store (n)	['haɪraɪz ˌræk 'stɔː]	das Hochregallager
intermediaries (n)	[ˌɪntə'miːdiəriz]	der Zwischenhändler, der Vermittler
intermediate warehouse (n)	[ˌɪntə'miːdiət 'weəhaʊs]	das Zwischenlager
likely (adj)	['laɪkli]	wahrscheinlich
manual warehouse (n)	['mænjuəl 'weəhaʊs]	das Handlager
material warehouse (n)	['mə'tɪəriəl 'weəhaʊs]	das Materiallager
open-air storage (n)	['əʊpən 'eə ˌstɔːrɪdʒ]	das offene Lager
order picking warehouse (n)	['ɔːdə 'pɪkɪŋ ˌweəhaʊs]	das Kommissionierlager
own warehouse	['əʊn ˌweəhaʊs]	das Eigenlager
production company	[prə'dʌkʃən 'kʌmpəni]	die Produktionsfirma
production warehouse	[prə'dʌkʃən 'weəhaʊs]	das Produktionslager
rack installation construction (n)	['ræk ɪnstə'leɪʃən kən'strʌkʃən]	die Einbauweise
rack storage (n)	['ræk ˌstɔːrɪdʒ]	die Regallagerung
reserve warehouse (n)	[rɪ'zɜːv ˌweəhaʊs]	das Reservelager
sales warehouse (n)	['seɪlz ˌweəhaʊs]	das Verkaufslager

sample warehouse (n)	['sɑːmpl 'weəhaʊs]	das Musterlager
silo construction	['saɪləʊ kən'strʌkʃən]	die Silobauweise
spare-parts warehouse (n)	['speə ˌpɑːts 'weəhaʊs]	das Werkzeug-/ Ersatzteillager
special storage area (n)	['speʃəl 'stɔːrɪdʒ 'eəriə]	das Sonderlager
special warehouse (n)	['speʃəl 'weəhaʊs]	das Speziallager
third-party warehouse (n)	[ˌθɜːd 'pɑːti ˌweəhaʊs]	das Fremdlager
wholesale company (n)	['həʊlseɪl 'kʌmpəni]	der Großhandel

Lifting, transporting and stacking goods

authorized (adj)	['ɔːθəraɪzd]	autorisiert, befugt, bevollmächtigt
belt conveyor (n)	['belt kənˌveɪə]	der Gurtförderer, das Laufband
block (v)	[blɒk]	abblocken, absperren, blockieren
bucket elevator (n)	['bʌkɪt ˌeləveɪtə]	das Becherwerk, der Kübelaufzug
classify (v)	['klæsɪfaɪ]	einordnen, klassifizieren, unterteilen
continuous acting handling and hoisting equipment (n)	[kən'tɪnjuəs ˌæktɪŋ 'hændlɪŋ ənd 'hɔɪstɪŋ ɪ'kwɪpmənt]	der Stetigförderer
counting scale (n)	['kaʊntɪŋ ˌskeɪl]	die Zählwaage
depend on (v)	[dɪ'pend ˌɒn]	abhängig sein, angewiesen sein
elevator (n)	['eləveɪtə]	der Aufzug, der Fahrstuhl
folding ruler (n)	['fəʊldɪŋ ˌruːlə]	der Gliedermaßstab, der Zollstock
ground conveyor (n)	['graʊnd kənˌveɪə]	das Flurförderzeug
handling (adj)	['hændlɪŋ]	handhabend
handling and hoisting equipment (n)	['hændlɪŋ ənd 'hɔɪstɪŋ ɪ'kwɪpmənt]	das Fördermittel
hoisting (adj)	['hɔɪstɪŋ]	hebend, hochziehend
hoisting device (n)	['hɔɪstɪŋ dɪˌvaɪs]	die Fördereinrichtung, die Hebevorrichtung
hoisting platform (n)	['hɔɪstɪŋ ˌplætfɔːm]	die Hebebühne, die Hubplattform
nail gun (n)	['neɪlgʌn]	der Druckluftnagler
overhead crane (n)	['əʊvəhed ˌkreɪn]	der Brückenkran, der Deckenlaufkran, der Laufkran
properly (adv)	['prɒpəli]	genau, passend, richtig
rack access equipment (n)	['ræk ˌækses ɪ'kwɪpmənt]	das Regalbediengerät, das Regalförderzeug
retail company (n)	['riːteɪl 'kʌmpəni]	der Einzelhandel
slide (n)	[slaɪd]	die Rutsche
sporadic acting handling and hoisting equipment	[spə'radik 'ak-tiŋ 'hændlɪŋ 'ænd 'hɔɪstɪŋ ɪ'kwɪpmənt]	der Unstetigförderer
tool (n)	[tuːl]	das Werkzeug

Racking systems

adjust (v)	[ə'dʒʌst]	adjustieren, anpassen, einstellen
aisle (n)	[aɪl]	der Gang
article (n)	['ɑːtɪkl]	der Artikel
braking system (n)	['breɪkɪŋ ˌsɪstəm]	das Bremssystem
carousel rack (n)	[ˌkærə'sel ˌræk]	das Umlaufregal
comb rack (n)	['kəʊm ˌræk]	das Kassettenregal, das Wabenregal

continuous rack (n)	[kənˌtɪnjuəs 'ræk]	das Durchlaufregal
conveyor (n)	[kən'veɪə]	die Förderanlage, das Förderband
crank (n)	[kræŋk]	die Kurbel
drive-in pallet rack (n)	[ˌdraɪv 'ɪn 'pælɪt ˌræk]	das Einfahrregal
dynamic (adj)	[daɪ'næmɪk]	bewegend, dynamisch
face side (n)	['feɪs ˌsaɪd]	die Stirnseite
high-rise rack (n)	['haɪraɪz ˌræk]	das Hochregal
input (n)	['ɪnpʊt]	die Eingabe, der Eingang
insert (v)	[ɪn'sɜːt]	einführen, einlegen, einschieben
lattice box (n)	['lætɪs ˌbɒks]	die Gitterbox
lift (v)	[lɪft]	anheben
mainly (adv)	['meɪnli]	hauptsächlich, überwiegend, vorwiegend
mobile rack (n)	[ˌməʊbaɪl 'ræk]	das Verschieberegal
modular rack (n)	[ˌmɒdjələ 'ræk]	das Fachbodenregal
multi-storey (adj)	[ˌmʌlti'stɔːri]	mehrgeschossig
non-palletised (adj)	[ˌnɒn'pælɪtaɪzd]	nicht palettiert
non-stackable (adj)	[ˌnɒn'stækəbl]	nicht stapelbar
output (n)	['aʊtpʊt]	die Ausgabe, der Ausgang
pallet rack (n)	['pælɪt ˌræk]	das Palettenregal
palletised (adj)	['pælɪtaɪzd]	palettiert
picking storage (n)	['pɪkɪŋ ˌstɔːrɪdʒ]	das Kommissionierlager
pipe (n)	[paɪp]	das Rohr
primarily (adv)	[praɪ'merəli]	hauptsächlich, vor allem
push-back pallet rack (n)	['pʊʃ ˌbæk 'pælɪt ˌræk]	das Einschubregal
racking system (n)	['rækɪŋ ˌsɪstəm]	die Regalart
rapid access (n)	[ˌræpɪd 'ækses]	der Schnellzugriff
roller conveyor (n)	['rəʊlə kənˌveɪə]	die Rollenbahn
rotating rack (n)	[rəʊ'teɪtɪŋ 'ræk]	das Umlaufregal
shelf board (n)	['ʃelfbɔːd]	der Regalboden
shelf life limit (n)	['ʃelf ˌlaɪf 'lɪmɪt]	das Mindesthaltbarkeitsdatum, die Lagerzeit
sideways (adv)	['saɪdweɪz]	seitlich, seitwärts
single-storey (adj)	['sɪŋgl ˌstɔːri]	eingeschossig
slope (n)	[sləʊp]	die Abschüssigkeit, das Gefälle
space-saving (adj)	['speɪs ˌseɪvɪŋ]	platzsparend, raumsparend
static (adj)	['stætɪk]	feststehend, stationär, statisch
stationary (adj)	['steɪʃənəri]	feststehend, stationär
stock placement (n)	['stɒk ˌpleɪsmənt]	die Einlagerung
stock removal (n)	['stɒk rɪˌmuːvəl]	die Auslagerung
suitable (adj)	['suːtəbl]	angemessen, geeignet, passend, tauglich
supporting beam (n)	[sə'pɔːtɪŋ ˌbiːm]	der Auflageträger
thread rod (n)	['θred ˌrɒd]	die Gewindestange
unit (n)	['juːnɪt]	das Bauteil, die Einheit
utilisation of available floorspace	[ˌjuːtəlaɪ'zeɪʃən ɒf ə'veɪləbl 'flɔːrspeɪs]	der Flächennutzungsgrad
utilisation of storage space (n)	[ˌjuːtəlaɪ'zeɪʃən ɒf 'stɔːrɪdʒ ˌspeɪs]	die Lagerraumnutzung
vary (v)	['veəri]	variieren, verändern

Different types of forklift trucks and their equipment

be patient (v)	[bi 'peɪʃənt]	sich gedulden
clamp (v)	[klæmp]	einklemmen, einspannen, klammern

machinery (n)	[mə'ʃiːnəri]	die maschinelle Einrichtung, die Maschinen
measure (n)	['meʒə]	das Maß, die Maßeinheit
of age (adj)	[ɒf 'eɪdʒ]	mündig sein, volljährig sein
operate (v)	['ɒpəreɪt]	arbeiten, bedienen, führen
pass (v)	[pɑːs]	absolvieren, bestehen
practical (adj)	['præktɪkəl]	praktisch
theoretical (adj)	[θɪə'retɪkəl]	theoretisch
weight (n)	[weɪt]	das Gewicht
attachment (n)	[ə'tætʃmənt]	das Anbaugerät, das Anbauteil, der Anhang
eager (adj)	['iːgə]	eifrig sein, erpicht sein, etwas unbedingt wollen
gantry crane (n)	['gæntri ˌkreɪn]	der Brückenkran, die Containerbrücke, der Portalkran
man-carrying platform (n)	['mæn ˌkæriɪŋ 'plætfɔːm]	die Arbeitsbühnen, der Personenbeförderungskotb
reach stacker (n)	['riːtʃ ˌstækə]	der Greifstapler
straddle carrier (n)	['strædl ˌkæriə]	der Portalhubwagen, der Van-Carrier (VC)
utility knife (n)	[ˌjuː'tɪləti ˌnaɪf]	das Cuttermesser, das Teppichmesser

Unit 5

Skills and competencies

introduce (v)	[ˌɪntrə'djuːs]	einführen, präsentieren, vorstellen
investment costs (n)	[ɪn'vestmənt ˌkɒsts]	die Investitionskosten
sensitivity (n)	[ˌsensɪ'tɪvəti]	die Empfindlichkeit
transshipment (n)	[træns'ʃɪpmənt]	der Güterumschlag

Order Picking

allocation of items (n)	[ˌælə'keɪʃən ɒf 'aɪtəmz]	die Bereitstellung der Ware
collect (v)	[kə'lekt]	abholen, einsammeln, zusammentragen
distance (n)	['dɪstəns]	die Distanz, die Entfernung, die Strecke
EDP (Electronic Data processing) (abbr)	[iː diː piː], [ˌelek'trɒnɪk 'deɪtə 'prəʊsesɪŋ]	die elektronische Datenverarbeitung (EDV)
goods to man (n)	[gʊdz tu mæn]	Ware zum Mann
man to goods (n)	[mæn tu gʊdz]	Mann zur Ware
order picker (n)	['ɔːdə ˌpɪkə]	der Kommissionierer
order picking (n)	['ɔːdə ˌpɪkɪŋ]	die Kommissionierung
pick to box (n)	[pɪk tu bɒks]	die auftragsorientierte serielle Kommissionierung mit Übergabesteller
picker to part method (n)	['pɪkə tu 'pɑːt ˌmeθəd]	auftragsorientierte serielle Kommissionierung
picking list (n)	['pɪkɪŋ ˌlɪst]	die Pickliste
piece picking (n)	['piːs ˌpɪkɪŋ]	auftragsorientierte serielle Kommissionierung
proceed (v)	[prə'siːd]	ablaufen, stattfinden, vorgehen
process (v)	['prəʊses]	aufbereiten, bearbeiten, prozessieren

productivity (n)	[ˌprɒdʌk'tɪvəti]	die Ergiebigkeit, die Leistungsfähigkeit, die Produktivität
real time (n)	['rɪəl ˌtaɪm]	die Echtzeit, die Realzeit
specific (adj)	[spə'sɪfɪk]	bestimmt, speziell, spezifisch
specified (adj)	['spesɪfaɪd]	angegeben, festgelegt, spezifiziert
wave picking method (n)	['weɪv ˌpɪkɪŋ 'meθəd]	die serienorientierte parallele Kommissionierung
zone (n)	[zəʊn]	der Bereich, das Gebiet, die Zone
zone picking method (n)	['zəʊn ˌpɪkɪŋ 'meθəd]	die auftragsorientierte parallele Kommissionierung

Paperless picking methods

accuracy (n)	['ækjərəsi]	die Akkuratesse, die Genauigkeit, die Fehlerfreiheit
accurate (adj)	['ækjərət]	akkurat, genau, sorgfältig
attach (v)	[ə'tætʃ]	anbringen, befestigen, beifügen
augmented (adj)	[ɔːg'mentɪd]	erweitert, vergrößert, vermehrt
based (adj)	[beɪst]	basierend, begründet, beruhend
batch (n)	[bætʃ]	das Batch, das Bündel, die Charge
bay (n)	[beɪ]	das Arbeitsfeld, die Bucht, das Feld
building (n)	['bɪldɪŋ]	das Bauwerk, das Gebäude, das Haus
button (n)	['bʌtən]	der Knopf
cart (n)	[kɑːt]	Einkaufswagen, Karre, Wagen
case (n)	[keɪs]	der Behälter, der Fall, die Kiste
check digit (n)	['tʃek ˌdɪdʒɪt]	die Kontrollziffer, die Prüfziffer
compartment (n)	[kəm'pɑːtmənt]	die Abteilung, das Fach, das Kompartiment
concerning (adj)	[kən'sɜːnɪŋ]	betreffend
configuration (n)	[kənˌfɪgjə'reɪʃən]	die Anordnung, die Einstellung, die Konfiguration
confirm (v)	[kən'fɜːm]	bestätigen, quittieren, zusagen
count back (n)	[ˌkaʊnt 'bæk]	das Korrekturzählen
data (n)	['deɪtə]	die Angaben, die Daten, die Informationen
directed (adj)	[dɪ'rektɪd]; [daɪ-]	adressiert, geleitet, gelenkt
e.g. (exempli gratia) (abbr)	[iː dʒiː], [ɪg'zæmplaɪ 'greɪʃiə]	zum Beispiel, beispielsweise
efficiency (n)	[ɪ'fɪʃənsi]	die Effizienz, die Leistung, die Wirtschaftlichkeit
enhanced (adj)	[ɪn'hɑːnst]	erweitert, vergrößert, verstärkt
expect (v)	[ɪk'spekt]	annehmen, erwarten, voraussetzen
extraction (n)	[ɪk'strækʃən]	die Entnahme, die Extraktion, die Gewinnung
glasses (n)	['glɑːsɪz]	die Brille

group (v)	[gruːp]	einteilen, gruppieren, unterteilen
guide (v)	[gaɪd]	führen, leiten, lotsen
headset (n)	['hedset]	der Kopfhörer, das Headset, die Sprechgarnitur
identify (v)	[aɪ'dentɪfaɪ]	ausweisen, erkennen, identifizieren
illuminated (adj)	[ɪ'luːmɪneɪtɪd]	beleuchtet, illuminiert
latest (adj)	['leɪtɪst]	aktuell, modernste, neueste
minimize (v)	['mɪnɪmaɪz]	herabmindern, minimieren, verkleinern
mobile data terminal (n)	['məʊbaɪl 'deɪtə ˌtɜːmɪnəl]	die mobile Datenstation, das mobile -Datenterminal
modification (n)	[ˌmɒdɪfɪ'keɪʃən]	die Modifikation, die Umrüstung, die Veränderung
packing slip (n)	['pækɪŋ ˌslɪp]	der Packzettel
pallet licence (n)	['pælɪt ˌlaɪsəns]	die Palettennummer
paperless (adj)	['peɪpələs]	beleglos, papierlos
paperwork (n)	['peɪpəwɜːk]	die Büroarbeit, die Dokumentation, der Papierkram
pick to light (n)	[pɪk tu laɪt]	die Kommissionierung per LED-Anzeigen
picking using bar code (n)	['pɪkɪŋ ˌjuːzɪŋ 'bɑː ˌkəʊd]	die Strichcodekommissionierung
picking using RFID (n)	['pɪkɪŋ ˌjuːzɪŋ ɑːr ef aɪ diː]	die Kommissionierung mit RFID
procedure (n)	[prə'siːdʒə]	die Handlungsweise, die Prozedur, der Vorgang
relevant (adj)	['reləvənt]	entsprechend, relevant, wichtig
reliably (adv)	[rɪ'laɪəbli]	betriebssicher, verlässlich, zuverlässig
RFID (Radio Frequency Identification) (abbr)	[ɑːr ef aɪ diː], ['reɪdiəʊ 'friːkwənsi aɪˌdentɪfɪ'keɪʃən]	die Radiofrequenz-Identifikation
simply (adv)	['sɪmpli]	einfach, schlicht, simpel
speed up (v)	[ˌspiːd 'ʌp]	beschleunigen, dynamisieren, schneller werden
switch on (v)	[ˌswɪtʃ 'ɒn]	anschalten, anstellen, einschalten
tag (n)	[tæg]	die Marke, das Schild, der Transponder
virtual (adj)	['vɜːtʃuəl]	gedacht, fiktiv, virtuell
voice directed warehousing (n)	['vɔɪs ˌdɪrektɪd 'weəhaʊzɪŋ]	die Kommissionierung per Sprachangaben
voice picking (n)	['vɔɪs ˌpɪkɪŋ]	die Kommissionierung per Sprachangaben

Vocabulary Trainer: Picking Policy – FiFo and LiFo

accounting (adj)	[ə'kaʊntɪŋ]	buchhaltungstechnisch
accounting purpose (n)	[ə'kaʊntɪŋ ˌpɜːpəs]	der Buchhaltungszweck
balance sheet (n)	['bæləns ˌʃiːt]	der Abschluss, die Bilanzaufstellung, der Jahresabschluss
expiry date (n)	[ɪk'spaɪəri ˌdeɪt]	das Ablaufdatum, das Fälligkeitsdatum, das Verfallsdatum
FiFo (first in, first out) (abbr)	['faɪfəʊ] [ˌfɜːst 'ɪn ˌfɜːst 'aʊt]	„zuerst rein, zuerst raus"
HiFo (highest in, first out) (abbr)	['haɪfəʊ] [ˌhaɪɪst 'ɪn ˌfɜːst 'aʊt]	„teuerste Ware zuerst raus"
LiFo (last in, first out) (abbr)	['laɪfəʊ] [ˌlɑːst 'ɪn ˌfɜːst 'aʊt]	„zuletzt rein, zuerst raus"

LoFo (lowest in, first out) (abbr)	['ləʊfəʊ] [ˌləʊɪst 'ɪn ˌfɜːst 'aʊt]	„günstigste Ware zuerst raus"
lower of cost or market (v)	['ləʊər ɒf 'kɒst ɔː 'mɑːkɪt]	das Niederstwertprinzip
opposite (n)	['ɒpəzɪt]	der Gegensatz, das Gegenteil
valuation (n)	[ˌvælju'eɪʃən]	die Bewertung, die Schätzung, die Wertermittlung
value (n)	['væljuː]	der Betrag, die Valuta, der Wert
value (v)	['væljuː]	bewerten, rechnen, schätzen

Unit 6

Skills and competencies

risk (n)	[rɪsk]	die Gefahr, das Risiko

Reasons for packing goods

adhesive tape (n)	[əd'hiːsɪv 'teɪp]	das Klebeband
bubble envelope (n)	['bʌbl ˌenvələʊp]	die Luftpolstertasche
corrugated cardboard	['kɒrəgeɪtɪd 'kɑːdbɔːd]	die Wellpappe
discover (v)	[dɪ'skʌvə]	erkennen, feststellen, herausfinden
ensure (v)	[ɪn'ʃɔː]	garantieren, gewährleisten, sicherstellen
handy (adj)	['hændi]	dienlich, nützlich, praktisch
namely (adv)	['neɪmli]	nämlich, und zwar
styrofoam (n)	['staɪərəfəʊm]	das Styropor

Different types of packing and packaging aids

carboy (n) die Korbflasche	['kɑːbɔɪ]	die Korbflasche
cardboard carton (n)	['kɑːdbɔːd ˌkɑːtən]	der Pappkarton, die Schachtel
cask (n)	[kɑːsk]	das Fass, die Tonne
chest (n)	[tʃest]	die Kiste, die Truhe
drum (n)	[drʌm]	die Trommel
euro-pallet (n)	['juːrəʊ ˌpælɪt]	die Euro-Palette
foam (n)	[fəʊm]	der Schaum
metal strapped (adj)	['metəl ˌstræpt]	stahlummantelt
package content (n)	['pækɪdʒ ˌkɒntent]	das Packgut
packaging (n)	['pækɪdʒɪŋ]	die Verkaufsverpackung
packaging aid (n)	['pækɪdʒɪŋ ˌeɪd]	das Packhilfsmittel
packaging material (n)	['pækɪdʒɪŋ məˌtɪəriəl]	der Packstoff
packaging means (n)	['pækɪdʒɪŋ ˌmiːnz]	das Packmittel
packing (n)	['pækɪŋ]	die Versandpackung
parcel (n)	['pɑːsəl]	das Packstück, das Paket
wooden box (n)	[ˌwʊdən 'bɒks]	die Holzkiste
bale (n)	[beɪl]	der Ballen
bubble wrap (n)	['bʌbl ˌræp]	die Luftpolsterfolie
foam peanut (n)	['fəʊm ˌpiːnʌt]	der Verpackungschip
hessian sack (n)	['hesiən ˌsæk]	der Jutesack
mould (n)	[məʊld]	die Form, die Gießform, die Gussform
plastic (n)	['plæstɪk]	der Kunststoff, das Plastik
plastic bag (n)	['plæstɪk ˌbæg]	der Plastikbeutel
polystyrene mould (n)	[ˌpɒlɪ'staɪriːn ˌməʊld]	die Styroporform
soft tissue (n)	[ˌsɒft 'tɪʃuː]	das Seidenpapier
wood wool (n)	['wʊdwʊl]	die Holzwolle
wrapping paper (n)	['ræpɪŋ ˌpeɪpə]	das Packpapier

Suitable packings for goods

barrel (n)	['bærəl]	das Fass
bunch (n)	[bʌntʃ]	das Bündel, das Gebinde, der Strauß
cotton (n)	['kɒtən]	Baumwolle
fragile (adj)	['frædʒaɪl]	fragil, zerbrechlich
screw (n)	[skruː]	die Schraube
tyre (n)	['taɪə]	der Reifen
seaworthy packing (n)	['siːˌwɜːði 'pækɪŋ]	die Seekiste
shipping document pouch (n)	['ʃɪpɪŋ ˌdɒkjəmənt 'paʊtʃ]	die Dokumententasche
big bag (n)	['bɪg ˌbæg]	der Big Bag
bundle (n) das Bündel	['bʌndl]	das Bündel
crate (n)	[kreɪt]	der Holzverschlag, die Lattenkiste
porcelain figure (n)	['pɔːsəlɪn ˌfɪgə]	die Porzellanfigur
reel (n)	[riːl]	die Rolle, die Spule

Unit 7

Skills and Competencies

dangerous goods (n)	['deɪndʒərəs 'gʊdz]	das Gefahrgut, der Gefahrstoff
dangerous goods safety advisor (n)	['deɪndʒərəs 'gʊdz 'seɪfti əd'vaɪzə]	Gefahrgutbeauftragter
dangerous goods safety mark (n)	['deɪndʒərəs 'gʊdz 'seɪfti ˌmɑːk]	der Gefahrenzettel
handling sign (n)	['hændlɪŋ ˌsaɪn]	das Handhabungszeichen
hazard (n)	['hæzəd]	die Gefahr
hazardous (adj)	['hæzədəs]	gefährlich
hazardous materials label (n)	['hæzədəs mə'tɪəriəlz ˌleɪbəl]	das Gefahrgutkennzeichen, das Gefahrgutlabel

The correct label for all goods

adviser (n)	[əd'vaɪzə]	der Advisor, der Beauftragte, der Berater
barrier (n)	['bæriə]	die Barriere, die Schutzabdeckung, die Sperrschicht
centre of gravity (n)	['sentər ɒf 'grævəti]	der Schwerpunkt
circle (n)	['sɜːkl]	der Kreis
combustion (n)	[kəm'bʌstʃən]	die Entzündung, die Verbrennung
contain (v)	[kən'teɪn]	beinhalten, enthalten
corrosion (n)	[kə'rəʊʒən]	die Korrosion, die Verätzung
duty (n)	['djuːti]	die Aufgabe, die Pflicht
electrostatic (adj)	[ɪˌlektrə'stætɪk]	elektrostatisch
emit (v)	[iː'mɪt]	absondern, ausstoßen, emittieren
environment (n)	[ɪn'vaɪrənmənt]	die Umwelt
environmental (adj)	[ɪnˌvaɪrən'məntəl]	hinsichtlich der Umwelt
essential (adj)	[ɪ'senʃəl]	erforderlich, essenziell, wichtig
exclamation mark (n)	[ekskl ə'meɪʃən ˌmɑːk]	das Ausrufungszeichen
fire brigade (n)	['faɪə brɪˌgeɪd]	die Feuerwehr
firework (n)	['faɪəwɜːk]	der Feuerwerksartikel, der Feuerwerkskörper
flame (n)	[fleɪm]	die Flamme
flammable (adj)	['flæməbl]	brennbar, entflammbar, feuergefährlich
frost (n)	[frɒst]	der Sammelpunkt, die Sammelstelle

gas cylinder (n)	['gæs ˌsɪlɪndə]	die Gasflasche
GHS (Globally Harmonised System of Classification and Labelling of Chemicals) (abbr)	[dʒiː eɪtʃ es], ['gləʊbəli ˌhɑːmənaɪzd 'sɪstəm ɒf ˌklæsɪfɪ'keɪʃən ænd 'leɪbəlɪŋ ɒf 'kemɪkəlz]	Global Harmonisiertes System zur Einstufung und Kennzeichnung von Chemikalien
hook (n)	[hʊk]	der Haken
keep away from (v)	[ˌkiːp ə'weɪ ˌfrɒm]	fernhalten
limitation (n)	[ˌlɪmɪ'teɪʃən]	die Beschränkung, die Einschränkung, die Grenze
petrol (n)	['petrəl]	das Benzin
proud (adj)	[praʊd]	stolz
responsible (adj)	[rɪ'spɒnsəbl]	verantwortlich, zuständig
sensitive (adj)	['sensɪtɪv]	empfindlich, sensibel, sensitiv
shave (v)	[ʃeɪv]	rasieren

Handling signs

desensitize (v)	[ˌdiː'sensɪtaɪz]	desensibilisieren, unempfindlich machen
health (n)	[helθ]	die Gesundheit
infectious (adj)	[ɪn'fekʃəs]	ansteckend, infektiös
liable to (adj)	['laɪəbl tu]	anfällig, neigend, verantwortlich
miscellaneous (adj)	[ˌmɪse'leɪəniəs]	divers, verschieden
organic (adj)	[ɔː'gænɪk]	biologisch, organisch
oxidizing (adj)	['ɒksɪdaɪzɪŋ]	oxidierend, rostend
peroxide (n)	[pə'rɒksaɪd]	das Peroxid, das Superoxid
physical (adj)	['fɪzɪkəl]	physikalisch
playground (n)	['pleɪgraʊnd]	der Spielplatz
safety mark (n)	['seɪfti ˌmɑːk]	die Sicherheitsmarkierung
self-reactive (adj)	['self rɪˌæktɪv]	selbsterhitzungsfähig, selbstzersetzlich
skull & crossbones (n)	['skʌl ænd 'krɒsbəʊnz]	das Totenkopfsymbol
solid (n)	['sɒlɪd]	der Festkörper, der Feststoff
spontaneous (adj)	[spɒn'teɪniəs]	spontan
substance (n)	['sʌbstəns]	die Materie, der Stoff, die Substanz
substitute (v)	['sʌbstɪtjuːt]	austauschen, ersetzen, substituieren
toxic (adj)	['tɒksɪk]	giftig, toxisch

Unit 8

Skills and Competencies

cargo (n)	['kɑːgəʊ]	die Fracht, die Ladung
external (adj)	[ɪk'stɜːnəl]	äußerlich, außen
measurement (n)	['meʒəmənt]	die Abmessung, die Größe, das Maß

The story of containers

circumference (n)	[sə'kʌmfərəns]	die Ausdehnung, der Umfang
container vessel (n)	[kən'teɪnə ˌvesəl]	das Containerschiff, das Versandschiff
equivalent (adj)	[ɪ'kwɪvələnt]	äquivalent, gleichviel, gleichwertig
fleet (n)	[fliːt]	die Flotte

foot (n)	[fʊt]	der Fuß (Längenmaß: 1′ (Fuß) = 30,48 cm)
French National Assembly (n)	[ˌfrenʃ ˈnæʃənəl əˈsembli]	die Französische Nationalversammlung
hay (n)	[heɪ]	das Heu
height (n)	[haɪt]	die Höhe
high (adj)	[haɪ]	hoch
human (adj)	[ˈhjuːmən]	human, menschlich
inch (n)	[ɪntʃ]	der Zoll (Längeneinheit: 1 Zoll = 2,54 cm)
initiative (n)	[ɪˈnɪʃətɪv]	der Anstoß, die Initiative
measure (v)	[ˈmeʒə]	messen
scrap iron (n)	[ˈskræp ˌaɪən]	das Alteisen, der Eisenschrott
standard (n)	[ˈstændəd]	die Norm, die Richtlinie, der Standard
TEU (Twenty Foot Equivalent Unit) (abbr)	[tiː iː juː], [ˌtwenti ˈfʊt ɪˈkwɪvələnt ˌjuːnɪt]	die 20′(Fuß)-Einheit
trade (n)	[treɪd]	der Handel
vessel (n)	[vesəl]	das Schiff, das Transportschiff
waste paper (n)	[ˈweɪstpeɪpə]	das Altpapier, der Papierabfall
yard (n) der Hof, das Yard	[jɑːd]	(Längenmaß: 1 Yard = 91,44 cm)

Measurements

by heart (adj)	[ˌbaɪ ˈhɑːt]	auswendig
capacity (n)	[kəˈpæsəti]	die Aufnahmefähigkeit, das Fassungsvermögen, die Kapazität
centrifugal force (n)	[ˌsentrɪˈfjuːgəl ˈfɔːs]	die Fliehkraft, die Zentrifugalkraft
consideration (n)	[kənˌsɪdəˈreɪʃən]	die Abwägung, die Berücksichtigung, die Erwägung
cu.cap. (cubic capacity) (abbr)	[ˈkjuːbɪk kəˈpæsəti]	der Nutzinhalt, der Rauminhalt
dead space (n)	[ˌded ˈspeɪs]	der ungenutzte Raum
force (n)	[fɔːs]	die Kraft
gravity (n)	[ˈgrævəti]	die Erdanziehungskraft, die Gravitationskraft, die Schwerkraft
gross (adj)	[grəʊs]	brutto
gross weight (n)	[ˈgrəʊs ˌweɪt]	das Bruttogewicht
internal (adj)	[ɪnˈtɜːnəl]	innen, intern
lashing material (n)	[ˈlæʃɪŋ məˌtɪəriəl]	das Laschmaterial
loose (adj)	[luːs]	locker, lose
m.g.w. (maximum gross weight) (abbr)	[em dʒiː ˈdʌblju], [ˈmæksɪməmˈgrəʊs ˌweɪt]	das maximale Bruttogewicht
tare (n)	[teə]	das Leergewicht, die Tara, das Verpackungsgewicht

Load securing

anti-slip mat (n)	[ˌæntɪ ˈslɪp ˌmæt]	die Antirutschmatte
cause (v)	[kɔːz]	bewirken, hervorrufen, verursachen
conclusion (n)	[kənˈkluːʒən]	das Ergebnis, das Fazit, die Schlussfolgerung
contract worker (n)	[ˈkɒntrækt ˌwɜːkə]	der Leiharbeiter, der Zeitarbeiter

edge protector (n)	['edʒ prə'tektə]	der Kantenschoner, der Kantenschutz
fine (n)	[faɪn]	das Bußgeld, die Geldstrafe
gang (n)	[gæŋ]	die Gang, die Gruppe
guarantee (v)	[ˌgærən'tiː]	garantieren, gewährleisten, sicherstellen
imprisonment (n)	[ɪm'prɪzənmənt]	die Freiheitsstrafe, die Inhaftierung
influence (n)	['ɪnfluəns]	der Einfluss, die Einwirkung
inspect (v)	[ɪn'spekt]	inspizieren, prüfen, untersuchen
insufficient (adj)	[ˌɪnsə'fɪʃənt]	insuffizient, nicht ausreichend, ungenügend
lashing point (n)	['læʃɪŋ ˌpɔɪnt]	der Laschpunkt
lashing strap (n)	['læʃɪŋ ˌstræp]	der Zurrgurt
leave (v)	[liːv]	fortfahren, verlassen
load balancing (n)	['ləʊd ˌbælənsɪŋ]	die Lastverteilung
loadmaster (n)	['ləʊdmɑːstə]	der Lademeister
net (adj)	[net]	nach Abzug von etwas, netto
observance (n)	[əb'zɜːvəns]	das Beachten, die Berücksichtigung, die Observanz
verification (n)	[ˌverɪfɪ'keɪʃən]	die Bestätigung, die Überprüfung, die Verifikation
wooden wedge (n)	[ˌwʊdən 'wedʒ]	der Holzkeil

Grammar: Adjective or Adverb - Asking questions

urgent (adj)	['ɜːdʒənt]	akut, dringend, zwingend
use (v)	[juːz]	benutzen, gebrauchen
wide (adj)	[waɪd]	breit

Packing pattern

concrete stone (n)	['kɒŋkriːt ˌstəʊn]	der Betonstein
cooperate (v)	[kəʊ'ɒpəreɪt]	kooperieren, zusammenarbeiten
i.e. (id est) (abbr)	[aɪ iː] [ɪd est]	das heißt
payload (n)	['peɪləʊd]	das Ladegewicht, die Nutzlast

Vocabulary trainer: Different types of containers and their cargo

bulk container (n)	['bʌlk kənˌteɪnə]	der Schüttgutcontainer
flatrack (flat) (n)	['flætræk], [flæt]	das Flat
grain (n)	[greɪn]	das Getreide
insulated (adj)	['ɪnsjəleɪtɪd]	gedämmt, isoliert
insulated container (n)	['ɪnsjəleɪtɪd kən'teɪnə]	der Isoliercontainer
length (n)	[leŋkθ]	die Länge
matter (n)	['mætə]	die Angelegenheit, die Materie, die Sache
platform (n)	['plætfɔːm]	die Plattform
refrigerated (adj)	[rɪ'frɪdʒəreɪtɪd]	gekühlt
refrigerated container (reefer) (n)	[rɪ'frɪdʒəreɪtɪd kən'teɪnə], ['riːfə]	der Kühlcontainer
tank container (n)	['tæŋk kənˌteɪnə]	der Tankcontainer
technical book (n)	['teknɪkəl ˌbʊk]	das Fachbuch
ventilated (adj)	['ventɪleɪtɪd]	belüftet, ventiliert
ventilated container (n)	['ventɪleɪtɪd kən'teɪnə]	der ventilierte Container
width (n)	[wɪdθ]	die Breite

Unit 9

The best way to send goods

combination (n)	[ˌkɒmbɪˈneɪʃən]	die Kombination, die Mischung
concentration (n)	[ˌkɒnsənˈtreɪʃən]	die Aufmerksamkeit, die Konzentration
crane (n)	[kreɪn]	der Kran
demand (v)	[dɪˈmɑːnd]	erfordern
mode of transport (n)	[ˌməʊd ɒf ˈtrænspɔːt]	die Beförderungsart, der Verkehrsträger
possible (adj)	[ˈpɒsɪbl]	möglich
reduce (v)	[rɪˈdjuːs]	reduzieren, vermindern, verringern
return (v)	[rɪˈtɜːn]	retournieren, zurückkehren, zurückschicken
roadtrain (n)	[ˈrəʊd ˌtreɪn]	der LKW-Zug
too (adv)	[tuː]	auch, ebenfalls, zu
train (n)	[treɪn]	der Eisenbahnzug
transport method (n)	[ˈtrænspɔːt ˌmeθəd]	die Transportmethode, die Transportmöglichkeit

Means and modes of transport

advantage (n)	[ədˈvɑːntɪdʒ]	der Vorteil
air (n)	[eə]	die Luft
aircraft (n)	[ˈeəkrɑːft]	das Flugzeug
corresponding (adj)	[ˌkɒrɪˈspɒndɪŋ]	dazugehörend, entsprechend, zugehörig
disadvantage (n)	[ˌdɪsədˈvɑːntɪdʒ]	der Nachteil
environmentally friendly (adj)	[ɪnˌvaɪərənˈmentəli ˈfrendli]	umweltfreundlich
environmentally unfriendly (adj)	[ɪnˌvaɪərənˈmentəli ʌnˈfrendli]	umweltschädlich
means of transport (n)	[ˌmiːnz ɒf ˈtrænspɔːt]	das Beförderungsmittel, das Transportmittel
punctual (adj)	[ˈpʌŋktʃuəl]	pünktlich, rechtzeitig
rail (n)	[reɪl]	die Eisenbahnschiene
railbound (adj)	[ˈreɪlbaʊnd]	schienengebunden
reliable (adj)	[rɪˈlaɪəbl]	verlässlich, zuverlässig
sea (n)	[siː]	das Meer
valuable (adj)	[ˈvæljuəbl]	nützlich, wertvoll

Documents in international trade

abroad (adv)	[əˈbrɔːd]	ins Ausland
air waybill (n)	[ˈeə ˌweɪbɪl]	der Luftfrachtbrief
bill of lading (n)	[ˌbɪl ɒf ˈleɪdɪŋ]	das Konnossement, der Seefrachtbrief
carrier (n)	[ˈkæriə]	der Frachtführer
certify (v)	[ˈsɜːtɪfaɪ]	bescheinigen, bestätigen, zertifizieren
certificate of origin (n)	[sɜːˈtɪfɪkət ɒf ˈɒrɪdʒɪn]	die Herkunftsbescheinigung, das Ursprungszeugnis
combined (adj)	[kəmˈbaɪnd]	kombiniert, zusammengesetzt
commercial invoice (n)	[kəˈmɜːʃəl ˈɪnvɔɪs]	die Handelsrechnung, die Warenrechnung
common (adj)	[ˈkɒmən]	gängig, gemeinsam
consignee (n)	[ˌkɒnsaɪˈniː]	der Empfänger

country (n)	['kʌntri]	das Land, der Staat
date of delivery (n)	[deɪt ɒf dɪ'lɪvəri]	das Lieferdatum
description of the consignment (n)	[dɪ'skrɪpʃən ɒf ðə kən'saɪnmənt]	die Beschreibung der Sendung
destination (n)	[ˌdestɪ'neɪʃən]	der Bestimmungsort
document of title (n)	['dɒkjəmənt ɒf 'taɪtl]	das Dispositionsdokument, die Legimitationsurkunde
holder (n)	['həʊldə]	der Halter, der Inhaber
insurance certificate (n)	[ɪn'ʃʊərəns sɜː'tɪfɪkət]	die Versicherungsbescheinigung
international trade (n)	[ˌɪntə'næʃənəl 'treɪd]	der internationale Handel, der Welthandel
lawful (adj)	['lɔːfʊl]	gesetzlich
leak (v)	[ˌliːk]	auslaufen
negotiable (adj)	[nɪ'gəʊʃiəbl]	übertragbar, verhandelbar, verkäuflich
owner (n)	['əʊnə]	der Besitzer, der Eigentümer
place of delivery (n)	[ˌpleɪs ɒf dɪ'lɪvəri]	der Lieferort
rail waybill (n)	[ˌreɪl 'weɪbɪl]	Frachtbrief der Bahn
rightful (adj)	['raɪtfʊl]	rechtmäßig
road waybill (n)	[ˌrəʊd 'weɪbɪl]	der Spediteurfrachtbrief
seller (n)	['selə]	der Verkäufer
shipper (n)	['ʃɪpə]	der Versender
waybill (n)	['weɪbɪl]	der Frachtbrief
weight of the cargo (n)	[weɪt ɒf ðə 'kɑːgəʊ]	das Gewicht der Fracht/der Ladung

Route Planning

expensive (adj)	[ɪk'spensɪv]	teuer
risky (adj)	['rɪski]	gefährlich, riskant
road (n)	[rəʊd]	die Straße

Incoterms®

calculate (v)	['kælkjəleɪt]	berechnen, ermitteln, errechnen
carriage (n)	['kærɪdʒ]	der Transport
CIF (cost, insurance and freight) (abbr)	[siː aɪ ef], [kɒst ɪn'ʃʊərəns ænd freɪt]	Kosten, Versicherung und Fracht
cost (n)	[kɒst]	die Kosten, der Preis
DDP (delivered duty paid) (abbr)	[di ːdiː piː], [dɪ'lɪvəd 'djuːti peɪd]	geliefert verzollt
differ (v)	['dɪfə]	differieren, unterscheiden
EXW (ex works) (abbr)	[iː eks 'dʌblju], [eks wɜːks]	ab Werk
FAS (free alongside ship) (abbr)	[ef eɪ es], [friː ə'lɒŋsaɪd ʃɪp]	frei Längsseite Schiff
FOB (free on board) (abbr)	[ef əʊ biː], [friː ɒn bɔːd]	frei an Bord
freight charges (n)	['freɪt ˌtʃɑːdʒɪz]	die Frachtkosten
Incoterms (n)	['ɪnkəʊtɜːmz]	die internationalen Handelsbedingungen der ICC, die Lieferbedingungen
loading costs (n)	['ləʊdɪŋ ˌkɒsts]	die Verladekosten
premises (n)	['premɪsɪz]	das Grundstück, das Firmengelände
send (v)	[send]	schicken, senden, versenden
ship (n)	[ʃɪp]	das Schiff
shipping costs (n)	['ʃɪpɪŋ ˌkɒsts]	die Versandkosten
unloading costs (n)	[ʌn'ləʊdɪŋ ˌkɒsts]	Kosten der Entladung, Kosten der Löschung

Vocabulary trainer: Damages to a shipment

bashed (adj)	[bæʃt]	ramponiert
burst (adj)	[bɜːst]	aufgeplatzt, gebrochen
compressed (adj)	[kəm'prest]	eingedrückt, gestaucht
condensation (n)	[ˌkɒnden'seɪʃən]	das Schwitzwasser
countable (adj)	['kaʊntəbl]	zählbar
deformed (adj)	[dɪ'fɔːmd]	deformiert
dented (adj)	['dentɪd]	eingedrückt, verbeult
heavily (adv)	['hevɪli]	stark
mouldy (adj)	['məʊldi]	moderig, muffig, schimmelig
newly (adv)	['njuːli]	neu
partly (adv)	['pɑːtli]	teils, teilweise
perforated (adj)	['pɜːfəreɪtɪd]	durchlöchert, löchrig, perforiert
plank (n)	[plæŋk]	das Brett
repack (v)	[ˌrɪ'pæk]	neu verpacken, umpacken
severely (adv)	[sɪ'vɪəli]	hart, schwer, streng
skid (n)	[skɪd]	das Ladegestell, die Palette
slightly (adv)	['slaɪtli]	etwas, geringfügig, leicht
sortable (adj)	['sɔːtəbl]	sortierbar
visible (adj)	['vɪzɪbl]	erkennbar, sichtbar

Skill Files Business Communication

Applying for an internship

apply (v)	[ə'plaɪ]	sich bewerben
applicant (n)	['æplɪkənt]	der Antragsteller, der Bewerber
challenge (n)	['tʃæləndʒ]	die Herausforderung
cv (curriculum vitae) (abbr)	[si :viː], [kə'rɪkjələm'viːtaɪ]; ['vaɪtiː]	der Lebenslauf
foreign (adj)	['fɒrɪn]	ausländisch, auswärtig, fremd
Latvia (n)	['lætviə]	Lettland
letter of application (n)	['letər ɒf ˌæplɪ'keɪʃən]	das Bewerbungsschreiben
middle (n)	['mɪdl]	Mitte, mittlerer Teil
neither … nor (conj)	['naɪðə … 'nɔː]	weder … noch
partnership (n)	['pɑːtnəʃɪp]	die Partnerschaft
qualification (n)	[ˌkwɒlɪfɪ'keɪʃən]	die Befähigung, die Eignung, die Qualifikation
share (v)	[ʃeə]	freigeben, mitbenutzen, teilen
take part (v)	[ˌteɪk 'pɑːt]	mitmachen, sich beteiligen, teilnehmen

Writing letters

acquisition (n)	[ˌækwɪ'zɪʃən]	die Akquisition, der Erwerb, die Übernahme
address (n)	['ædrəs]	die Adresse
application (n)	[ˌæplɪ'keɪʃən]	die Anwendung, die Bewerbungsunterlagen, die Verwendung
authentic (adj)	[ɔː'θentɪk]	authentisch, echt
body of the letter (n)	['bɒdi ɒf ðə 'letə]	der Hauptteil des Briefes
concerning (prep)	[kən'sɜːnɪŋ]	bezüglich, hinsichtlich, wegen
difficulty (n)	['dɪfɪkəlti]	das Problem, die Schwierigkeit
due (adj)	[djuː]	fällig
fear (n)	[fɪə]	die Angst, die Befürchtung, die Furcht

for the attention of (n)	[fɔː ði ə'tenʃən ɒf]	zu Händen
ideally (adv)	[aɪ'diəli]	ideal, idealerweise
increase (v)	[ɪn'kriːs]	erhöhen, steigern, vergrößern
job advertisement (n)	['dʒɒb əd,vɜːtɪsmənt]	die Stellenanzeige, die Stellenausschreibung
language ability (n)	['læŋgwɪdʒ ə,bɪləti]	die Sprachkenntnis
likes (n)	['laɪks]	die Vorlieben
might (v)	[maɪt]	könnte
mixed up (adj)	[,mɪkst 'ʌp]	durcheinander
operating (adj)	['ɒpəreɪtɪŋ]	agierend, operierend, wirkend
opportunity (n)	[,ɒpə'tjuːnəti]	die Gelegenheit, die Möglichkeit
pay scale (n)	['peɪ ,skeɪl]	die Lohntabelle
payment (n)	['peɪmənt]	die Bezahlung, die Vergütung
phrasing (n)	['freɪzɪŋ]	die Ausdrucksweise, der Stil
route planning (n)	['ruːt ,plænɪŋ]	die Routenplanung, die Tourenplanung
salutation (n)	[,sæljə'teɪʃən]	die Anrede, der Gruß
sincerely (adv)	[sɪ'sɪəli]	aufrichtig, ergebenst
successfully (adv)	[sək'sesfʊli]	erfolgreich
unfinished (adj)	[,ʌn'fɪnɪʃt]	unerledigt, unfertig, unvollendet
welcome (v)	['welkəm]	begrüßen, willkommen heißen

The job interview

appearance (n)	[ə'pɪərəns]	das Auftreten, das Aussehen, das Erscheinungsbild
body language (n)	['bɒdi ,læŋgwɪdʒ]	die Körpersprache
confident (adj)	['kɒnfɪdənt]	selbstbewusst, sicher, zuversichtlich
criticise (v)	['krɪtɪsaɪz]	bemängeln, kritisieren, mäkeln
customer contact (n)	['kʌstəmə 'kɒntækt]	der Kundenkontakt
demonstrate (v)	['demənstreɪt]	demonstrieren, zeigen
dress (v)	[dres]	ankleiden, anziehen
fidget (v)	['fɪdʒɪt]	hampeln, zappeln
honest (adj)	['ɒnɪst]	aufrichtig, ehrlich
improve (v)	[ɪm'pruːv]	steigern, verbessern
in general (adj)	[ɪn 'dʒenərəl]	im Allgemeinen, üblich
interviewee (n)	[,ɪntəvju'iː]	der Befragte, der Interviewte
interviewer (n)	['ɪntəvjuːə]	der Befrager, der Interviewer
job interview (n)	['dʒɒb ,ɪntəvjuː]	das Bewerbungsgespräch, das Vorstellungsgespräch
listener (n)	['lɪsənə]	der Zuhörer
mandatory (adj)	['mændətəri]	obligatorisch, verbindlich, zwingend
nervous (adj)	['nɜːvəs]	aufgeregt, nervös
permanent position (n)	['pɜːmənənt pə'zɪʃən]	die Festanstellung
representative (n)	[,reprɪ'zentətɪv]	der Beauftragte, der Repräsentant, der Vertreter
self-confidence (n)	[,self 'kɒnfɪdəns]	das Selbstbewusstsein, die Selbstsicherheit, das Selbstvertrauen
sheet of paper (n)	[,ʃiːt əf 'peɪpə]	das Blatt Papier, der Papierbogen

slump down (v)	[ˌslʌmp 'daʊn]	in sich zusammensacken
starting salary (n)	['stɑːtɪŋ 'sæləri]	das Anfangsgehalt
statement (n)	['steɪtmənt]	die Äußerung, die Erklärung, die Feststellung, das Statement
tutor (n)	['tjuːtə]	der Betreuer, der Lehrer, der Tutor
unprepared (adj)	[ˌʌnprɪ'peəd]	unvorbereitet

Meet & Greet

administrative department (n)	[əd'mɪnɪstrətɪv dɪ'pɑːtmənt]	die Verwaltung
apricot pie (n)	['eɪprɪkɒt ˌpaɪ]	die Aprikosenpastete
awkward (adj)	['ɔːkwəd]	peinlich, unangenehm, unbehaglich
broccoli pie (n)	['brɒkəli ˌpaɪ]	die Brokkolipastete
caramelized (adj)	['kærəməlaɪzd]	karamellisiert
chips (n)	[tʃɪps]	AE: die Kartoffelchips, BE: die Pommes frites
chopped (adj)	['tʃɒpt]	gehackt, zerkleinert
creamy (adj)	['kriːmi]	sahnig
diced (adj)	['daɪst]	gewürfelt
dipping (adj)	['dɪpɪŋ]	eintauchend, tunkend
facial expression (n)	['feɪʃəl ɪk'spreʃən]	der Gesichtsausdruck, die Mimik
greet (v)	[griːt]	begrüßen
impression (n)	[ɪm'preʃən]	der Eindruck, die Impression, die Wirkung
leg of lamb (n)	[leg ɒf læm]	die Lammkeule
mashed potatoes (n)	[ˌmæʃt pə'teɪtəʊz]	das Kartoffelpüree
menu (n)	['menjuː]	die Speisekarte
mint (n)	[mɪnt]	die Pfefferminze
mushroom pie (n)	['mʌʃrʊm ˌpaɪ]	die Pilzpastete
official (adj)	[ə'fɪʃəl]	förmlich, formell, offiziell
onion and cider soup (n)	['ʌnjən ænd 'saɪdə ˌsuːp]	die Zwiebelsuppe mit Apfelwein
Oyster card (n)	['ɔɪstə ˌkɑːd]	elektronische Fahrkarte in England
participate (v)	[pɑː'tɪsɪpeɪt]	mitmachen, partizipieren, teilnehmen
pepper (n)	['pepə]	die Paprika, der Pfeffer
proper (adj)	['prɒpə]	angemessen, geeignet, ordnungsgemäß
residence (n)	['rezɪdəns]	die Residenz, der Wohnort, der Wohnsitz
rice (n)	[raɪs]	der Reis
roast (v)	[rəʊst]	braten, rösten
role play (n)	['rəʊl ˌpleɪ]	das Rollenspiel
roughly (adv)	['rʌfli]	derb, grob, ungefähr
small talk (n)	['smɔːl ˌtɔːk]	das Geplauder, die oberflächliche Unterhaltung, der Smalltalk
somewhat (adv)	['sʌmwɒt]	ein wenig, etwas
spicy (adj)	['spaɪsi]	pikant, scharf, würzig
toasted (adj)	['təʊstɪd]	geröstet
topic (n)	['tɒpɪk]	der Inhalt, das Thema, die Thematik
top with (v)	['tɒp ˌwɪð]	bedecken

treat (v)	[triːt]	behandeln
unhelpful (adj)	[ˌʌn'helpfʊl]	nicht hilfreich, nicht hilfsbereit
unwelcoming (adj)	[ˌʌn'welkəmɪŋ]	unerwünscht, unlieb, unwillkommen

Commercial correspondence

commercial correspondence (n)	[kə'mɜːʃəl ˌkɒrɪ'spɒndəns]	die Handelskorrespondenz, der kaufmännische Schriftverkehr
apologize (v)	[ə'pɑlədʒaɪz]	Abbitte leisten, sich entschuldigen
appreciate (v)	[ə'priːʃieɪt]	begrüßen, schätzen, würdigen
appropriate (adj)	[ə'prəʊpriət]	angemessen, geeignet, passend
assure (v)	[ə'ʃʊə]	garantieren, gewährleisten, zusichern
available (adj)	[ə'veɪləbl]	erhältlich, lieferbar, verfügbar
business letter (n)	['bɪznəs ˌletə]	der Geschäftsbrief
complimentary close (n)	[ˌkɒmplɪ'mentəri ˌkləʊz]	die Grußformel, die Schlussformel
concession (n)	[kən'seʃən]	die Erlaubnis, die Konzession, das Zugeständnis
consider (v)	[kən'sɪdə]	ansehen, betrachten, berücksichtigen
consignment (n)	[kən'saɪnmənt]	die Konsignation, die Lieferung, die Sendung
consignor (n)	[kən'saɪnə]	der Konsignant, der Verfrachter, der Versender
consultation (n)	[ˌkɒnsəl'teɪʃən]	die Beratung, die Konsultation, die Rücksprache
deadline (n)	['dedlaɪn]	die Deadline, die Frist, der Termin
delighted (adj)	[dɪ'laɪtɪd]	begeistert, beglückt, erfreut
distribution (n)	[ˌdɪstrɪ'bjuːʃən]	die Ausgabe, die Distribution, die Verteilung
distribution system (n)	[ˌdɪstrɪ'bjuːʃən ˌsɪstəm]	das Distributionssystem, das Verteilsystem
enable (v)	[ɪn'eɪbl]	befähigen, ermöglichen
enclosing (adj)	[ɪn'kləʊzɪŋ]	anfügend, beiliegend, enthaltend
established (adj)	[ɪ'stæblɪʃt]	eingeführt, etabliert, feststehend
fax transmission (n)	['fæks trænsˌmɪʃən]	die Faxtransmission, die Faxübermittlung, die Faxübertragung
future (adj)	['fjuːtʃə]	angehend, kommend, zukünftig
grant (v)	[grɑːnt]	bewilligen, erteilen, gewähren
hesitate (v)	['hezɪteɪt]	unsicher sein, zögern
in particular (adj)	[ɪn pə'tɪkjələ]	ausdrücklich, im Besonderen, speziell
inform (v)	[ɪn'fɔːm]	informieren, in Kenntnis setzen, unterrichten
inquiry (n)	[ɪn'kwaɪəri]	die Anfrage, die Nachfrage

insist on (v)	[ɪn'sɪst ɒn]	beharren auf, insistieren auf, pochen auf
malfunctioning (adj)	[ˌmæl'fʌŋkʃənɪŋ]	gestört, nicht richtig arbeitend, schlecht funktionierend
mend (v)	[mend]	ausbessern, instand setzen, reparieren
on behalf of (adj)	[ɒn bɪ'hɑːf ˌɒf]	im Auftrag von, im Namen von
particular (adj)	[pə'tɪkjələ]	besonders, bestimmt
provide (v)	[prə'vaɪd]	bereitstellen, bieten, zur Verfügung stellen
purpose (n)	['pɜːpəs]	der Absicht, die Bestimmung, der Zweck
refer to (v)	[rɪ'fɜː tu]	beziehen, hinweisen, verweisen
reference (n)	['refərəns]	der Bezug, der Hinweis, die Referenz
regarding (prep)	[rɪ'gɑːdɪŋ]	betreffend, bezüglich
request (n)	[rɪ'kwest]	die Anfrage, das Ersuchen, das Gesuch
structure (n)	['strʌktʃə]	der Aufbau, die Gliederung, die Struktur
subject line (n)	['sʌbdʒɪkt ˌlaɪn]	die Betreffzeile
threaten (v)	['θretən]	androhen, drohen
topic of the email (n)	['tɒpɪk ɒf ðə 'iˌmeɪl]	das Thema der E-Mail
urgently (adj)	['ɜːdʒəntli]	dringend, nötig
utmost (adj)	['ʌtməʊst]	äußerst, höchst
via (prep)	['vaɪə]	durch, per, über

Telephone Training

enquiry (n)	[ɪn'kwaɪəri]	die Abfrage, die Anfrage, die Erkundigung
aviation alphabet (n)	[ˌeɪvi'eɪʃən 'ælfəbət]	das Luftfahrt-Alphabet
deal (v)	[diːl]	austeilen, handeln, tätigen
manufacturer (n)	[ˌmænjə'fæktʃərə]	der Erzeuger, der Hersteller, der Produzent
put through (v)	[ˌpʊt 'θruː]	durchstellen, verbinden
serial number (n)	['sɪəriəl 'nʌmbə]	die Seriennummer
similar (adj)	['sɪmɪlə]	ähnlich, gleich

Skill Files Grammar

on board (prep)	[ˌɒn 'bɔːd]	an Bord
harbour (n)	['hɑːbə]	der Hafen

Vokabelverzeichnis

a

a.m. (ante meridiem) (abbr)	vor dem Mittag
abroad (adv)	ins Ausland
accept (v)	akzeptieren, annehmen
accident (n)	der Unfall
accident report (n)	der Unfallbericht
according to (prep)	entsprechend, gemäß
accountant (n)	der Buchhalter
accounting (adj)	buchhaltungstechnisch
accounting purpose (n)	der Buchhaltungszweck
accounts department (n)	die Buchhaltung
accuracy (n)	die Akkuratesse, die Genauigkeit, die Fehlerfreiheit
accurate (adj)	akkurat, genau, sorgfältig
achieve (v)	erlangen, erreichen, erzielen
acquisition (n)	die Akquisition, der Erwerb, die Übernahme
add (v)	addieren
address (n)	die Adresse
adhesive tape (n)	das Klebeband
adjust (v)	adjustieren, anpassen, einstellen
administrative department (n)	die Verwaltung
advantage (n)	der Vorteil
advice (n)	die Empfehlung, der Hinweis, der Ratschlag
adviser (n)	der Advisor, der Beauftragte, der Berater
air (n)	die Luft
air waybill (n)	der Luftfrachtbrief
aircraft (n)	das Flugzeug
airhall store (n)	Traglufthallenlager
aisle (n)	der Gang
allocation of items (n)	die Bereitstellung der Ware
amount (n)	die Anzahl, die Menge
answer (v)	beantworten
anti-slip mat (n)	die Antirutschmatte
apologize (v)	Abbitte leisten, sich entschuldigen
apparently (adv)	anscheinend, offensichtlich
appearance (n)	das Auftreten, das Aussehen, das Erscheinungsbild
applicant (n)	der Antragsteller, der Bewerber
application (n)	die Anwendung, die Bewerbungsunterlagen, die Verwendung
apply (v)	sich bewerben
appreciate (v)	begrüßen, schätzen, würdigen
apprentice (n)	der Auszubildende
apprenticeship (n)	die Ausbildung
appropriate (adj)	angemessen, geeignet, passend
apricot pie (n)	die Aprikosenpastete
arrival (n)	die Ankunft
arrive (v)	ankommen
article (n)	der Artikel
article number (n)	die Artikelnummer
aspect (n)	der Aspekt
assistance (n)	die Unterstützung, die Hilfe
assure (v)	garantieren, gewährleisten, zusichern
attach (v)	anbringen, befestigen, beifügen
attachment (n)	das Anbaugerät, das Anbauteil, der Anhang
augmented (adj)	erweitert, vergrößert, vermehrt
authentic (adj)	authentisch, echt
authorized (adj)	autorisiert, befugt, bevollmächtigt
available (adj)	erhältlich, lieferbar, verfügbar
aviation alphabet (n)	das Luftfahrt-Alphabet
avoid (v)	verhindern, vermeiden
awkward (adj)	peinlich, unangenehm, unbehaglich

b

background (n)	der Hintergrund
balance sheet (n)	der Abschluss, die Bilanzaufstellung, der Jahresabschluss
bale (n)	der Ballen
barrel (n)	das Fass
barrier (n)	die Barriere, die Schutzabdeckung, die Sperrschicht
based (adj)	basierend, begründet, beruhend

bashed (adj) ramponiert
batch (n) das Batch, das Bündel, die Charge
bay (n) das Arbeitsfeld, die Bucht, das Feld
be patient (v) sich gedulden
belt conveyor (n) der Gurtförderer, das Laufband
big bag (n) der Big Bag
bill of lading (n) das Konnossement, der Seefrachtbrief
bleeding (n) das Bluten, die Blutung
block (v) abblocken, absperren, blockieren
body language (n) die Körpersprache
body of the letter (n) der Hauptteil des Briefes
border (n) der Rahmen, der Rand
box (n) die Schachtel
braking system (n) das Bremssystem
broccoli pie (n) die Brokkolipastete
broken (adj) beschädigt, gebrochen, kaputt
bubble envelope (n) die Luftpolstertasche
bubble wrap (n) die Luftpolsterfolie
bucket elevator (n) das Becherwerk, der Kübelaufzug
building (n) das Bauwerk, das Gebäude, das Haus
bulk container (n) der Schüttgutcontainer
bunch (n) das Bündel, das Gebinde, der Strauß
bundle (n) das Bündel das Bündel
bunker/silo/tank store (n) Bunker-/Silo-/Tanklager
burst (adj) aufgeplatzt, gebrochen
business letter (n) der Geschäftsbrief
button (n) der Knopf
by heart (adj) auswendig

C

calculate (v) berechnen, ermitteln, errechnen
call (v) anrufen, nennen
call the emergency (v) den Notruf anrufen
can (n) die Dose, der Kanister, die Kanne
capacity (n) die Aufnahmefähigkeit, das Fassungsvermögen, die Kapazität
caramelized (adj) karamellisiert
carboy (n) die Korbflasche die Korbflasche
cardboard carton (n) der Pappkarton, die Schachtel
cardiac pacemaker (n) der Herzschrittmacher
carelessness (n) die Nachlässigkeit, die Unachtsamkeit
cargo (n) die Fracht, die Ladung
cargo tours (n) die Frachtrouten
carousel rack (n) das Umlaufregal
carriage (n) der Transport
carrier (n) der Frachtführer
cart (n) Einkaufswagen, Karre, Wagen
case (n) der Behälter, der Fall, die Kiste
cask (n) das Fass, die Tonne
cause (v) bewirken, hervorrufen, verursachen
central (adj) zentral
centre of gravity (n) der Schwerpunkt
centrifugal force (n) die Fliehkraft, die Zentrifugalkraft
certificate of origin (n) die Herkunftsbescheinigung, das Ursprungszeugnis
certify (v) bescheinigen, bestätigen, zertifizieren
challenge (n) die Herausforderung
cheap (adj) billig, kostengünstig, preiswert
check (v) kontrollieren, -überprüfen
check digit (n) die Kontrollziffer, die Prüfziffer
chest (n) die Kiste, die Truhe
chief storekeeper (n) der Lagermeister
chips (n) AE: die Kartoffelchips, BE: die Pommes frites
chopped (adj) gehackt, zerkleinert
CIF (cost, insurance and freight) (abbr) Kosten, Versicherung und Fracht
circle (n) der Kreis
circumference (n) die Ausdehnung, der Umfang
circumstance (n) der Umstand, die Sachlage
clamp (v) einklemmen, einspannen, klammern
classify (v) einordnen, klassifizieren, unterteilen
colleague (n) der Arbeitskollege

collect (v)	abholen, einsammeln, zusammentragen
comb rack (n)	das Kassettenregal, das Wabenregal
combination (n)	die Kombination, die Mischung
combined (adj)	kombiniert, zusammengesetzt
combustion (n)	die Entzündung, die Verbrennung
commercial correspondence (n)	die Handelskorrespondenz, der kaufmännische Schriftverkehr
commercial invoice (n)	die Handelsrechnung, die Warenrechnung
commission (v)	kommissionieren, zusammenstellen
commission (v)	kommissionieren, zusammenstellen
commission agent (n)	der Kommissionär
commission warehouse (n)	das Kommissionslager
common (adj)	gängig, gemeinsam
company (n)	die Firma
compare (v)	vergleichen
comparison (n)	der Vergleich
compartment (n)	die Abteilung, das Fach, das Kompartiment
complaint (n)	die Beschwerde
complimentary close (n)	die Grußformel, die Schlussformel
compressed (adj)	eingedrückt, gestaucht
concentration (n)	die Aufmerksamkeit, die Konzentration
concerning (adj)	betreffend
concerning (prep)	bezüglich, hinsichtlich, wegen
concession (n)	die Erlaubnis, die Konzession, das Zugeständnis
conclusion (n)	das Ergebnis, das Fazit, die Schlussfolgerung
concrete stone (n)	der Betonstein
condensation (n)	das Schwitzwasser
condition (n)	die Beschaffenheit
conference (n)	die Konferenz, die Sitzung
confident (adj)	selbstbewusst, sicher, zuversichtlich
configuration (n)	die Anordnung, die Einstellung, die Konfiguration
confirm (v)	bestätigen, quittieren, zusagen
connect (v)	verbinden
consider (v)	ansehen, betrachten, berücksichtigen
consideration (n)	die Abwägung, die Berücksichtigung, die Erwägung
consignee (n)	der Empfänger
consignment (n)	die Konsignation, die Lieferung, die Sendung
consignment warehouse (n)	das Konsignationslager
consignor (n)	der Konsignant, der Verfrachter, der Versender
consultation (n)	die Beratung, die Konsultation, die Rücksprache
contain (v)	beinhalten, enthalten
container (n)	der Container
container vessel (n)	das Containerschiff, das Versandschiff
contents (n)	der Inhalt
continuous acting handling and hoisting equipment (n)	der Stetigförderer
continuous rack (n)	das Durchlaufregal
contract worker (n)	der Leiharbeiter, der Zeitarbeiter
conveyor (n)	die Förderanlage, das Förderband
cooperate (v)	kooperieren, zusammenarbeiten
correspond to (v)	entsprechen
correspondence (n)	Korrespondenz, Schriftverkehr
corresponding (adj)	dazugehörend, entsprechend, zugehörig
corrosion (n)	die Korrosion, die Verätzung
corrugated cardboard	die Wellpappe
cost (n)	die Kosten, der Preis
cotton (adj)	baumwoll
cotton (n)	die Baumwolle
count back (n)	das Korrekturzählen
countable (adj)	zählbar
counting scale (n)	die Zählwaage
country (n)	das Land, der Staat
course of events (n)	der Gang der Ereignisse, der Hergang
cover (v)	abdecken, bedecken

crafts enterprise (n) der Handwerksbetrieb
crane (n) der Kran
crank (n) die Kurbel
crate (n) der Holzverschlag, die Lattenkiste
creamy (adj) sahnig
criticise (v) bemängeln, kritisieren, mäkeln
crossbar (n) der Querbalken
cu.cap. (cubic capacity) (abbr) der Nutzinhalt, der Rauminhalt
customer (n) der Kunde
customer contact (n) der Kundenkontakt
customer service department (n) der Kundendienst, die Kundendienstabteilung
cv (curriculum vitae) (abbr) der Lebenslauf

d

daily routine (n) der Tagesablauf
damage (n) der Schaden
dangerous goods (n) das Gefahrgut, der Gefahrstoff
dangerous goods safety advisor (n) Gefahrgutbeauftragter
dangerous goods and safety mark der Gefahrenzettel
data (n) die Angaben, die Daten, die Informationen
date of delivery (n) das Lieferdatum
DDP (delivered duty paid) (abbr) geliefert verzollt
dead space (n) der ungenutzte Raum
deadline (n) die Deadline, die Frist, der Termin
deal (v) austeilen, handeln, tätigen
decentralized (adj) dezentral
declare (v) angeben, anmelden, deklarieren
deformed (adj) deformiert
delighted (adj) begeistert, beglückt, erfreut
deliver (v) liefern
delivery (n) die Lieferung
delivery note (n) der Lieferschein
demand (v) erfordern
demonstrate (v) demonstrieren, zeigen
dented (adj) eingedrückt, verbeult
department (n) die Abteilung
depend on (v) abhängig sein, angewiesen sein
describe (v) beschreiben, darstellen, wiedergeben
description of the consignment (n) die Beschreibung der Sendung
desensitize (v) desensibilisieren, unempfindlich machen
desperate to do something (adj) etwas unbedingt tun wollen
destination (n) der Bestimmungsort
diced (adj) gewürfelt
differ (v) differieren, unterscheiden
difference (n) der Unterschied
difficulty (n) das Problem, die Schwierigkeit
dipping (adj) eintauchend, tunkend
directed (adj) adressiert, geleitet, gelenkt
disadvantage (n) der Nachteil
discover (v) erkennen, feststellen, herausfinden
dispatch warehouse (n) das Absatzlager
distance (n) die Distanz, die Entfernung, die Strecke
distributing warehouse (n) das Versandlager, das Auslieferungslager
distribution (n) die Ausgabe, die Distribution, die Verteilung
distribution system (n) das Distributionssystem, das Verteilsystem
divide (v) aufgliedern, dividieren, unterteilen
document (n) das Dokument
document of title (n) das Dispositionsdokument, die Legimitationsurkunde
dress (v) ankleiden, anziehen
drive-in pallet rack (n) das Einfahrregal
driver's license (n) der Führerschein
drum (n) die Trommel
due (adj) fällig
due to (sth.) (prep) wegen, aufgrund
duration (n) die Dauer
duty (n) die Aufgabe, die Pflicht
dynamic (adj) bewegend, dynamisch

e

e.g. (exempli gratia) (abbr) zum Beispiel, beispielsweise
eager (adj) eifrig sein, erpicht sein, etwas unbedingt wollen
edge protector (n) der Kantenschoner, der Kantenschutz

EDP (Electronic Data processing) (abbr)	die elektronische Datenverarbeitung (EDV)
efficiency (n)	die Effizienz, die Leistung, die Wirtschaftlichkeit
efficient (adj)	effizient, leistungsfähig, wirtschaftlich
electrostatic (adj)	elektrostatisch
elevator (n)	der Aufzug, der Fahrstuhl
emergency call (n)	der Notruf
emergency sign (n)	das Rettungszeichen
emit (v)	absondern, ausstoßen, emittieren
enable (v)	befähigen, ermöglichen
enclosing (adj)	anfügend, beiliegend, enthaltend
enhanced (adj)	erweitert, vergrößert, verstärkt
enquiry (n)	die Abfrage, die Anfrage, die Erkundigung
ensure (v)	garantieren, gewährleisten, sicherstellen
enter (v)	eingeben, hereinkommen
environment (n)	die Umwelt
environmental (adj)	hinsichtlich der Umwelt
environmentally friendly (adj)	umweltfreundlich
environmentally unfriendly (adj)	umweltschädlich
equipment (n)	die Ausrüstung
equivalent (adj)	äquivalent, gleichviel, gleichwertig
error analysis (n)	die Fehleranalyse
essential (adj)	erforderlich, essenziell, wichtig
established (adj)	eingeführt, etabliert, feststehend
euro-pallet (n)	die Euro-Palette
exclamation mark (n)	das Ausrufungszeichen
expect (v)	annehmen, erwarten, voraussetzen
expensive (adj)	teuer
experience (n)	die Erfahrung
expiry date (n)	das Ablaufdatum, das Fälligkeitsdatum, das Verfallsdatum
explosive (n)	der Explosivstoff, der Sprengstoff
external (adj)	äußerlich, außen
extract (v)	entnehmen, extrahieren
extraction (n)	die Entnahme, die Extraktion, die Gewinnung
EXW (ex works) (abbr)	ab Werk
eye shower (n)	die Augendusche

f

face side (n)	die Stirnseite
facial expression (n)	der Gesichtsausdruck, die Mimik
FAS (free alongside ship) (abbr)	frei Längsseite Schiff
fast armature (n)	der Schnellläufer
fax transmission (n)	die Faxtransmission, die Faxübermittlung, die Faxübertragung
fear (n)	die Angst, die Befürchtung, die Furcht
feature (n)	der Bestandteil, die Eigenschaft, das Merkmal
fetch something/ someone (v)	etwas/jemanden abholen
fidget (v)	hampeln, zappeln
field of activity (n)	das Arbeitsgebiet, der Tätigkeitsbereich
FiFo (first in, first out) (abbr)	„zuerst rein, zuerst raus"
financial accounting (n)	die Finanzbuchhaltung
fine (n)	das Bußgeld, die Geldstrafe
finished goods warehouse (n)	das Fertigwaren-/ Erzeugnislager
fire alarm (n)	der Feueralarm, der Feuermelder
fire brigade (n)	die Feuerwehr
fire extinguisher (n)	der Feuerlöscher
fire fighting equipment (n)	die Brandschutzausrüstung, das Feuerlöschgerät
fire hose (n)	der Feuerlöschschlauch
fire safety sign (n)	das Brandschutzzeichen
firework (n)	der Feuerwerksartikel, der Feuerwerkskörper
first-aid (n)	Erste Hilfe
first-aid kit (n)	der Erste-Hilfe-Kasten
flame (n)	die Flamme
flammable (adj)	brennbar, entflammbar, feuergefährlich
flat store (n)	das Flachlager
flatrack (flat) (n)	das Flat
fleet (n)	die Flotte
floating (adj)	schwebend, schwimmend
floor storage (n)	die Bodenlagerung
floor store (n)	das Etagenlager

flow of goods (n)	der Warenfluss
foam (n)	der Schaum
foam peanut (n)	der Verpackungschip
FOB (free on board) (abbr)	frei an Bord
folding ruler (n)	der Gliedermaßstab, der Zollstock
foot (n)	der Fuß (Längenmaß: 1′ (Fuß) = 30,48 cm)
for the attention of (n)	zu Händen
forbid (v)	untersagen, verbieten, verhindern
force (n)	die Kraft
foreign (adj)	ausländisch, auswärtig, fremd
foreign language terminology (n)	die fremdsprachlichen Fachausdrücke
forklift truck (n)	der Gabelstapler
formulate (v)	abfassen, formulieren
fortnight (n)	14 Tage
forwarding agency (n)	die Spedition
forwarding company (n)	die Spedition
forwarding document (n)	das Frachtpapier
fragile (adj)	fragil, zerbrechlich
freight charges (n)	die Frachtkosten
French National Assembly (n)	die Französische Nationalversammlung
frost (n)	der Sammelpunkt, die Sammelstelle
further (adj)	anderweitig, zusätzlich
future (adj)	angehend, kommend, zukünftig
g	
gang (n)	die Gang, die Gruppe
gantry crane (n)	der Brückenkran, die Containerbrücke, der Portalkran
gas cylinder (n)	die Gasflasche
gathering point (n)	der Frost
generate (v)	entwickeln, erstellen, generieren
gesture (v)	eine Handbewegung machen, gestikulieren
GHS (Globally Harmonised System of Classification and Labelling of Chemicals) (abbr)	Global Harmonisiertes System zur Einstufung und Kennzeichnung von Chemikalien
glasses (n)	die Brille
goggles	die Schutzbrille
goods (n)	die Güter, die Ware
goods receiving warehouse (n)	das Wareneingangslager
goods to man (n)	Ware zum Mann
grain (n)	das Getreide
grant (v)	bewilligen, erteilen, gewähren
gravity (n)	die Erdanziehungskraft, die Gravitationskraft, die Schwerkraft
greet (v)	begrüßen
gross (adj)	brutto
gross weight (n)	das Bruttogewicht
ground conveyor (n)	das Flurförderzeug
group (v)	einteilen, gruppieren, unterteilen
guarantee (v)	garantieren, gewährleisten, sicherstellen
guide (v)	führen, leiten, lotsen
h	
hand forklift truck (n)	der Handhubwagen
handle (v)	abfertigen, bearbeiten, handhaben
handling (adj)	handhabend
handling and hoisting equipment (n)	das Fördermittel
handling sign (n)	das Handhabungszeichen
handy (adj)	dienlich, nützlich, praktisch
harbour (n)	der Hafen
hard hat (n)	der Schutzhelm, der Sicherheitshelm
harm (v)	schädigen, verletzen
hay (n)	das Heu
hazard (n)	die Gefahr
hazardous (adj)	gefährlich
hazardous (adj)	gefährlich
hazardous materials label (n)	das Gefahrgutkennzeichen, das Gefahrgutlabel
headset (n)	der Kopfhörer, das Headset, die Sprechgarnitur
health (n)	die Gesundheit
health insurance (n)	die Krankenversicherung
heart defibrillator (n)	der Defibrillator
heavily (adv)	stark
height (n)	die Höhe
hesitate (v)	unsicher sein, zögern

hessian sack (n)	der Jutesack
HiFo (highest in, first out) (abbr)	„teuerste Ware zuerst raus“
high (adj)	hoch
high voltage (n)	die Hochspannung
high-rise rack (n)	das Hochregal
highrise rack store (n)	das Hochregallager
hoisting (adj)	hebend, hochziehend
hoisting device (n)	die Fördereinrichtung, die Hebevorrichtung
hoisting platform (n)	die Hebebühne, die Hubplattform
holder (n)	der Halter, der Inhaber
honest (adj)	aufrichtig, ehrlich
hook (n)	der Haken
horizontal (adj)	horizontal, waagerecht
human (adj)	human, menschlich

i

i.e. (id est) (abbr)	das heißt
ideally (adv)	ideal, idealerweise
identify (v)	ausweisen, erkennen, identifizieren
identity (n)	die Identität
ignore (v)	ignorieren, übergehen, vernachlässigen
illuminated (adj)	beleuchtet, illuminiert
immediate (adj)	direkt, sofortig, unverzüglich
impression (n)	der Eindruck, die Impression, die Wirkung
imprisonment (n)	die Freiheitsstrafe, die Inhaftierung
improve (v)	steigern, verbessern
in general (adj)	im Allgemeinen, üblich
in particular (adj)	ausdrücklich, im Besonderen, speziell
inch (n)	der Zoll (Längeneinheit: 1 Zoll = 2,54 cm)
incoming (adj)	eingehend, hereinkommend
incoming goods department (n)	der Wareneingang
Incoterms (n)	die internationalen Handelsbedingungen der ICC, die Lieferbedingungen
increase (v)	erhöhen, steigern, vergrößern
indicate (v)	angeben, hinweisen, zeigen
industrial company (n)	der Industriebetrieb
industrial estate (n)	das Industriegebiet
industrial truck (n)	das Flurförderzeug
infectious (adj)	ansteckend, infektiös
influence (n)	der Einfluss, die Einwirkung
inform (v)	informieren, in Kenntnis setzen, unterrichten
informal (adj)	formlos, informell, ungezwungen
initial medical examination (n)	die Erstuntersuchung
initiative (n)	der Anstoß, die Initiative
injure (v)	beschädigen, verletzen
input (n)	die Eingabe, der Eingang
inquiry (n)	die Anfrage, die Nachfrage
insert (v)	einführen, einlegen, einschieben
insist on (v)	beharren auf, insistieren auf, pochen auf
inspect (v)	inspizieren, prüfen, untersuchen
instruction (n)	die Anweisung, die Instruktion
insufficient (adj)	insuffizient, nicht ausreichend, ungenügend
insulated (adj)	gedämmt, isoliert
insulated container (n)	der Isoliercontainer
insurance (n)	die Versicherung
insurance certificate (n)	die Versicherungsbescheinigung
intermediaries (n)	der Zwischenhändler, der Vermittler
intermediate warehouse (n)	das Zwischenlager
intern (n)	der Praktikant
internal (adj)	innen, intern
international trade (n)	der internationale Handel, der Welthandel
internship (n)	das Praktikum
interviewee (n)	der Befragte, der Interviewte
interviewer (n)	der Befrager, der Interviewer
introduce (v)	einführen, präsentieren, vorstellen
inventory	der Bestand, das Inventar, der Vorrat
inventory department (n)	die Bestandsabteilung

investment costs (n)	die Investitionskosten
invoice (n)	die Rechnung
involve (v)	beteiligen, involvieren
item (n)	der Artikel, der Gegenstand

j

job advertisement (n)	die Stellenanzeige, die Stellenausschreibung
job interview (n)	das Bewerbungsgespräch, das Vorstellungsgespräch
job title (n)	die Berufsbezeichnung

k

keep away from (v)	fernhalten
keyword (n)	das Stichwort

l

label (n)	die Beschriftung, das Etikett
label (v)	etikettieren, kennzeichnen, markieren
lacking (adj)	fehlend, mangelnd
language (n)	die Sprache
language ability (n)	die Sprachkenntnis
lashing material (n)	das Laschmaterial
lashing point (n)	der Laschpunkt
lashing strap (n)	der Zurrgurt
latest (adj)	aktuell, modernste, neueste
lattice box (n)	die Gitterbox
Latvia (n)	Lettland
lawful (adj)	gesetzlich
leak (v)	auslaufen
learn by heart (v)	etwas auswendig lernen
leave (v)	fortfahren, verlassen
leg of lamb (n)	die Lammkeule
length (n)	die Länge
letter of application (n)	das Bewerbungsschreiben
liable to (adj)	anfällig, neigend, verantwortlich
LiFo (last in, first out) (abbr)	„zuletzt rein, zuerst raus“
lift (v)	anheben
likely (adj)	wahrscheinlich
likes (n)	die Vorlieben
limitation (n)	die Beschränkung, die Einschränkung, die Grenze
liquid (n)	die Flüssigkeit
listener (n)	der Zuhörer
load (v)	beladen
load balancing (n)	die Lastverteilung
loading costs (n)	die Verladekosten
loadmaster (n)	der Lademeister
located (adj)	angesiedelt, ansässig, lokalisiert
LoFo (lowest in, first out) (abbr)	„günstigste Ware zuerst raus“
loose (adj)	locker, lose
lorry (n)	der LKW
lower of cost or market (v)	das Niederstwertprinzip

m

m.g.w. (maximum gross weight) (abbr)	das maximale Bruttogewicht
machinery (n)	die maschinelle Einrichtung, die Maschinen
mainly (adv)	hauptsächlich, überwiegend, vorwiegend
malfunctioning (adj)	gestört, nicht richtig arbeitend, schlecht funktionierend
man to goods (n)	Mann zur Ware
manage (v)	erledigen, verwalten
man-carrying platform (n)	die Arbeitsbühnen, der Personenbeförderungskorb
mandatory (adj)	obligatorisch, verbindlich, zwingend
mandatory sign (n)	das Gebotszeichen
manual warehouse (n)	das Handlager
manufacturer (n)	der Erzeuger, der Hersteller, der Produzent
mashed potatoes (n)	das Kartoffelpüree
material warehouse (n)	das Materiallager
matter (n)	die Angelegenheit, die Materie, die Sache
meaning (n)	die Bedeutung
means of transport (n)	das Beförderungsmittel, das Transportmittel
measure (n)	das Maß, die Maßeinheit
measure (v)	messen
measurement (n)	die Abmessung, die Größe, das Maß
meeting room (n)	das Besprechungszimmer, der Konferenzraum
mend (v)	ausbessern, instand setzen, reparieren

mention (v) erwähnen, vermerken
menu (n) die Speisekarte
metal strapped (adj) stahlummantelt
middle (n) Mitte, mittlerer Teil
might (v) könnte
minimize (v) herabmindern, minimieren, verkleinern
mint (n) die Pfefferminze
miscellaneous (adj) divers, verschieden
miserable (adj) elendig, jämmerlich
mistake (n) der Fehler
mixed up (adj) durcheinander
mobile data terminal (n) die mobile Datenstation, das mobile -Datenterminal
mobile phone (n) das Funktelefon, das Mobiltelefon
mobile rack (n) das Verschieberegal
mode of transport (n) die Beförderungsart, der Verkehrsträger
modification (n) die Modifikation, die Umrüstung, die Veränderung
modular rack (n) das Fachbodenregal
mould (n) die Form, die Gießform, die Gussform
mouldy (adj) moderig, muffig, schimmelig
multi-storey (adj) mehrgeschossig
mushroom pie (n) die Pilzpastete

n

nail gun (n) der Druckluftnagler
namely (adv) nämlich, und zwar
necessary (adj) erforderlich, notwendig
negotiable (adj) übertragbar, verhandelbar, verkäuflich
neither … nor (conj) weder … noch
nervous (adj) aufgeregt, nervös
net (adj) nach Abzug von etwas, netto
nevertheless (adv) dennoch, trotzdem
newly (adv) neu
non-occupied (adj) frei, nicht besetzt
non-palletised (adj) nicht palettiert
non-stackable (adj) nicht stapelbar
normally (adv) normalerweise, üblicherweise

o

obey (v) ausführen, befolgen, gehorchen
observance (n) das Beachten, die Berücksichtigung, die Observanz
occupational skills (n) die beruflichen Fähigkeiten
occur (v) auftreten, geschehen, passieren
of age (adj) mündig sein, volljährig sein
offer (n) das Angebot
office (n) das Büro
official (adj) förmlich, formell, offiziell
on behalf of (adj) im Auftrag von, im Namen von
on board (prep) an Bord
onion and cider soup (n) die Zwiebelsuppe mit Apfelwein
open-air storage (n) das offene Lager
operate (v) arbeiten, bedienen, führen
operating (adj) agierend, operierend, wirkend
operator (n) der Bediener, der Betreiber, der Telefonist
opportunity (n) die Gelegenheit, die Möglichkeit
opposite (n) der Gegensatz, das Gegenteil
order (n) die Bestellung
order (v) bestellen
order picker (n) der Kommissionierer
order picking (n) die Kommissionierung
order picking warehouse (n) das Kommissionierlager
organic (adj) biologisch, organisch
organise (v) organisieren
otherwise (adv) andernfalls, ansonsten
outgoing goods department (n) der Warenausgang
output (n) die Ausgabe, der Ausgang
overcome (v) überwinden
over-delivery (n) die Mehrlieferung
overhead crane (n) der Brückenkran, der Deckenlaufkran, der Laufkran
own warehouse das Eigenlager

owner (n) der Besitzer, der Eigentümer
oxidizing (adj) oxidierend, rostend
Oyster card (n) elektronische Fahrkarte in England

p

p.m. (post meridiem) (abbr) nach dem Mittag
pack (v) packen
package (n) das Packstück, das Paket
package content (n) das Packgut
packaging (n) die Verkaufsverpackung
packaging aid (n) das Packhilfsmittel
packaging material (n) der Packstoff
packaging means (n) das Packmittel
packing (n) die Versandpackung
packing list (n) die Packliste
packing slip (n) der Packzettel
pallet (n) die Palette
pallet licence (n) die Palettennummer
pallet rack (n) das Palettenregal
palletised (adj) palettiert
paperless (adj) beleglos, papierlos
paperwork (n) die Büroarbeit, die Dokumentation, der Papierkram
parcel (n) das Packstück, das Paket
part (n) das Teil
participate (v) mitmachen, partizipieren, teilnehmen
particular (adj) besonders, bestimmt
partly (adv) teils, teilweise
partnership (n) die Partnerschaft
part-time (adj) teilzeitlich
pass (v) absolvieren, bestehen
pay scale (n) die Lohntabelle
payload (n) das Ladegewicht, die Nutzlast
payment (n) die Bezahlung, die Vergütung
pedestrian (n) der Fußgänger
pepper (n) die Paprika, der Pfeffer
perforated (adj) durchlöchert, löchrig, perforiert
perform (v) ausführen, durchführen
permanent position (n) die Festanstellung
peroxide (n) das Peroxid, das Superoxid
personnel department (n) die Personalabteilung
petrol (n) das Benzin
phrasing (n) die Ausdrucksweise, der Stil
physical (adj) physikalisch
pick out (v) herausgreifen, heraussuchen
pick to box (n) die auftragsorientierte serielle Kommissionierung mit Übergabestellen
pick to light (n) die Kommissionierung per LED-Anzeigen
pick up (v) abheben, aufnehmen, abholen
picker to part method (n) auftragsorientierte serielle Kommissionierung
picking department (n) die Kommissionier-abteilung
picking list (n) die Pickliste
picking storage (n) das Kommissionierlager
picking using bar code (n) die Strichcode-kommissionierung
picking using RFID (n) die Kommissionierung mit RFID
piece picking (n) auftragsorientierte serielle Kommissionierung
pipe (n) das Rohr
place (v) legen, setzen, stellen, unterbringen
place of delivery (n) der Lieferort
plan (v) planen
plank (n) das Brett
plastic (n) der Kunststoff, das Plastik
plastic bag (n) der Plastikbeutel
platform (n) die Plattform
playground (n) der Spielplatz
polystyrene mould (n) die Styroporform
porcelain figure (n) die Porzellanfigur
possible (adj) möglich
pour out (v) ausgießen, ausschütten
practical (adj) praktisch
practise (v) trainieren, üben
premises (n) das Grundstück, das Firmengelände
price (n) der Preis
primarily (adv) hauptsächlich, vor allem
procedure (n) die Handlungsweise, die Prozedur, der Vorgang

proceed (v)	ablaufen, stattfinden, vorgehen
process (v)	aufbereiten, bearbeiten, prozessieren
product testing (n)	Warenprüfung
production company	die Produktionsfirma
production warehouse	das Produktionslager
productivity (n)	die Ergiebigkeit, die Leistungsfähigkeit, die Produktivität
profession (n)	der Beruf
prohibition sign (n)	das Verbotszeichen
proper (adj)	angemessen, geeignet, ordnungsgemäß
properly (adv)	genau, passend, richtig
protect (v)	schützen, sichern
protection (n)	der Schutz
proud (adj)	stolz
provide (v)	bereitstellen, bieten, zur Verfügung stellen
punctual (adj)	pünktlich, rechtzeitig
purpose (n)	der Absicht, die Bestimmung, der Zweck
push-back pallet rack (n)	das Einschubregal
put through (v)	durchstellen, verbinden

q

qualification (n)	die Befähigung, die Eignung, die Qualifikation
quality (n)	die Qualität
quality control department (n)	die Qualitätskontrolle
quantity (n)	die Quantität

r

rack access equipment (n)	das Regalbediengerät, das Regalförderzeug
rack installation construction (n)	die Einbauweise
rack storage (n)	die Regallagerung
racking system (n)	die Regalart
rail (n)	die Eisenbahnschiene
rail waybill (n)	Frachtbrief der Bahn
railbound (adj)	schienengebunden
ramp (n)	die Rampe
random sampling (n)	die Stichprobe
rapid access (n)	der Schnellzugriff
reach stacker (n)	der Greifstapler
read (v)	lesen
real time (n)	die Echtzeit, die Realzeit
receipt of goods (n)	die Warenannahme
receive (v)	erhalten
rectangular (adj)	rechteckig
reduce (v)	reduzieren, vermindern, verringern
reel (n)	die Rolle, die Spule
refer to (v)	beziehen, hinweisen, verweisen
reference (n)	der Bezug, der Hinweis, die Referenz
refrigerated (adj)	gekühlt
refrigerated container (reefer) (n)	der Kühlcontainer
regarding (prep)	betreffend, bezüglich
relevant (adj)	entsprechend, relevant, wichtig
reliable (adj)	verlässlich, zuverlässig
reliably (adv)	betriebssicher, verlässlich, zuverlässig
reminder (n)	die Erinnerung, der Mahnbrief, die Mahnung
repack (v)	neu verpacken, umpacken
representative (n)	der Beauftragte, der Repräsentant, der Vertreter
request (n)	die Anfrage, das Ersuchen, das Gesuch
require (v)	benötigen, brauchen, erfordern
reserve warehouse (n)	das Reservelager
residence (n)	die Residenz, der Wohnort, der Wohnsitz
responsible (adj)	verantwortlich, zuständig
result (n)	das Ergebnis
result (v)	entstehen, ergeben, resultieren
retail company (n)	der Einzelhandel
return (v)	retournieren, zurückkehren, zurückschicken
RFID (Radio Frequency Identification) (abbr)	die Radiofrequenz-Identifikation
rice (n)	der Reis
rightful (adj)	rechtmäßig
risk (n)	die Gefahr, das Risiko
risky (adj)	gefährlich, riskant
road (n)	die Straße
road waybill (n)	der Spediteurfrachtbrief
roadtrain (n)	der LKW-Zug
roast (v)	braten, rösten

role play (n) das Rollenspiel
roller conveyor (n) die Rollenbahn
rotating rack (n) das Umlaufregal
roughly (adv) derb, grob, ungefähr
route planning (n) die Routenplanung, die Tourenplanung
rule (n) die Regel, die Richtlinie, die Vorschrift

S

safety belt (n) der Sicherheitsgurt
safety boot (n) der Sicherheitsstiefel
safety glove (n) der Sicherheitshandschuh
safety mark (n) die Sicherheitsmarkierung
safety sign (n) das Sicherheitszeichen
sales warehouse (n) das Verkaufslager
salutation (n) die Anrede, der Gruß
sample warehouse (n) das Musterlager
scrap iron (n) das Alteisen, der Eisenschrott
screw (n) die Schraube
sea (n) das Meer
seaworthy packing (n) die Seekiste
seem (v) erscheinen, scheinen, wirken
self-confidence (n) das Selbstbewusstsein, die Selbstsicherheit, das Selbstvertrauen
self-reactive (adj) selbsterhitzungsfähig, selbstzersetzlich
seller (n) der Verkäufer
send (v) schicken, senden, versenden
sensitive (adj) empfindlich, sensibel, sensitiv
sensitivity (n) die Empfindlichkeit
serial number (n) die Seriennummer
service company (n) die Dienstleistungsfirma
severely (adv) hart, schwer, streng
share (v) freigeben, mitbenutzen, teilen
shave (v) rasieren
sheet of paper (n) das Blatt Papier, der Papierbogen
shelf (n) das Regal
shelf board (n) der Regalboden
shelf life limit (n) das Mindesthaltbarkeitsdatum, die Lagerzeit
shelves (n) die Regale
ship (n) das Schiff
ship (v) liefern, senden, verschiffen
shipment (n) die Lieferung, die Sendung
shipper (n) der Versender
shipping costs (n) die Versandkosten
shipping document pouch (n) die Dokumententasche
short delivery (n) die Minderlieferung
sideways (adv) seitlich, seitwärts
sign (v) unterschreiben
signature (n) die Unterschrift
silo construction die Silobauweise
similar (adj) ähnlich, gleich
simply (adv) einfach, schlicht, simpel
sincerely (adv) aufrichtig, ergebenst
single-storey (adj) eingeschossig
skid (n) das Ladegestell, die Palette
skip (v) auslassen, hüpfen, springen
skull & crossbones (n) das Totenkopfsymbol
slide (n) die Rutsche
slightly (adv) etwas, geringfügig, leicht
slip (v) entgleiten, rutschen
slippery (adj) glatt, rutschig
slope (n) die Abschüssigkeit, das Gefälle
slump down (v) in sich zusammensacken
small talk (n) das Geplauder, die oberflächliche Unterhaltung, der Smalltalk
social insurance identity card (n) der Sozialversicherungsausweis
soft tissue (n) das Seidenpapier
solid (n) der Festkörper, der Feststoff
sometimes (adv) manchmal, mitunter
somewhat (adv) ein wenig, etwas
sort (v) ordnen, sortieren
sortable (adj) sortierbar
space-saving (adj) platzsparend, raumsparend
spare-parts warehouse (n) das Werkzeug-/Ersatzteillager
special storage area (n) das Sonderlager
special warehouse (n) das Speziallager
specific (adj) bestimmt, speziell, spezifisch
specified (adj) angegeben, festgelegt, spezifiziert

speed up (v) beschleunigen, dynamisieren, schneller werden
spicy (adj) pikant, scharf, würzig
spontaneous (adj) spontan
sporadic acting handling and hoisting equipment der Unstetigförderer
square (adj) quadratisch
stack (v) schichten, stapeln
stamp (v) abstempeln
standard (n) die Norm, die Richtlinie, der Standard
starting salary (n) das Anfangsgehalt
statement (n) die Äußerung, die Erklärung, die Feststellung, das Statement
static (adj) feststehend, stationär, statisch
stationary (adj) feststehend, stationär
stock list (n) die Lagerliste, die Warenbestandsliste
stock placement (n) die Einlagerung
stock records (n) der Lagerbestand, der Warenbestand
stock removal (n) die Auslagerung
storage (n) das Lager, die Lagerhalle
storage document (n) die Bestandsdokumentation, die Lagerdokumentation
storage equipment (n) die Lagerausrüstung
store (v) einlagern
store superintendent (n) der Lagermeister
straddle carrier (n) der Portalhubwagen, der Van-Carrier (VC)
stretch foil (n) die Stretchfolie
structure (n) der Aufbau, die Gliederung, die Struktur
styrofoam (n) das Styropor
subject line (n) die Betreffzeile
subsection (n) die Unterabteilung
substance (n) die Materie, der Stoff, die Substanz
substitute (v) austauschen, ersetzen, substituieren
successful (adj) erfolgreich
successfully (adv) erfolgreich
suddenly (adj) abrupt, plötzlich, unvermittelt
suggest (v) empfehlen, vorschlagen
suitable (adj) angemessen, geeignet, passend, tauglich
sum up (v) zusammenfassen
supplier (n) der Lieferant
supporting beam (n) der Auflageträger
switch on (v) anschalten, anstellen, einschalten

t

tag (n) die Marke, das Schild, der Transponder
take part (v) mitmachen, sich beteiligen, teilnehmen
tank container (n) der Tankcontainer
tare (n) das Leergewicht, die Tara, das Verpackungsgewicht
task (n) die Aufgabe
tax identification number (n) die Steuer-Identifikationsnummer
technical book (n) das Fachbuch
TEU (Twenty Foot Equivalent Unit) (abbr) die 20'(Fuß)-Einheit
theoretical (adj) theoretisch
third-party warehouse (n) das Fremdlager
thread rod (n) die Gewindestange
threaten (v) androhen, drohen
tissue (n) das Gewebe, das Taschentuch
toasted (adj) geröstet
too (adv) auch, ebenfalls, zu
tool (n) das Werkzeug
top with (v) bedecken
topic (n) der Inhalt, das Thema, die Thematik
topic of the email (n) das Thema der E-Mail
toxic (adj) giftig, toxisch
trade (n) der Handel
trade (v) handeln, tauschen
trading company (n) die Großhandelsfirma
train (n) der Eisenbahnzug
train (v) anlernen, einweisen, trainieren
transport (v) befördern, transportieren
transport method (n) die Transportmethode, die Transportmöglichkeit
transshipment (n) der Güterumschlag
treat (v) behandeln
triangular (adj) dreieckig
truck dispatch (n) die Hebestelle
tutor (n) der Betreuer, der Lehrer, der Tutor
tyre (n) der Reifen

u

unconscious (adj)	bewusstlos, ohnmächtig
unfinished (adj)	unerledigt, unfertig, unvollendet
unhelpful (adj)	nicht hilfreich, nicht hilfsbereit
unit (n)	das Bauteil, die Einheit
unload (v)	entladen
unloading costs (n)	Kosten der Entladung, Kosten der Löschung
unpack (v)	entpacken
unprepared (adj)	unvorbereitet
unwelcoming (adj)	unerwünscht, unlieb, unwillkommen
urgent (adj)	akut, dringend, zwingend
urgently (adj)	dringend, nötig
use (v)	benutzen, gebrauchen
usually (adj)	gewöhnlich, normalerweise
utilisation of available floorspace	der Flächennutzungsgrad
utilisation of storage space (n)	die Lagerraumnutzung
utility knife (n)	das Cuttermesser, das Teppichmesser
utmost (adj)	äußerst, höchst

v

valuable (adj)	nützlich, wertvoll
valuation (n)	die Bewertung, die Schätzung, die Wertermittlung
value (n)	der Betrag, die Valuta, der Wert
value (v)	bewerten, rechnen, schätzen
vary (v)	variieren, verändern
vehicle (n)	das Fahrzeug
ventilated (adj)	belüftet, ventiliert
ventilated container (n)	der ventilierte Container
verification (n)	die Bestätigung, die Überprüfung, die Verifikation
vertical (adj)	senkrecht, vertikal
vessel (n)	das Schiff, das Transportschiff
via (prep)	durch, per, über
virtual (adj)	gedacht, fiktiv, virtuell
visible (adj)	erkennbar, sichtbar
visual check (n)	die Sichtkontrolle
vocational school (n)	die Berufsschule
voice directed warehousing (n)	die Kommissionierung per Sprachangaben
voice picking (n)	die Kommissionierung per Sprachangaben

w

wage (n)	der Lohn
wage accounting (n)	die Lohnbuchhaltung
warehouse (n)	das Lager, die Lagerhalle
warehouse logistics operator (n)	die Fachkraft für Lagerlogistik
warehouse operator (n)	der Fachlagerist
warehouse system (n)	das Lagerverwaltungssystem
warn (v)	warnen
warning sign (n)	das Warnzeichen
waste paper (n)	das Altpapier, der Papierabfall
wave picking method (n)	die serienorientierte parallele Kommissionierung
waybill (n)	der Frachtbrief
weariness (n)	die Müdigkeit
weigh (v)	wiegen
weight (n)	das Gewicht
weight of the cargo (n)	das Gewicht der Fracht/der Ladung
welcome (v)	begrüßen, willkommen heißen
wholesale company (n)	der Großhandel
wide (adj)	breit
width (n)	die Breite
witness (n)	der Zeuge
wood wool (n)	die Holzwolle
wooden box (n)	die Holzkiste
wooden wedge (n)	der Holzkeil
wrapping paper (n)	das Packpapier

y

yard (n)	der Hof, das Yard (Längenmaß: 1 Yard = 91,44 cm)

z

zone (n)	der Bereich, das Gebiet, die Zone
zone picking method (n)	die auftragsorientierte parallele Kommissionierung

Bildquellenverzeichnis

Dreamstime.com: S. 12 (Viktor Levi), S. 26.5 (Duncan Noakes), 27.2 (Timothy Large), S. 28 (Yakim19), S. 30 (Graça Victoria), S. 51.2 (Fallostupido), S. 53.2 (Monkey Business Images), S. 59 (Texelart), S. 60.15 (Karayuschij), S. 61 (Scanrail), S. 63 (Monkey Business Images), S. 64.1 (Monkey Business Images), S. 74.1 (Corepics Vof), S. 74.2 (Petarneychev), S. 75.1 (Raghuramaswamy), S. 89.1 (Madpixblue), S. 105.10 (Katarzyna Bialasiewicz), S. 119 (Milan Kopcok), S. 123 (Gumpanat Thavankitdumrong)

Fotolia.com: S. 9 (Uwe Annas), S. 11 (auremar), S. 13 (industrieblick), S. 14 (Marie-Thérèse GUIHAL), S. 15 (Picture-Factory), S. 16 (Texelart), S. 18.1 (Robert Kneschke), S. 18.2 (robu_s), S. 19.1 (Maksym Yemelyanov), S. 19.2 (fineart-collection), S. 19.3 (industrieblick), S. 20 (jojje11), S. 21 (TTstudio), S. 22 (contrastwerkstatt), S. 23 (Blend Images), S. 25 (tiero), S. 26.1 (Photographee.eu), S. 26.2 (Waler), S. 26.3 (lucassg83), S. 26.4 (Photographee.eu), S. 31 (Andres Rodriguez), S. 33 (Juice Images), S. 34.1 (mahey), S. 34.2 (Inok), S. 34.3 (BillionPhotos.com), S. 35.1 (pitb_1), S. 35.2 (viperagp), S. 36 (Christian Schwier), S. 37.1 (industrieblick), S. 37.2 (Robert Kneschke), S. 38.1 (sergeevspb), S. 39.5 (Elenathewise), S. 39.6 (djama), S. 39.13 (Fotogrund), S. 39.14 (Fotogrund), S. 40 (industrieblick), S. 41.3 (AKS), S. 42.1 (Marie-Thérèse GUIHAL), S. 42.2 (furuoda), S. 42.3 (Moreno Soppelsa), S. 42.4 (arska n), S. 43.1–2 (Zelfit), S. 44.1–6 (Zelfit), S. 45 (Nejron Photo), S. 46 (Texelart), S. 48 (fineart-collection), S. 49 (Monkey Business), S. 51.1 (Spencer), S. 51.4 (Benjamin Haas), 51.6 (Ideeah Studio), S. 51.7 (iconshow), S. 52 (Gstudio Group), S. 53. 1 (Nejron Photo), S. 54.1–2 (stanciuc), S. 56. (Nejron Photo), S. 58.1 (Monkey Business), S. 58.2 (Maxal Tamor), S. 60.1 (koya79), S. 60.2 (PRILL Mediendesign), S. 60.3 (Guido Vrola), S. 60.4 (vladischern), S. 60.5 (J.M.), S. 60.6 (Zelfit), S. 60.7 (PRILL Mediendesign), S. 60.8 (Irina Fischer), S. 60.9 (topae), S. 60.10 (euthymia), S. 60.11 (miket), S. 60.12 (Reena), S. 60.13 (ILYA AKINSHIN), S. 60.14 (Björn Wylezich), S. 60.15 (Macro), S. 62 (Syda Productions), S. 64.2–5 (texelart), S. 64.6–7 (coramax), S. 65 (Rido), S. 66 (Cybrain), S. 69 (VRD), S. 70 (Andres Rodriguez), S. 71.1 (Andreas Hilger), S. 71.2 (Sven Bähren), S. 71.3 (Frank Täubel), S. 71.4 (Africa Studio), S. 73 (Binkski), S. 75.2 (zhu difeng), S. 76 (ake1150), S. 77.2 (KirstyPargeter), S. 79 (beketoff), S. 80 (Photographee.eu), S. 83.1 (kamonrat), S. 83.2 (lassedesignen), S. 84 (ikuvshinov), S. 85.1 (Jakob Kamender), S. 85.2 (Diezer), S. 85.3 (scanrail), S. 86 (Christos Georghiou), S. 87 (Nightman1965), S. 88 (macrovector), S. 89.2 (Marco Saracco), S. 92.1 (gcpics), S. 92.2 (roopert), S. 92.3 (Klaus Eppele), S. 92.4 (Roman Sigaev), S. 92.5 (RNG), S. 92.6 (Andre Bonn), S. 93.1–2 (picsfive), S. 94 (Arsel), S. 95.1 (Picture-Factory), S. 95.2 (Andres Rodriguez), S. 96 (Robert Kneschke), S. 97 (Andres Rodriguez), S. 98 (Picture-Factory), S. 99 (tashatuvango), S. 102 (auremar), S. 103 (iQoncept), S. 104.1 (Picture-Factory), S. 104.2 (Monkey Business), S. 104.3 (PhotoSG), S. 104.4 (Bernd Jürgens), S. 104.5 (Barbara Pheby), S. 104.6 (Paulista), S. 105.1 (Jacek Chabraszewski), S. 105.2 (gerald schilling), S. 105.3 (Jacek Chabraszewski), S. 105.4 (LianeM), S. 105.5 (Jacek Chabraszewski), S. 105.6 (Nessi), S. 105.7 (CandyBox Images), S. 105.8 (Lucky Dragon), S. 105.9 (unpict), S. 106.1 (Kaarsten), S. 106.2 (yanlev), S. 106.3 (auremar), S. 106.4 (Picture-Factory), S. 106.5–6 (Robert Kneschke), S. 106.7 (Elenathewise), S. 106.8 (francovolpato), S. 106.9–13 (auremar), S. 107 (Mimi Potter), S. 110 (Andres Rodriguez), S. 111 (contrastwerkstatt), S. 112.1–2 (contrastwerkstatt), S. 114 (contrastwerkstatt), S. 115.1 (Picture-Factory), S. 115.2 (contrastwerkstatt), S. 116 (fotomek), S. 117 (contrastwerkstatt)

Elisabeth Galas, Bad Breisig / Bildungsverlag EINS, Köln: S. 27.1–7
Identisys GmbH, Stadtallendorf: S. 51.3
Joh. Friedrich Behrens AG, Ahrensburg: 39.9–10
Jungfalk GmbH & Co. KG, Engen: S. 78.1
MEV Verlag GmbH, Augsburg: S. 38.2

KBS Industrieelektronik GmbH, Freiburg: S. 51.8
Klaus-Peter Zander GmbH, Hamburg: S. 39.8
Vocollect by Honeywell, Pittsburgh (USA): S. 51.5

Umschlagfoto: Fotolia.com (Nejron Photo)